His Majesty's Grand Conceit

Robert Barclay

Also by Robert Barclay

Non-fiction

The Art of the Trumpet-maker
The Preservation and Use of Historic Musical Instruments
Making a Natural Trumpet

Fiction

Triple Take: A Museum Story
Death at the Podium
Ask Me About My Bombshells
Jacob the Trumpeter

His Majesty's Grand Conceit

Being *firfthand* defcriptions by the *dramatis perfonæ* of all the machinations, plots, subterfuges, craft and wiles undertaken in bringing about His Royal Highnefs King George II's FIREWORK SPECTACLE of April 27, in the year of Our Lord 1749 at the *Green Park* in London in celebration of the Peace of Aix-la-Chapelle, clofing the War of the Auftrian Succefsion

As told to Robert Barclay *efq.*

Printed and sold at the sign of the *Loofe Cannon*
GLOUCESTER
MMXX

LIBRARY AND ARCHIVES CANADA CATALOGUING IN PUBLICATION

Title: His Majesty's grand conceit / Robert Barclay.
Names: Barclay, R. L., author.
Description: Includes bibliographical references.
Identifiers: Canadiana 20200281666 | ISBN 9781988657196 (softcover)
Classification: LCC PS8603.A7244 H57 2020 | DDC C813/.6 – dc23ISBN

Copyright © 2020 Robert Barclay

All rights reserved. Except for use in any review or critical article, the reproduction or use of this work, in whole or in part, in any form by any electronic, mechanical or other means—including xerography, photocopying, scanning and recording—or in any information or storage retrieval system, is forbidden without express permission of the publisher

Cover art: Loose Cannon Designs

Published by
LOOSE CANNON PRESS

www.loosecannonpress.com

DEDICATION

During research for this story I was especially surprised by two historical characters who emerged from my reading: one, a man who was prosecuted, sentenced to death and then exiled for his sexual orientation; and the other, the child of a deceased African slave living in a cold and alien land. Captain Robert Jones was a dabbler in fireworks, invented the modern ice skate and perfected its sport, and came against an intolerant society that treated people of his kind as criminals. Charles Ignatius Sancho had the good fortune to be saved, cherished and nurtured, enabling him to express his creative powers in a milieu that more often regarded people of his race as scarcely human.

To Captain Robert Jones and to Charles Ignatius Sancho: your lives are remembered.

Dramatis Personæ
In Order of Appearance

John Byrom, 4th Earl of Orford
    Poet and Inventor
King George II
    King of Great Britain and Ireland, Duke of Brunswick-Lüneburg and Prince-Elector of the Holy Roman Empire
John, 2nd Duke of Montagu
    Master-General of His Majesty's Ordnance
Charles Frederick
    Surveyor-General of the Ordnance
Captain Thomas Desaguliers
    Chief Firemaster of His Majesty's Royal Laboratory
James Morris
    Master Carpenter to the Office of Ordnance
Giovanni Niccolò Servandoni
    Architect, Artist and Theatre Designer
Gaetano Ruggieri
    Pyrotechnician
Jonathan Tyers
    Impresario, Businessman and Proprietor
George Frideric Handel
    Composer and Impresario

SETTING THE SCENE

Late in 1748, a great edifice in the form of a classical temple arose in the Green Park in London's west end, opposite St. James's Palace, King George II's residence. This edifice would be the launching pad for the fireworks to celebrate the Peace of Aix-la-Chapelle, a festive occasion which would take place the following April on the anniversary of the signing. The preparations for the extravaganza were the rage amongst Londoners, and the popular press made great sport of it all. The construction spawned announcements of progress on the site and many firsthand descriptions of the subsequent spectacle. Newspapers of the period abound with ribald satires and highly pointed criticism, while comical pamphlets, letters and memoirs mercilessly lampoon the entire grand conceit. Division, disagreement, misunderstanding and folly enrich the literature of this extraordinary event. There is much to draw upon, making the documentation a gold mine for the historian and for the writer of historical fiction. To add to the fun, I don't know another period in English history when the satire was so pointed, so well-honed, and done with such panache.

I have summoned ten eyewitnesses, all of whom were engaged on this incredible project, so I can record their impressions and memories. All these characters lived and breathed, and several of them left records of their doings. But all their documentary material only comes alive when the tale is told in the first person. It is only when we hear the characters' voices that we are truly drawn into the narrative. I feel privileged to have been their conduit so their interlocking stories may be passed along. But did it all transpire as these ten narrators have related it to me? Well, in the greater part, yes, but if not quite, they probably think it should have. And over a span of two centuries and more, I can hardly argue with their views and memories.

Occasionally, these raconteurs make passing mention of details from their everyday experiences and the milieu in which they lived. These references might be obscure to the modern reader, so I have included endnotes for clarification and sometimes enlightenment. You may refer to these as you wish, or leave them alone, because they add nothing to the immediate flow of their stories. I have made no conscious adjustments to the timeframe, allowing the historical record and its witnesses to dictate the unfolding of events. I'm sure you will appreciate the contemporary illustrations on the opposite page of the "machine" for launching the fireworks—the Temple of Peace—and the map of its location. Further in the narrative you will find the official drawing of the machine and the frontispiece of the subsequent publication. All these, together, give some idea of the vast scale of this extraordinary achievement.

Now let us proceed forthwith to the Green Park and meet our first eyewitness, so he can tell us what all the fuss is about.

The Scene of the Action

The Temple of Peace, the temporary "machine" for launching the fireworks, erected in five months in the Green Park. (Image courtesy of the Gerald Coke Handel Foundation.)

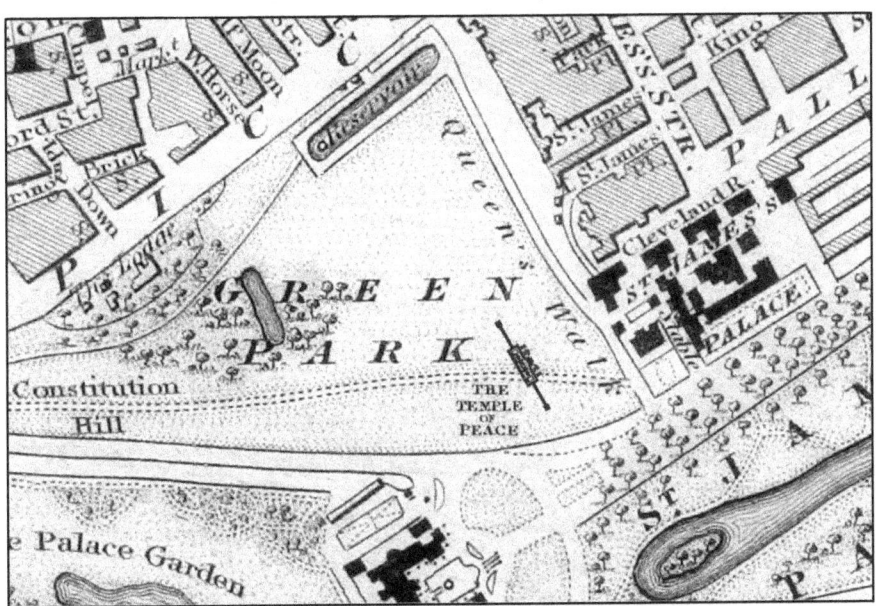

The position of the Temple of Peace in the Green Park, facing St. James's Palace. The temple has been added graphically to a contemporary map.

Prelude

John Byrom, 4th Earl of Orford (1692 to 1763)
Fellow of the Royal Society, Poet and Inventor

In which the first eyewitness opens our story

It was an astonishing spectacle, supreme amongst any other that season, or for many a year, truth to tell. But the celebration of peace between our German king and the damned Austrians and French and whatnot was hardly the reason I went to the Green Park. I care not a damp fart upon squabbles across the Channel. I'm English through and through, and damned proud of it, although 'tis more than unwise to hold in public a view that Hanover is less legitimate than Stuart. Besides, the so-called peace that our oh-so-English George had wrought at Aix-la-Chapelle was stale news by April of 1749. No, for me, 'twas purely for the spectacle, for 'tis not often one can have music, cannon and fireworks all laid on in one evening. 'Twas indeed a grand conceit.

I perforce left my carriage in charge of the driver far down James Street, a fair walk from the gates of the Green Park, because of a crowd of like-minded gentry milling forward. I say gentry, for those were the ones I mixed with, but in truth, anyone in London with a lust for spectacle was there, from the highest to the lowest. This is the great vexation of laying on spectacles at no charge. It is not pleasant to go far afoot in the London streets, for one sees the filth of humanity closer than is desirable. On this night, the risk of being accosted by cut-purses, beggars or the gin-sodden refuse of the lower sort was greater in the press of people.

As I stepped quickly through the east gate of the park, happily unmolested, I encountered Horace Walpole, a chance acquaintance. I had met him recently on this visit to London, and we found we shared a kindred wit even though he was a Whig Member of Parliament. He represented somewhere in Cornwall at that time, although he never set a foot farther west than Twickenham that I know of. He knew not a hint of my political views, for I hold them to be mine and no one else's. In truth, Whig or not, we were united only by our wit and a fondness for coffee, snuff and fine drink. That's plenty enough acquaintance for a stroll together in the park.

'Damnable press of bodies,' I remarked as we came away from the crowd. 'Hard put not to be set upon and robbed.'

'I hear tell Fielding hath designs for a force of constabulary.'

'Aye, from his Bow Street office. Cannot come sooner.'

'Assuming they will be sufficient.'

We walked side by side into the greenspace as the sun was falling before us, and there was the great erection we had heard so much of, silhouetted by the last of the light. This gigantic Temple of Peace designed upon classical lines had been built upon the grass of the park facing the Queen's Library of St. James's Palace. Some 400 and more feet long it was, and rising to at least a quarter that height. And soaring even above that, a gigantic sun figure, a vast firework wheel with VIVAT REX writ at its centre, to be picked out in fires when the show was to be played off. And this was no thing of stagecraft, this temple, being as thin as canvas and propped at the rear; no, 'twas a full building in its depth, with front, sides and back. It is quite remarkable what can be done with timber, plaister, canvas and paint, especially in the short few months since the start of its erection. It was extremely neat and pretty and grand to look at, and a world of fireworks were placed in an order that promised a most amazing scene when it was all to be in full display. His Majesty and other great folks were walking to see the machinery, but it was all railed about there, where the lords, ladies, commons, et cetera were sat under a scaffolding. They seemed to be under confinement in comparison to us mobility, who were enjoying the free air.

Accompanying the king was his youngest son William, Duke of Cumberland—him they call the Butcher for his bloody pursuit of the ragged Highlanders after Culloden—with Lady Yarmouth, the sovereign's mattress bounce, Princess Emilia, Lady Pembroke and old John, Duke of Montagu, whose nose had been in the whole pie from the start. The fence about the structure was picketed with fusiliers who stood at the ready with their weapons at their sides, preventing trespass of those who had not tickets.

'What think you of this squib castle?' I asked Walpole with a smile after we had surveyed its immensity.

'Oh, I don't doubt but 'twill be a fine spectacle. But the Peace gives not the least joy; the stocks do not rise, and the merchants are unsatisfied. And here, to rub their noses in it, the government is to give a magnificent firework.'

'Aye, and one designed and fired off by foreigners. But you'd not deny yourself the entertainment?'

'Oh, for myself, I enjoy a spectacle as much as the next man. Doth not signify that I subscribe to the principle.'

The Peace of Aix-la-Chapelle had been signed the November past, and although His Majesty had long planned these festivities, their execution needs must wait until the ink was dry. And it was hardly opportune to stage such a spectacle in the winter months. We strolled closer to the fenced area where we could see the musicians on the platform of the machine, preparing the Grand Overture under the eyes of Mr Handel, who was standing upon a raised podium of wood. Trumpets, horns, reeds, drums and such, all warlike instruments for a peaceful occasion, but no one apparently taking this with any irony.

'And Tweedledum is contracted to provide the music,' I observed, seeing Mr Handel waving irascibly at his band of musicians.

He laughed at that. My rhyme lampooning George Frideric Handel, when he and Giovanni Bononcini were matching opera for opera like duelling puppets, was now common currency.[1]

'Ah, but Tweedledee had the last laugh, did he not?' said Walpole. 'His *Te Deum* was performed last year at the signing of the Peace, which I am sure must have exercised Handel.'

'Hardly. Pleased him, surely, Bononcini being dead these two years!'

We laughed again and shared a pinch of snuff from my pouch. I placed my pinch just so at the junction of my thumb and index finger, as did Walpole, and together we sniffed and sneezed almost simultaneous. There is nothing that more induces a kindred spirit amongst men than to expel one's air explosively in unison. I sneezed again, returned my square of cambric to my vest pocket, and together we strode to the front of the structure. I was once more taken with the elaborateness of it all. The entire front of the pavilion was adorned with frets, gilding, artificial flowers, inscriptions, carvings and allegorical pictures. I counted at least twenty statues in relief, many friezes, festoons and medallions, and texts in Latin throughout. The principal text, which occupied a high place at the front and centre, amused me in particular. Here, rendered in English, is said:

> George II, the Assertor of our Liberty, the Establisher of our Tranquility, the Father of his People.[2]

Oh, there was such irony in the father of our people being this man who took himself off overseas, fought battles for his Hanoverian holdings, and in so doing ran up a bill that he then foisted off upon the English people's Parliament. On one side of the façade, there was another depiction that also gave me wry amusement: His Majesty Giving Peace to Britannia. Fine sentiment... but for the fact that we'd had peace all along; damned if the warring frogs and cabbages and whoever on the Continent had spilled onto Britannia's soil, and the king and his butcher had done with the Scots long since.

That the sole function of this great erection was for this one occasion, and that it would be torn down thereafter, was a symbol to me of the extent to which our beloved sovereign will go to curry favour with his English subjects. And the extent, also, to which he most seriously misunderstands the people over whom he rules. I had never seen such a flurry of ribald pamphlets, lampoons and adverse press opinions as spewed forth since the public first learned of this regal folly. We had been laughing over the papers for months, yet were also titillated by the lure of it, so whatever one's politics, one was drawn to it and captivated by anticipation of it.

Behind the structure, ranged along Constitution Hill, were the guns of the Royal Train of Artillery, which were to fire the royal salute of 101 shots. Six pounders, twelve-pounders and great twenty-four-pound guns were ready blank-shotted, their gun captains and matrosses in attendance with ramrods, swabs and matches. Mr Charles Frederick, the Surveyor-General of the Ordnance, stood close by the viewing stand with a kerchief in his hand, ready to signal the start of the spectacle before riding forth to join his gunners on the hill.

The sun had long since slid behind the dwellings of Grosvenor Place when a single rocket was fired to call attention and bring all to order. At the rocket's report, Mr Handel on his podium bowed deeply to the king and the court, turned to his musicians with raised arms, and swept them down...

CHAPTER ONE

His Majesty King George II (1683 to 1760)
King of Great Britain and Ireland, Duke of Brunswick-Lüneburg and Prince-Elector of the Holy Roman Empire

In which King George hatches his scheme for a grand firework and John, Duke of Montagu, finds himself cast upon the bonfire

I have lately made John, 2nd Duke of Montagu Master-General of my Board of Ordnance. Poor John thinks it a sinecure and treats it as such, but if there were ever one who could organise the spectacle I have in mind, it is he. It is often questioned why I, as did my father before me, give such preferments to the jester and wag he hath proved himself to be. But he is a man of many and varied talents, and of great diplomatic skill, and I have promoted him far and awarded him many duties in our household. Even so, he is becoming prone in his advancing age to seek the easy life. I decided to shake him out of his indolence. I summoned the man to St James's Palace to administer my great surprise. I had him come up to the library, not the great reception room. That one's too filled with damned flunkies and hangers-on and all the nuisances of state that make decisions longer and more tedious in the execution. Besides, the library looks out upon the park.

'Montagu! Come sit yourself down here.' He is a tall, long-nosed fellow with a serious mien that is but skin-deep. Indeed, a roguish twinkle in his eye belies the countenance of first impression. He is a man who always dresses immaculately; this day his coat was well brushed, his hose and shirt spotless, and a fine shine to the shoe buckles. Withal, his wig was somewhat crooked, and he was a little out of breath from the few stairs to the library, so I waved my man to pull forward a chair at the other side of the work table, then sent him from the room.

'I trust I find you well?'

'Indeed, Your Majesty,' he puffed as he straightened his apparel and twitched his wig, 'I am as well as might be, though this November weather doth so work at my joints.'

'Aye, these last few days have been the coldest for many years. I hope 'tis not presaging the winter to come.'

'I hope not, Your Majesty,' he answered, with an expression of anticipation.

'Listen, John. It's damnable. I am sick of vulgar disrespect.'

You may wonder to hear a mighty king, duke and prince-elector speak thus to one of his subjects. Where is gravitas? you ask; where the dignity of high office? Truth to tell, there is none in my court to open my heart to, so John Montagu sees a privy side of me that none other knows, nor even suspects. He respects this bond, so whilst we may be intimate when we are quite alone, he is formal and precise when in company, as he must ever be in the respect due his royal sovereign. Not one crack in my imperial armour shall any other see.

'I was ever disrespected,' I complained, 'by those who hold that their throne is a British prerogative and that only British born and bred need apply. Their history shows them Normans, French, Dutch and yokel Scots amongst their so-called island purity, yet still I am mocked as a foreigner.'

'Your Majesty, I beg you to set aside the vulgar…'

'My heart still burns from that vile pamphlet pinned to the gates of this palace: "Lost or strayed out of this house, a man who hath left a wife and six children on the parish." Vile calumny! Just so I spent some time in Brunswick-Lüneburg!'

'Oh, I had hoped that scurrilous slur did not still rankle. 'Twas years past.'

'Aye, mayhap it was, but nothing is repaired! Nothing! I speak their language a hundred times more fluently than my father ever tried to, Lucifer roast his soul. I choose *not* to spend half the year in Brunswick-Lüneburg, I leave policy and decisions on Britain to their own Parliament, and I've prised the Catholic Stuart pretenders off their backs, yet still they despise me.'

'I am sure it is but a noisy few…' I paid him no heed. My choler was fully risen, and Montagu was the prime vessel for my spleen.

'They have it that this late war more benefitted Hanover than

England and that the Peace of Aix-la-Chapelle sold them to the French. Damn it! I finally have the French recognise the legitimacy of my throne—*my throne!*—I have them kick the Papist Scots out of France, and all the English people do is whine and satirise. Eight bloody years of war, for what? Mine is a *Hanoverian* throne by Protestant right, and it is our own Parliament that passed the Act of Succession to make it so. Blast those who would seek to have it otherwise. Oh, it is damnable!'

'I am ever your servant, Your Majesty,' he replied, in no way put out by my venting. 'If there is any duty I may perform…'

'Yes, you may!' I said, fixing his attention and reining in my choler. 'You know, quite before the Peace was finally signed, that we had plans for a spectacle.'

'Aye, Your Majesty. It hath been the talk for some time, and we have even discussed possible venues. After all, The Hague, Paris, Dublin, all are putting on great spectacles to honour the Peace. So must we.'

'Enough talk. Now we act! What I conceive will be a vast show of prestige. We need to turn the English head, show my people our might, our authority, our will. A gigantic spectacle of pomp and guns and a great machine for fireworks to celebrate the Peace in magnificence; one such as hath never before been seen in this land. I will see to it.'

'Where shall this spectacle take place?' he asked. 'You recall we had mooted Lincoln's Inn Fields as a suitable site.'

'Oh, that was ill-thought nonsense! Besides, have the Duke of Newcastle reap the benefits? Never.'

'Aye, truly, he owns the land thereabouts. Besides, the tenants of the place were much up in arms about it.'

'Bugger the tenants! It's Newcastle who exercises me!'

'Where then, sire?'

'It needs be in the closest proximity to this palace as possible. The association between the Crown and the Peace is paramount.'

'Then, there,' he waved at the window. 'In the Green Park.'

'Of course, in the Green Park! Five hundred feet from the Queen's Walk, no more. As directly and as closely adjacent to this dwelling as is possible. Those are my very words.'

And when I speak such words, my subjects do my bidding. Montagu's curiosity as to why he had been summoned was patent on his face, but there was now a worm of thought as to what I intended to charge him with. I rang for my man and had him pour two glasses of claret, then sent him for a large sheet of paper and writing instruments; medium folio at least, for I wanted space.

'To the continuing good health of your joints,' I toasted. We drank in silence until my man returned and laid the paper and instruments on my work table.

'Look you, John,' I said, 'here's what's in my mind.'

I dismissed my man, and once the door closed behind him, I sketched quickly: there would be a great machine for the launching of the fireworks, a vast structure along classical lines with Doric columns and pediments, arches and all manner of architectural and decorative devices. I'd seen these things in French papers and knew what store their King Louis set by pomp and theatre and show. Well, we'd employ their best artificers away from them, bring them to this land, and top them at their own game! I reckoned a length of 400 feet would impress the world; then, say, a hundred high, so I wrote the sizes in. There would be inscriptions celebrating the Peace, there would be passages from the classics, there would be encomiums to my warlike greatness. I sketched 'em in roughly as well. After a while, I put my pencil aside and imagined the thunderous cannonades to split the ears with my prowess and my victory. My crown; my kingdom.

'More rockets, wheels, fountains and aerial fire effects than have ever been seen, here or anywhere else on earth, John. Anywhere else on earth! Y' hear me? And there will be cannon for a mighty salute; 101 of them, as is customary! Aye, I can see in my mind's eye the Train of Artillery ranged along Constitution Hill.' I swept my arm along the skyline visible through the window.

'I am in awe of this conceit, Your Majesty,' he said slowly, 'and feel privileged to be the first to whom you have expressed it.'

'So you should be. This will be finer, larger, more elaborate than anything those puffed-up French clods could call forth.'

'And what you have sketched here is the form of the machine for the fireworks... the structure from which they will be launched?'

'Just so.'

'But, 'tis enormous. 'Twould dwarf the proposition we made for Lincoln's Inn Fields...'

'Of course! Bigger, better, grander! And there shall be a viewing scaffold with as many seats as may be for the court, for the gentry and the merchants of the city. Now, tell me, John, do you know of Giovanni Niccolò Servandoni?'

'Of course, Your Majesty. A Frenchman who designs theatrical structures. A highly regarded designer who hath done much work here in England.' His face was the picture of expectation.

'What of the Ruggieri family?'

'Why, the Ruggieri are the finest artisans of fireworks in the whole of Europe. The new pyrotechnicians.' His expression became even more one of bated anticipation.

'Yes. *Pyrotechnicians.*' I pronounced the new word with some relish. 'I would employ them.'

'And so you should…' Now I could see comprehension beginning to run across the wrinkles of his face.

'Yes, employ. And,' I continued, launching my bombshell, 'I am given to believe that it is you alone who will be capable of bringing about my grand spectacle.'

His horror at the thought of such onerous duty, the labours and responsibilities of the undertaking, was writ large upon his face. He looked for all the world like a Guy Fawkes effigy flung upon the bonfire.

'I see this comes as a great surprise.' I relish always the expressions of those who must do my bidding, waver as they will.

'Aye, Your Majesty,' he waffled, 'but… but I am sure my talent is but insignificant, and perhaps those who have given you to believe my capability exaggerate my usefulness in this endeavour.'

'Your modesty, sir, might well be taken for reluctance to do my bidding.' I was waspish because he needed to know his place.

'Oh, no, no, Your Majesty!' he cried in a dither, the scurrilous bastard, imagining my favours of a sudden withdrawn. 'Far from it for me to hint that your judgement is in any way wanting…'

'Good. Let it be settled then. You will immediately contact Charles Frederick of the Ordnance, have him muster his staff at the Laboratory in Woolwich and the Master Carpenter. You will communicate forthwith to Servandoni, offering him work and, with the Ruggieri family, indicating that it will be our pleasure to employ one of them as soon as might be convenient.'

'They are all, I believe, to be found in Paris....'

'You must inform them directly, and in plain words, that we want the greatest, the best, the most extravagant.'

He finished his glass at a gulp, and I poured him more. Oh, yes, I love to watch a face when its owner is given unwanted but incontrovertible instruction. There begins perplexity, followed by the dawn of comprehension, then horror, brief intransigence quickly masked by probity, and so succeeded by resignation and finally acceptance with a false willingness to serve. 'Tis a comedic peep-show.

'When will this be accomplished? How long do we... I... have to get it done?'

'Well, damn it to Hades, it should have been done ere this! The Peace was so long in the signing that the good weather slipped away.' By God, the delays and fiddle-faddling these past months had driven me nigh to distraction. 'But time is of essence. It must take place in the spring of next year, at all costs before the end of April. The anniversary.'

'That's... that's scarce...' his fingers counted off, '...five months away, Your Majesty!'

'Then it would be well to act now. In faith, it would have been well to have acted sooner. Off with you, and see to the organising of it. Take this paper with you, and we will meet at some time convenient to draw it up in detail.'

He stood a while, not moving towards the door as I had waved at him, and looked expectantly at me.

'What then?'

'It is the matter, Your Majesty, of the ah... fiscal aspect of the endeavour...'

'All works will be undertaken by the Board of Ordnance. How else? Powder, firework fabrication, erection of the structure and assignment of working men. All of it. Frederick will inform William Earle, Clerk of the Cheque, of our pleasure in this matter.'

'And your chosen contractors... to bring them from overseas and to supply their wants?'

'Yes, yes, of course. I'd quite forgot. See Richard Arundel's flunkies at the office of the Treasurer of Chamber. I may not be troubled with detail. They will have you control a purse. But mark my words,' I warned him, 'I've told Arundel not to spare the purse—nor you the

Ordnance—for want of a few guineas. This must be done well! Lavish. Spectacular. Royal!'

He bowed and scurried out, willing as always to do our bidding. Damned certain it was the old scoundrel would find a way to line his purse at the Crown's expense, but damned certain also was that a shower of coin was a sovereign physic and a spur to the flanks of my servants. I knew damned well that the cost of my fireworks would look well on paper, that the figures would balance to a nicety, but that the executors thereof would be well served by it. It was ever thus in this world.

Even though damnable betimes, 'tis good to be king.

Chapter Two

John, 2nd Duke of Montagu (1690 to 1749)
Master-General of His Majesty's Ordnance, Fellow of the Royal College of Physicians, Knight of the Garter, &c. &c.

In which the Duke of Montagu sets about the organising of the spectacle

I pulled that one off quite well, I felt! The king knows not of my theatrical talent, although the way I masked my foreknowledge with fear and fawning would do credit to Sadler's Wells. And my supposèd ignorance as well. Great surprise, my arse! His Majesty's household keeps secrets as my bladder holds water; sparingly and with much spillage. There had been talk of such a celebration long since—the absurd plans for Lincoln's Inn Fields, the need for spectacle, and so on—and I knew only too well that His Majesty would point his imperious finger in my direction. Who else? I was privy long since to my role in his grand design, having had words with his secretary, who hath been a confidant of mine for some time. Ah, wheels within wheels. Surprise, my nether aperture!

So, I took on the king's grand plan, seemingly unwilling, though in truth I take on with gusto all tasks and honours the Crown sends my way, both of His Majesty King George II and his father before him. Over the years, I have been awarded numerous appointments. I was but twenty-seven when I was made a Fellow of the Royal College of Physicians. I was Knight of the Garter a scant two years later, and I got the Order of the Bath and a Fellowship of the Royal Society in 1725. Then I became Grand Master of the Premier Grand Lodge of England. So, you see, the trust His Majesty has in me is warranted. I've accumulated a West Indies fortune and pissed it all away—yet still keeping the royal favour, mark you—I've mounted and equipped my own troop of cavalry, and now, of course, I'm Master-General of His Majesty's Ordnance.

The king knows that I am a versatile, able and willing servant; I am courageous, energetic and very well-connected indeed. In short, I am a man to be reckoned with. But in all things, y' know, I've lived life to the fullest and treated it all as a great infernal jape. There are those who dislike my handicraft jokes, especially those victims whose sense of fun is not as sharp as mine. But it is all done in pleasantness and, I am sure, quite forgivable. Nobody, I believe, can say I am an unkind man.

From all these things I have taken on, though, I've profited mightily. And this grand Royal Fireworks to celebrate the Peace would be no exception. If I could not feather my nest from the king's purse, I'm not the man I think I am. (And I'll mix a metaphor with the best of 'em, too.) But I did wonder if this late enterprise that His Majesty had thrown in my lap might well take more than I could give it. Y' see, being Master-General of His Majesty's Ordnance ought to be the sort of position whose duties naturally fall to underlings. Such is the case with my elevation to the Captaincy of the Gentlemen Pensioners and my duties as Master of the Great Wardrobe. (Forgot to mention those before, did I not?) None of these duties should be onerous, and I see to it that they are not. One employs clerks and scriveners and overseers to attend to the minutiae and merely pockets the generous pension. That's how one builds houses and maintains style.

Thus, it should be honorary, this post with the Ordnance, and I have always treated it as such. Charles Frederick's the Surveyor-General, Andrew Wilkinson keeps the stores, and William Rawlinson Earle does the books. So, all I'm obliged to do—or should be obliged to do, in God's name—is have Chas, Andrew and William round for a bottle of claret and a pipe every so often and not even think of talking shop. Jesting and laughing, fooling with each other, that's our sport. Gentlemanly frivolity.

So, I don't captain His Majesty's Ordnance any more than the figurehead of a man-o'-war captains the ship. It is titular only or should be. But at fifty-nine years of age, I have joints that plague me when 'tis cold and moist, and pissing these winter months is down to a trickle—"by their *boots* shall ye know them"—so I suspected that organising these grand fireworks would be a taxing thing. I might be obliged to work for my living, damn it all. And now His Majesty had summoned me and, in no uncertain terms, loaded upon my shoulders the execution of it. He had laid it out that success or failure rested upon my head. Even though forewarned, I was yet dizzy with thoughts of what needed to be brought together in the endeavour. It was clear that, until this scheme was over and finished, I would see precious little of Boughton House in Northamptonshire or my dear wife, Mary, at our country house on Blackheath; I needs must work from my more modest mansion in Whitehall. This last is most conveniently close to the centre of parliamentary activity and not far from the king's chief residence at St. James's Palace.

I have to record, though, that if His Majesty desired by this spectacle to curry favour with the English populace, I feel he was sorely misleading himself. My ear to the general tenor of discussion in the coffee houses and taverns of this nation (which I fondly frequent) would lead me to conclude otherwise. By my reckoning, your average man in the street would forego vast wastage on pomp and spectacle when the solid Christian virtues of hard work, thrift and modesty were so grossly debased in this land. All around him was ostentation, vulgarity, immorality and extravagance. He would see that England had lately emerged from a costly European war that was none of her doing and that capitulation to France and Spain provided no commercial advantage whatsoever. In short, Mr London Town was far more concerned with godly English pursuits than flamboyant foreign entertainment inimical to his solid, pragmatic constitution. Why waste money burning gunpowder at the hands of foreigners when limbless soldiers from the late war went starving on the London streets for want of alms? Widespread was the contempt for overseas influences on the affairs of our island, and great was the desire to retrench within our own domain.

Certain it was that the Ruggieri and our fine friend Servandoni might be called upon by the Crown to entertain the nation, but it must be kept to all appearances a solidly English affair. In all essence, it must bear the mark of our Royal Laboratory, our Master Carpenter and our Train of Artillery. It is *our* celebration of the Peace and, to my way of thinking, we must make it a paean to God upon the existence of the English Channel. And here lay a balancing act that would rival that of a tightrope walker; my balancing act. How to keep English, French and Italian harmonious yet still hold Britannia front and centre.

As a first step in guiding the king's grand conceit, I visited the office of the Treasurer of the Chamber to assure the necessary flow of coin, for without this promise at the outset, nothing would be achieved. The Ordnance would foot the larger part of the bill, but ready money in coin was of essence. A thin rail of a man with a skew wig and pince-nez spectacles sat behind a high desk surrounded by writing instruments, papers and parchments. Behind him, cubbyholes held ledger books, rolled papers bound with tape, and folders and dossiers of many shapes and sizes. It all looked very ordered and methodical. He had been apprised of the king's grand spectacle and was well prepared for me.

'A purse hath been set aside at Barclay's in Lombard Street in your name,' this scrivener sniffed. 'You will withdraw funds as needed and keep a record of all outgoings no matter how trifling. My master, Richard Arundel, hath told me that no expense should be spared, and whilst I do my sovereign's bidding, I also keep tight watch upon his purse.'

'Oh, I am quite sure you do,' I said with icy politeness. Damned smellfungus. But the look in his magnified eye, as he tilted his head back and settled his glasses on his nose with a forefinger, reeked of mistrust and focused probity.

'The money is to be spent only upon the foreigners His Majesty is employing. All other expenses are with your department, the Ordnance, and may not be confused.'

'Well, there will be expenses to tradesmen that are made in coin,' I snapped. 'Some of these may well be reimbursed by paper bank note from the Ordnance, for the Ordnance, for your information, doth not dish out specie. The two accounts will necessarily cross!'

'As long as the paper and the coin balance in the records at Barclay's, you will not be held to account.'

'Held to account?' I cried. 'Damn your impudence! Who d' ye think you're addressing?'

'The purse is voted by Parliament annually,' he wagged, ignoring my outburst, 'and it is not bottomless.'

He dashed off a note to the bank, instructing them to honour my requirements, sanded it quickly and thrust it to me over the desk. Business concluded, I left the room, not without a qualm for the microscope my affairs would be under. If this enterprise were to profit me, I would need to be circumspect.

It is not every day that a king's purse opens for one of his servants, and I think a man would be a fool to let opportunity pass him by when 'tis there for the taking. Were I exceptional in this, I would be branded a scoundrel, but all know that if advantage is to be made, one should seize the day. The king knows this; he is nobody's fool (but his own, but let that matter rest), and he knows that crumbs fall from his table. All are enriched by his largess, the money trickles down from the high to the low, and a royal blind eye ensures the willing execution of his designs. None of those with whom I share coffee and a pipe would hold from lining his purse should the occasion offer, and none would think the worse of a friend who carried it off. One winks and shakes hands, and all is well. It was ever thus in this world.

But, let me say this: I do not *need* the money. I am as well off as I need to be, so if I reap extra rewards *sub tabula*, as it were, it is more for the sport than for the gain.

As soon as I had returned by cabriolet to my Whitehall office, I set my staff the task of seeking the whereabouts of our selected contractors so I could write letters to them post haste. We must find and then commission Servandoni, the designer of the machine for the fireworks. So as to apprise him of the king's designs, I drew a small sketch copied from His Majesty's drawing of what I thought was expected, this to be included in my letter. And the design and firing of the display needs must be in the hands of the Ruggieri, the so-called pyrotechnicians, so we must find them as well, and bring one of 'em here. Again, a small sketch would apprise them of the king's demands.

Foremost amongst all my duties, and one not to be put off too long, would be to inform Charles Frederick, the Surveyor-General of the Ordnance, of these machinations, for 'twas upon his shoulders that the king's great incubus would roost. That duty I would do on the morrow. Though highly competent—and I'd not have recommended him for the post to the prime minister else—Frederick is not the most commanding of figures. He is a scholarly man of slight stature who is more at home with books than cannon, but yet he is of a flexible nature and learns quickly.[3] I was in no way anxious that the load would tax him o'er much, but I did feel even then that he would benefit from my firm support and guidance. Done well, this enterprise might well net him a knighthood, and I would see to it that the slips for his launching would be well greased.

Charles would need many artificers to build the great machine and merchants to procure the materials for it. He would need craftsmen to execute the king's designs, though I was certain that Servandoni would agree upon the men I had in mind. And how ever much gunpowder and other combustible materials would be required? Was there enough in store? And what skills had we at the Laboratory in Woolwich to see to the fabrication of the rockets, and the fountains, wheels, gerbs and whatnot? And Charles would need cannon for the salute, although that might be the easiest of his tasks, the gunners being stood-down and eating half-pay pudding. And, though the king had not said so, should there not be music?

I have connections everywhere in the city to draw upon, so I set my machine in motion, and a great deal of busyness started to take place. I made lists of all the requirements for the execution of the plan and determined to see to each entry thereon by visiting the specialists in question. I took myself off to Lombard Street to apprise the bank of my account and to arrange the issue of bank notes of fifty guineas to defray the expenses of Servandoni and the Ruggieri in their travels. The bank notes would also act as promissory of our intentions. Dangling coin is ever the way to snare the fish. I would need to call soon on Captain Thomas Desaguliers, the Chief Firemaster, to apprise him of the plan and to enlist the people at the Armoury in procuring supplies of materials. And, oh my God, the great wooden structure the king had sketched out! And I would need long audiences with His Majesty so we could work out in greater detail the elements of the design he had in mind. Much, much more I would need to accomplish in the weeks that followed, feeling all the time the pressing need for haste. All this I would be obliged to record meticulously so that at the end of the day, the books being examined, all would be seen to be in order.

'Don't spare the purse for want of a few guineas,' I had heard His Majesty say. I would not, and the books *would* balance.

Chapter Three

Charles Frederick (1709 to 1785)
Surveyor-General of the Ordnance

In which the Surveyor-General of the Ordnance is apprised of his role

I am a scholar, an artist and an antiquary. I am neither politician nor military man, yet I represent the influential burghers of New Shoreham as their Member of Parliament—though they scarce see me—and I am the Surveyor-General of the Ordnance. How *did* this all come about? Well, everyone knows that if the various departments of the government are to run well and smoothly, the prime minister needs must approve the royal appointment of an educated man of the right position and standing. I was given the nod by Henry Pelham on the recommendation of John Montagu, who knows this function only too well. Montagu is the kindliest and most thoughtful man I know, and even though there is the air of a rascal about him, he is solid, reliable and true.

In the Ordnance, we have our staff beneath us to organise the affairs of our departments, and all sails on as well as might be. And I intend by this service to the country and the Crown to see my way to a title. But, it doth seem to me that if one is charged with the office of Surveyor-General of the Ordnance, it would do well to do one's homework and learn a thing or two of the business. So, I would visit the Tower of London and the Arsenal at Woolwich on occasion, inspect the tools and materials, and ask as many questions as I considered fit to give me knowledge of the workings of the artillery. I have been particularly enamoured of gunpowder and all its multifarious uses, not the least of which is the making of fireworks. News of the sovereign's great plan had trickled down to me, of course, but it was not 'til Montagu strode into my office in

Whitehall that I became apprised of the extent of it.

I was delighted when, shaking the rain off his cape and splashing the papers and notes upon my desk, he plunked himself down and unrolled a paper wrapped in oilskin. Sweeping my work aside, he spread out the king's grand firework plan.

'This is but a sketch; 'twill change as the king and I work upon it, but take it as the plan.'

My delight grew boundless when I saw before me a classical temple upon Doric lines, which must be constructed to display the fireworks. I delight in the architecture of the ancients; whilst yet young, my brother John and I took a Grand Tour to Rome and Constantinople, laying the ground for an enduring passion and also learning much of the language and habits of those climes.[4] To be involved in the re-creation of such a classical structure here in London was heaven indeed.

'Ah, this is excellent!' I cried. ''Tis much bruited about in Whitehall, and Woolwich knows of it, though here we see the meat of it!'

'Aye, just so. The meat, the vegetables, the poultry, the whole damned banquet of it.'

'And when is this wanted?' I asked.

'It must be all ready by the end of April next year at the latest. For then is the anniversary of the Peace.'

I was dumbstruck for a moment at this news, for it seemed to me precipitate in the extreme.

'Fireworks,' he continued into my silence, 'will be under the direction of one of the Ruggieri brothers, Bolognaise gentlemen who work in Paris, and decoration of the edifice will be the charge of Chevalier Servandoni, a Frenchman also invited from Paris. I see you nod.'

'Oh, aye, I know of 'em, Servandoni particularly; who in architecture and theatre doth not? Foreigners both of 'em.'

'What of that?'

'Diplomacy, eh?' I replied. 'Seems to me there might be friction…'

'Not between the two of 'em; they've worked together for years.'

'You slip sideways from my meaning, sir. Us. English, frogs, maccaronis, there's where you'll see friction.'

I felt I'd hit a sore point, but I saw that John Montagu was not to be so deflected. 'Now, there are two aspects of this construction that will engage you,' he cried, all business. 'First, the firing of the display will be under the direction of Signor Ruggieri, who will, of course, require workers to make the fireworks and set fire to the damned things or whatever it is they do. This function will be under the charge of Tom Desaguliers of the Laboratory, but it will be your artillerymen who will need drilling and instruction. Until Ruggieri is here, though, naught can be done in that regard.'

'Thomas Desaguliers is to work with Ruggieri?'

'Yes. That is precisely what I said. Why so quizzical?'

'There have been long discussions at the Laboratory regarding the nature of royal fireworks, particularly their military versus er… entertainment role. Captain Desaguliers is of the opinion that…'

'Now, look 'e here, Charles. You spend o'er much interest in the workings of those beneath you. Feathers can be ruffled and backs put up by too much… aye, I won't call it interference quite but interest certainly.'

'But should I not show *some* interest at least?' I asked.

'Yes, but no. 'Tis a sinecure, this post of Surveyor-General. The ship is well enough in the water without extra puffs of wayward wind or, God help us, another man at the tiller. The workings of government are such that smooth running is assured, not by *doing* something but by quite the reverse process.'

'So, the Laboratory and Ruggieri are expected to cooperate?' He nodded. 'With no intervention from me?' He nodded again. 'So, there is nothing to do now… except perhaps fret.'

'Fret why?' he sniffed.

'The friction of which we just spoke…'

'Will *not* be permitted to interfere with the expedition of this endeavour. And there's an end to 't.' His arms crossed over his chest signalled a closed paragraph in our discourse.

'And the other aspect?' It was his turn to look quizzical. 'Of my engagement?'

'Yes, yes. This thing…' and he slapped the paper with his

fingers, 'will need to be built in the Green Park. Jas Morris, our Master Carpenter, will need mustering to the park with tools and materials, for it's a vast undertaking. The ground must be surveyed and levelled and preparations made.'

'I will have him here to give instruction. I'll also need to apprise Wilkinson and Earle.' Andrew Wilkinson was the Storekeeper of the Ordnance, and William Rawlinson Earle was the Clerk of the Cheque. One would see to the supplies and the other the financing.

'Set an appointment with Wilkinson and Earle, and apprise me. Then send Morris a summons. I will furnish you with a copy of this paper. See that he makes a start on the ground and begins to consider his requirements. We have the size of the machine and its placing in the Green Park. That's all that's needed at present. The rest must wait for Servandoni and Ruggieri.'

'This needs expedition on my part,' said I with an air of industriousness and zeal, albeit more theatre than substance.

'Charles, Charles, Charles.' He wagged a finger. 'How oft must I tell you that nothing in your purview *ever* requires expedition? Should there be a need for haste, you will have your underlings do the hastening. Morris hath need of haste; you do not.' He paused. 'There is, however, another matter that will need thought.'

'But not *expeditious* thought?'

'Just so. Not expeditious. His Majesty expects the Train of Artillery for a 101-gun salute, so you shall be responsible for that when the time comes.'

'So be it. Nothing to be done at this instant.'

'No, nothing. Well… not quite nothing,' he said, rolling up his paper and pulling his watch out of its fob. 'I feel 'tis time for a far more important matter. Never too early for coffee and a pipe. Let's away.'

I looked a little nervously at my scattered papers, reasoned that they, too, could benefit from a studied lack of expediency, and accompanied him out of the office and down the stairs.

Chapter Four

Captain Thomas Desaguliers (1721 to 1780)
Chief Firemaster of His Majesty's Royal Laboratory

In which the disposition of the fireworks becomes a matter of dispute

I dislike Montagu. Blasted popinjay! Here's a man filled with frivolity and ribaldry, with not one original thought to cross his brow. Everything to him is a jest, and everyone with whom he is in contact is a target for his japes. He salts his guests' beds with irritating powders, he foists frauds and hoaxes upon the public, and soaks colleagues and visitors with squirts of water. Why, even his mother-in-law said that he is a fifteen-year-old in the frame of a man. Then there was the lunatic troop of cavalry he got up for Culloden, by the mercy of God, so ill trained they were never mustered. A boy playing with soldiers. And now, in damnation, he's playing soldiers with me! 'Tis bad enough that I am subservient to him in my duties at the Arsenal in Woolwich, but in God's name, his post is but a sinecure, and everybody knows it. The king favours him too far, giving him the pension of posts for which he is both ill-equipped and indifferent. The man knows naught of my craft, though 'til now, he's had at least wit enough not to interfere.

That's more than can be said of that meddling nuisance Charles Frederick, the newly-appointed Surveyor-General of the Ordnance. He would do well to enjoy his sinecure, stay rooted in Whitehall, and keep his nose out of Woolwich and the Tower. Leave the true work of the Ordnance to the professionals who make a life study of it. I've heard tell that since Frederick learned of the king's design for a great firework display, he hath been enamoured of gunpowder, squibs and rockets, and regales all and sundry with tales of how this vast show will rival the spectacles of Rome. For God's sake, a few fireworks, a machine to launch 'em from, a few hours of fire and smoke; nothing the Laboratory hath not done before and will likely do again without all the fuss.

But Frederick—and Montagu above him—are my superiors, and I would do well to reflect upon how fortunate I am to be in this position. I know I am yet young, being not yet five-and-twenty and a mere captain, but that makes me in no way inferior or callow. Certainly, the Board of Ordnance placed me in this position through my family's position, but such an appointment would never have been made if they knew not my worth. I'm like my late-lamented father in this respect, that I take on my craft with an analytical and serious intent and make advances in it by reason and study. There is no improvement to be made in artillery without sound knowledge of principles and stern practice. And that comes from me, not some titled nincompoops in London.

And now Montagu had written to me on a matter of some urgency regarding the fireworks. I knew he'd raise it before long, for it's been the talk of the Laboratory for some time. You can be sure that if Frederick knows it, all and sundry down to the cleaners of privies know of it. I wrote back straightway that I was busy upon some matter of cannon founding and measurement, which was not susceptible of interruption. I was too occupied to attend him, so let him take a boat to Woolwich if the matter be so urgent. But why in God's name the king hath given the charge of the affair to Montagu is beyond my comprehension. Why, 'tis below his station; 'tis even below Frederick's. It is clearly the role of the Royal Laboratory to stage firework demonstrations, as we have done in Hyde Park for many a year.

The cock's-comb came to Laboratory Square a day in November with a roll of paper tucked under his arm. I met him at my office door in the Warren, which is what they call the mess of buildings that have grown up around here. Montagu fussed in, removed his cape, sat himself down in *my* chair and crossed his legs. As I took his cape to hang, I clenched my jaw and ground my teeth hard, for I wished to present as polite a countenance as I could. It doth one's advancement and career no good to cross with those who have the ear of the king.

'To what great pleasure may I attribute your visit?' I asked, all gun oil and with face a mask, whilst I poured him a glass of Madeira. I knew damned well; the whole Laboratory did.

'As you know, His Majesty hath charged me with the organisation of his fireworks, which will take place this coming April in the Green

Park next his palace.'

'Of course. We talk of nothing else.' My irony appeared lost on him. 'I will provide lists of firework products, their kind and the number of them, and I will instruct the hands at the Laboratory to begin their fabrication. I suspect we must place a special order at the mill at Waltham for the correct powders.'

'Ah, it is perhaps not quite so straightforward.' I detected a reticence in his face and in the eyes that failed to meet mine.

'It will be all in hand,' I assured him. 'Not unlike any other royal occasion for which we provide the entertainment, surely?'

'Ah, but the king hath created a grand design; a vast temple of classical proportions...' And here he rolled out the paper he had with him onto my desk. 'This is His Majesty's sketch. It is to be decorated and furnished by Giovanni Servandoni, a Frenchman, and the fireworks to be placed upon it.'

I understood his reticence. Laying out our mortars, rocket frames, fountains and gerbs upon the ground was our style, but this was clearly to be on a scale vaster than any we had accomplished thus far. It looked to be an enormous structure of great height, though yet only a sketch. I had heard of these things in France and Russia, of course, but our gunners always resisted the meddling influence of the theatre; putting artistry into artillery, for God's sake. But thinking deeper, I had great misgivings. How would we contrive to ignite our fireworks on such a structure? How could we coordinate and compose our sequences and our timing? In my visit to St Petersburg, I had seen plans and manifests for the extravagant firework celebrations of the Empress Elizabeth's coronation, a thoroughly French affair, as was everything they did in Russia. But we could not possibly rival those, and I prayed we would not have to.

'It rivals those great erections of the King of France...'

'Betters them...'

'Even so, nothing we can not accomplish,' I replied, swallowing hard and telling perhaps the biggest lie of my short career, then falling back upon the practicalities of the structure itself. 'The building of it may be placed in the charge of James Morris, the Master Carpenter to this office. Though in the past, he hath built frames and structures of a modest sort, this is far from beyond his capabilities. He hath been called upon to raise the masts of ships. He will need better than this sketch, though.'

'That will be furnished. And Frederick will apprise Morris of this directly.' He paused as if steeling himself. 'As to the number and disposition of the fireworks, that decision will not be in the Laboratory's hands.'

'Not? Why not, pray?' Now I knew the true source of his reticence; 'twas spelt on his guileless face. 'Surely, not Benjamin Brock? Or Mr Pain? They are small fry and, besides, they flirt with the law.'[5]

'Flirt, sir? How so?'

'There is a statute on the books that expressly forbids the making of squibs, rockets or any other gunpowder devices save by the Royal Laboratory.'

'But honoured more in the breach than the observance, surely?' He smiled, somewhat archly, I thought. 'Look at the entertainments at Cuper's, Ranelagh, Vauxhall…'

'Aye, but this is a *royal* endeavour. If it will not be in the Laboratory's hands, it will certainly not be in the hands of scofflaws. Then in whose?'

He took a long, slow breath through his nose. 'The firework is to be in the design of Signor Gaetano Ruggieri, who the king hath contracted in this endeavour.'

Ruggieri! Of course. I kept my face immobile.

'His family,' he continued, 'has answered His Majesty's letter and has nominated Gaetano to attend us.'

The Ruggieri family were everywhere; Bolognaise by extraction but adopted by the French, dominating King Louis's entertainments these twenty years. But did our king not value his Chief Firemaster? Why did he think to bring this Italian mountebank to teach us our own craft? Gunners have ever controlled all uses of royal gunpowder in this entire realm, and there was no need to change that now. Though I confess I had seen this coming for some time, and Montagu's news was no surprise to me, it came like a cannonade nonetheless. The whole of Europe was enamoured of these Italian artificers who weave artistry into the pyrotechnical arts, calling 'emselves pyrotechnicians. Everywhere the art of the gunners was being supplanted by specialists who do nothing else but put on spectacles. I would stand firm; I would not have our secrets, our specific craft, our knowledge of powders and the art of fire, go to naught in an onslaught from France.

Yet, whilst I vowed to stand firm, there was a strange conflict within me. Firstly, there was my strong concern as to how we would bring this about ourselves, if we so insisted. It would be an enormous undertaking with techniques never tried by us. But, secondly, and perhaps more difficult to reconcile, was a deep curiosity. How did they arrange their displays, how was the timing effected, what systems of fusing and ignition did they employ? In short, what secrets might we at Woolwich not become privy to? Nevertheless, the firm stance remained foremost, young fool that I was.

'What truck do we have with the French in this matter?'

'His Majesty hath it that they are the best at this craft and must be brought here to serve him.'

'Is he not satisfied, then, with the displays Woolwich hath staged?'

'Oh, yes, yes! Of course,' he fuffed. 'But he sees this as a spectacle of far greater compass…'

'…than his own men are capable of putting on,' I finished for him, insecure in my confidence and doubting that we would be able to pull it off ourselves.

'I knew not there would be such a conflict,' he sighed, though I was certain he knew only too well what might come to pass between us. Who could fail to ignore the ribaldry in the pamphlets and news-papers upon all things foreign?

'Besides,' he continued, 'the matter is settled. Ruggieri is already sent for from France.'

'The same nation we were lately at war with, and now we must fall over ourselves to give them favour?'

'We are now at peace…'

'Oh, aye, I'd quite forgot we had signed a paper this last year. So, all is now serene.'

'Do you, sir, gainsay your king?'

'No, I do not, *sir!*' The foolish man had squeezed my trigger. 'And don't you dare imply so. I fought with Cumberland at Fontenoy; I fought for my king and for my nation whilst others fussed with papers in Whitehall or went to the play in Drury Lane. We were beaten then, and I'm damned if they'll beat us now!'

'You, young man, are impertinent!'

'And you, sir, are forward!'

'Oh, come, come.' He flapped his hands as if trying to douse the flames he had unwittingly ignited, though 'twas more like to fan them. ''Tis but a firework show…' Indeed, the firework show was right there in my office.

'It is a matter of solid principle,' I replied, 'which you, as a politician, might perhaps find hard to grasp.' I was treading close to that very line I had earlier eschewed.

'But, the king…'

'The matter is between you and he. I will serve His Majesty in this endeavour, as I have ever done. Ruggieri may select the number and disposition of the fireworks, but their fabrication and their firing are to be in the hands of the Chief Firemaster and no other.'

'I don't doubt but the king will be most displeased…'

'That is for you to see to. 'Tis no concern of mine. You, sir, are the diplomat; I am but His Majesty's humble servant. Come, let me help you with your cloak.'

As soon as he left the room, I paced a while, then stood before my window chin in hand. I considered myself fortunate that a mere captain had spoken in this fashion to his superior and remained unscathed. I was foolish to have so lost mastery of myself. But no mistake, I was twixt Scylla and Charybdis; should I bow to this Italian from France and put all the tools of the Laboratory at his disposal, or should I stand by our craft and strive to have Woolwich pull off the staging of it?

Had I a choice? Was my stand to Montagu mere bluster?

Damnation!

CHAPTER FIVE

James Morris (c. 1700 to c. 1760)
Master Carpenter to the Office of the Ordnance

In which the Master Carpenter comes to the realisation of the enormity of his task

I am a man of my hands. Even so, my position with the Ordnance is quite raised from my family's humble roots. My grandfather was a simple bricklayer, who passed his craft on to his son, Roger Morris.[6] Now, my father got his start by building his own house, and such a job he made of it that gentlemen were asking after him. Building and selling, building and selling; that's what helped him work his way up, but then he was employed by Colen Campbell and Henry Herbert. After that the work came thick and fast, and he rose in the ranks of society. Such was his standing, he was granted the place of Master Carpenter before me, and though 'twas more an honorary position, he knew the craft backwards and forwards. And he'd brought me up with tools and materials since I was in frocks. So, when he took to his bed—not likely to rise again until he meets our immortal Maker, rest his soul—he sued the Ordnance for my preferment in his stead.

They pay me near £3,000 a year as Master Carpenter, but I don't do a damned bit of woodwork. I do, though, know how 'tis done and how it ought to be done. I oversee, organise and instruct, which is a lot more than most in these preferred positions can put their hands to. Captain Desaguliers is one like me; he won his preferment through his father, but by God, he knows what's what. Half my age, well tried in battle and now Chief Firemaster! Quite often, with the rank of captain and above, it's some rich pa who's paid for his son's commission—most likely to keep 'im out of the way—and a useless shower of incompetent arse-wipes they are. The army couldn't perform without its NCOs giving "advice" to those fops above 'em who've bought their colours and know nothing. With them 'tis the exact contrary to merit: appointments are made by *who* you know and what you *don't* know. As I say, though, Desaguliers is cut of a different cloth altogether.

I oversee all the woodwork for the Office of Ordnance—mostly gun carriages and limbers, though the work comes and goes with the need—reporting to Charles Frederick, although that's a formality. He wouldn't know an auger from his own arsehole, but give him his due, he leaves me alone to run my department, and that's fine by me. Or, at least, he did until this damned firework thing. Normally, I have more business with Captain Desaguliers, mostly in the development of artillery carriages to his design because his research in the Laboratory encompasses all aspects of the operation of cannon. We've built sheds and warehouses for the Storekeeper's Department as well and divers racks and shelves. Anything made of wood, my workshop takes it on. We've also built frames of various kinds for the captain's firework devices, and that's where the story began for me.

Charles Frederick summoned me to Whitehall early in November to have me fully informed of the firework plans. It was all the talk of the Warren, and some wild ideas were flying about. But it was certain that whatever came to pass, we would be deeply into it before too long. I rose early and took a boat up from Woolwich in a cold, pissing rain, alighting at a jetty a stone's throw from the new Westminster Bridge, not yet open and crawling with workmen effecting repairs. I heard tell one of the piers had subsided, doubtless due to the ignorance of the Swiss chap tasked with the project. It's taken years to get this bridge of fools open, and still it waits. Wants a stout Englishman at the helm, in my opinion.

I strode up from the river, getting to the Whitehall building late in the forenoon. I was shown up to Frederick's office where some lackey of his took my cape away for drying out. Frederick rolled a sketch plan out onto a table, and I have to tell you right off, I was stricken terrified. Yes, sheds and warehouses, certainly racks for rockets, I can build them. But nothing like this! The thing was monstrous; more 'n 400 feet long by a hundred high, and all in wood.

'And where is this to be built, sir?'

''Tis to be built upon the Green Park in front of St. James's Palace,' he told me. 'Five hundred feet from the palace at most. Is it not the most remarkable thing?' He positively bubbled. 'We shall rival—nay, exceed—the pomp and spectacle of the ancients!'

I nodded simply, looking over the plan in silence whilst I thought how like my father's designs this thing would be. He took the forms of classical architecture, using mostly the Doric order, and refined them with good English taste and sensibility. As I mulled this over, I was doing a rough calculation of what lumber might be needed, how the scaffolding would go, what great swathes of sailcloth would cover it, and what ironwork and suchlike we'd have to find to hold the damned thing together. 'Twas, at first flush, a highly pessimistic evaluation, let me tell you.

'Well, Mr Morris? What say you?' he said into my silence. 'Is it not wonderful that we are charged with creating such a structure?' I was a bit worried about the "we." I knew the man was an antiquary and dabbled in all sorts of ancient matters, but I'd rather be left on my own to see to the building of this. Enthusiasm misdirected is a chisel in the hands of a babe.

'Aye, 'tis a fine conceit, sir. As 'tis but a temporary structure, 'twould be sufficient to frame it in wood and sheet in with canvas white-washed to suit…'

'The details you may decide in good time,' he interrupted, 'for it is no business of mine. I have only to report that this thing can be done and that we at the Ordnance are fit to undertake it. Well?'

'When is this wanted, sir?' I asked, for that was the question that trumped all others.

'Not later than the middle of April.' Now that news, I can swear to you, liked to shrivel the hairs off my bum. Impossible!

'But that's scarcely more 'n five months away, sir,' I said, rather blurting my thoughts instead of keeping me trap shut. 'And we must work through the most ill of weathers.'

'Then 'twere best to be expeditious,' he replied, rolling the word "expeditious" around his mouth like he was savouring it. 'You must first examine the site. This plan is but preliminary, though it will suffice for the present. I will not accompany you,' he continued, glancing at the streaming window pane with little else visible beyond it, 'for I have important work to conduct for this office. Report here later.'

I wasn't where I'd got to by shirking a challenge, and, besides, you don't disobey orders no matter how foolish they are or how foolish the mouths they issue from. So, I took myself off without delay in the pouring rain, with my cape scarce slightly dried, passed through Horse Guards and walked the length of St. James's Park. The Green Park opens off St. James's to the north and is roughly triangular, with the Queen's walk and Piccadilly as two of the sides. I turned onto the Queen's Walk and then, facing away from the palace, I paced out my guess of 500 feet on the grass. Where I stopped, the ground rose somewhat to the north and fell slightly to the south, but this would take slight effort to level, removing half the overburden and using it as fill for the other half. There were no trees of any size, as this land had been long laid out as a promenade. Preparation, at least, would take no trouble. Turning to face the palace, I was apprised of the view of the fireworks to be gotten from its windows.

I had the vision of a stray rocket…

Aye, well.

I squelched back to Whitehall to report what few findings I had. The more I thought on it, the more fantastical it seemed. I imagined me and my men working in conditions such as these and perhaps even sleet or snow. Better not to dwell upon it, I thought, but to buckle down and see it through. I dripped and slopped my way into Frederick's office, slyly amused at his face when he saw my puddles all over his fine floor.

'Well, Morris, what are your thoughts?'

''Tis an easy site to prepare, sir, but all the stores I have at Woolwich lack enough timber for the job. We'll have to search far and wide for more, especially at this stormy season, as most comes from the Dutch.'

'Dutch? Why? Do we not have enough timber here, but we must bring it from the Low Countries?'

'There's not a lot of big stands of timber in England nowadays, sir. The Dutch bring it from the Baltic, and 'tis cheaper.'

'Cheaper, how?'

'We use pit sawyers, sir, whereas the Dutch mill it mechanical.'

'Well, you know best, but see to it we have enough,' said he, ridding himself of a problem he didn't have the wit to comprehend. 'You would do well to begin in the park as soon as may be, for we are driven by His Majesty's will.'

He showed me quickly to the door and gave me the king's plan to take away to Woolwich, much good such a sketch would do at this stage, but it was a start.

Where in the name of Jesus' nose would I begin?

Chapter Six

Captain Thomas Desaguliers (1721 to 1780)
Chief Firemaster of His Majesty's Royal Laboratory

In which the captain is pestered upon the nature of fireworks and becomes a reluctant tutor, though in philosophical opposition

I wish to God that Thomas Lascelles had not resigned his post as Chief Royal Engineer last year, though I know he was failing in health. He was a man of enormous experience and expertise, and he knew the operations of this Laboratory intimately. But he had this attribute, that with all these sterling qualifications—and of a matter quite paradoxical—he left the Laboratory to its own devices. He was ever my champion, and though he underpinned the work of this division, he was never one to interfere, control or direct according to his own will. It is the character of a true leader that he sees the worth of those below him yet gives that worth full rein. This is utterly contrary to our present leaders, for our figureheads are now politicians, not fighting men. The cock's-comb Montagu I discount, for his appointment hath no bearing upon us either at Woolwich or the Tower.

Mr Frederick, on the other hand, is closer to our workings and hath the view that he must have his nose into our doings. That is his failing; a military man who knows our workings is one thing, but a man of letters who knows nothing would far better hold off. He shows an immense and driving curiosity, but, unlike us at the Laboratory, he is of such a contrary philosophical bent that all his delving and researching is worthless. For him, knowledge is a thing and an end unto itself; he seeks to know for the satisfaction of knowing, not for the use to which he can put the knowledge. He is an authority on old French coins, he publishes monographs upon ancient architecture, he engraves drawings of churches and monuments. All of this is knowledge, acquired, sifted and disseminated but in essence useless; it is of the past, and its accumulation changes nothing. This is contrary to the work of the

Laboratory—my work—which seeks to understand our world, dissect it, and learn from it. This is why, when Mr Frederick beards me, I shudder to waste my time, for I know that nothing constructive will come of it.

It was not long after Montagu sprang the Ruggieri trap upon me that Frederick sent a note that he would visit my office in the Warren. He'd been waxing lyrical about fireworks and spectacles and ancient monuments to anyone who would listen but, until now, confined it to the bored ears of cronies in Whitehall and the clubs and coffee houses of the city. As soon as I read his note, my heart sank into my boots. The boat journey down the Thames to Woolwich provides a very valuable degree of quarantine, so I knew that whatever mission he was upon, it must have some great importance. Supplies for the project were in the care of the Storekeeper, Andrew Wilkinson, and Jas Morris was building the machine, so that just left the fireworks, the making of which was in my capable hands. No technical conversation upon that subject was warranted, and whilst Ruggieri was still on his way, clearly nothing was left to discuss.

He entered my office, and I anticipated a swift solution to the mystery of his presence. He hung his wet topcoat and hat on the hook by the door and took a seat. I was busy with the measurements of three rocket cases and had the measuring tools, notepad and pencil laid out upon my desk. His eyes lit up when he saw them.

'I bid you welcome, sir,' I said, and seeing the wet patches where his coat had failed to cover him, I added, 'and I hope your river passage was tolerable.'

"Tis never more than tolerable. Today 'twas hateful, but such is the urgency of my mission I needs must do it.' But withal he didn't sound at all put out; quite the reverse.

'Urgency, sir?' What in God's name could be so urgent as to bring him here under duress and yet happily?

'Yes, urgency!' His face showed some inner fire. 'I would know the nature of gunpowder, for it fascinates the scholar in me. How it is formed, whence come the earths that make it, the whole art of it. That is my urgency!'

Relief that there was no real urgency—no critical passage that needed my attention—was coupled with irritation at the time I might well waste on a thing which was to me frivolous. Frederick's boundless enthusiasm and thirst for mere knowledge were what was to be foisted upon me this day. Damnation to be overseen by a busybody! This was worse than that nuisance Robert Jones, a lieutenant in the Artillery who haunts the Laboratory in his off-duty hours, which are far too many, in my estimation.[7] Unlike Jones, I was obliged to treat Frederick with politeness, for, whatever his qualities, he must be answered to.

'Surely, sir,' I replied, perhaps a little too forthrightly, 'is it not beneath your station to so enquire?'

'No, no, Captain! If I am charged with the Ordnance, it is fitting that I know all its workings. Gunpowder is no exception.'

'True, sir, but 'tis an arcane craft…'

'*Arcane,* you say?' and his eyes veritably lit up. 'Then I would have you tell me all!'

I tried not to betray my sigh for the idiot choice of words, for I knew that with one who knew nothing, I was in for a long discourse. 'I suppose one starts with the receipt. Gunpowder is made of but three elements: saltpetre, charcoal and brimstone…'

'How doth the deflagration pass so swiftly in it?'

'The saltpetre, which we also call nitre, contains proportions of both air and water, and it is violently rarified by the burning of the charcoal and brimstone, so giving a kind of fiery explosive blast.'

'So, these elements are driven from each other?'

'Forcibly. As the saltpetre vaporises, so its elements act like a bellows, swiftly blowing off the brimstone and charcoal in flame and vapour.'

'The key to the quintessence!' he breathed. 'Earth, air and water passing into fire!'

I forbore explaining that recent natural philosophy finds much wanting in the general understanding of the elements. That way lay arcane speculation consuming more time than I was prepared to afford.

'To us, sir, 'tis but gunpowder, to wield to our advantage in both war and peace.'

'Just so,' said he, coming down from his elevation. 'That is what goes into these?' he asked, picking up one of the rocket shells from the desk.

'No, sir.' God grant me forbearance, I thought, and guide my face into a look of tolerance. 'Gunpowder is made for use in guns.' As wig powder is for wigs and face powder for faces, I near as damn it said. 'We do use gunpowder for the reports and for passing fire quickly between pieces.'

'So, these contain what then?' He peered down the end, looking slightly disappointed that he found it empty.

'They do contain those three elements, but they are merely mixed, whereas gunpowder is milled with water, dried and mealed.'

'Mealed?'

'Yes, sir. It is ground to a range of fineness, depending upon its use. Finely mealed for muskets and pistols, coarser for larger guns, and in bigger grains still for cannon.'

'I would know more of this mealing.'

'It would be best, then, to visit the powder mill at Waltham Abbey, for that is where all our powder is prepared.' And they would welcome, I doubted not, the time he would waste upon them there.

'And the fireworks? What of their receipts?'

'The three elements are merely mixed finely together,' I said, 'and other elements are added to modify their properties. For example, if a rocket were to be packed with mealed gunpowder, its fire would progress too fast. It would burst. Thus, to the three elements, we add more charcoal in greater or lesser amounts as the size and weight require.'

'You slow the deflagration! But how do you determine this?'

'That is the job of the Laboratory, sir, although we possess many receipts and books that date from earlier times. That is why I say 'tis arcane, sir, for there is much lore and experience passed down from elders to journeymen.'

'And what of the sparkles and twinkles in the fire of candles?' Was there no end to the questions? I wondered.

'We add other elements to the powder, sir. Steel shavings produce fine sparks, and filings of iron will produce sparks of another kind. And lampblack and salt will change the colour of the fire, also.'

There was a great deal more questioning of this sort, too tedious to detail here, whilst my thoughts strayed to the task I had before me on my table, now long delayed. It was nearer two hours than one before he rose from his seat.

'Thank you, Captain. You have helped me a great deal.' He clapped his hands together with great zeal. 'Now, let me see the Laboratory. Lead the way.'

'Just across the quadrangle, sir.' I handed him his well-dried coat from the hook and led the way, creeping most reluctant.

'And then, I'll sit with you and make a firework of my own.'

God grant me the patience of Job, thought I, and smite me with a rash of boils, for such an affliction would be the Balm of Gilead by comparison. Then I thought of a ruse to rid myself of this pest by foisting him off on another. Jones! As we entered the Laboratory, I called to the fore-man.

'Sergeant Jason, find Lieutenant Jones, and bring him here.'

After a wait of some ten minutes, whilst Frederick dabbled around the room in coupled awe and curiosity, Robert Jones reported to us. He is a tall, willowy Welshman of fair complexion and looks not a bit like a soldier of the Crown. His enthusiasm for gunpowder and fireworks is disproportionate, and though his nosiness is irksome, I have not the heart to have him posted elsewhere lest he be of some future use.

I performed the introductions. 'Lieutenant Jones is a keen student of our craft,' I told Frederick, 'and will serve you better than I in instruction.'

With that bare-faced falsehood, I left 'em to 't and got back to the real work of the Ordnance, blast the delay. 'Twas not 'til a week later that Frederick wrote me a note insisting, so impressed was he, that Jones be assigned to the Artillery team that would set the show. Thus was I rewarded for my cleverness. An itch that could not be scratched.

CHAPTER SEVEN

James Morris (c. 1700 to c. 1760)
Master Carpenter to the Office of the Ordnance

In which the ground is surveyed for the great machine, but wood is found wanting

'T was all a bit precipitate. I like best to work from plans, but heeding Fredrick's order that work must start in the Green Park as soon as may be, I took the king's sketch and made a fair copy of it with ruler and pen, lining it out with dimensions. The original would have to go back to the palace, and I wouldn't miss it because, quite honestly, King George was no draughtsman. I figured that to give fair proportion, the central temple structure must be around 140 feet wide. Then the flanking colonnades and the end pavilions would bring it all to around four hundred and ten. A bloody monster and no mistake. Later I would have to calculate the amount of timber I'd need (God help me), but for now the job was to get out to the site as quick as possible and get a start made.

There's no limit to the resources we can muster at the Office of the Ordnance if the king commands it, so within a day, the Corps of Engineers had set things in motion. I would be supplied with an Artificer Company, which was composed of artisans and labourers not in uniform but all commanded by non-commissioned and commissioned officers. For the survey of the site, I had ready all the tools we'd need for a measuring and staking out. On this foray, I'd take a small squad of men. There were tents and cooking stoves, as well as barrels of drink and sacks of meal and dried meat, and so on. 'Twas clear we'd be on site from here on, so farewell Woolwich and my home life until this was done. I mind it was the seventh of November when we threw the lot into a sail barge and set off at the turn of the tide with a reaching wind. We hauled up just downriver of London Bridge—for there was no way a barge could be drawn between the piers in the strong current—loaded a dray drawn up at the jetty, and trundled off to the

Green Park. It was a whole day of toil before we had all the equipment on site. Of course, it was fuckin' raining the whole time, wasn't it? Better, I suppose, than the awful cold that had gripped us earlier in the month.

Now here's a thing: when I'm working in Woolwich, I'm not overseen all that much. I know what I'm doing, the chain of command knows what I'm doing, and I'm left to get on with it. Here, right out in the Green Park, right under the library windows, anyone could see that work was afoot. And, certain it was, the king would have his eye upon his great project. He would have his eye upon me! Now, I don't lack for confidence—didn't get where I am without it—but even so, 'twas quite disconcerting to think that my every move was watched and even remarked upon. I felt all the while like an animalcule under a lens.

The first order of business was to set stakes in the ground to limn out the shape of the beast. This meant an oblong in the middle where the main pavilion would be, then two arms going north and south, with small pavilions at each end. I made the main pavilion dead centre with the library windows. We tapped wood stakes into the ground with a mallet, then stretched a knotted measuring line along to locate the next spot; another stake driven in and so forth. Looking at the lie of the land again whilst we were doing this, I had second thoughts about the levelling. 'Twould be a lot of labour and not much benefit, as there was not above a foot-and-a-half of rise along the whole 410 feet of the thing. Only Constitution Hill rose more above the level, and that was maybe a quarter mile distant. If it were a structure that was meant to last, you'd need a sturdy foundation of some kind, but for a temporary thing, wooden baulks buried in the ground like piles would do. If the wood were to be buried long, it would rot away, but for a few months, it didn't matter a damn.

Staking was all done as dusk came on, and I took the extra trouble of stringing linen tapes between the stakes. Not so I knew the shape, which was passing obvious, but so the shape could be seen from afar by eyes untrained. That was the first day's work, and I hoped the royal eyes drilling into the back of my neck would be happy enough come the early hours of the morrow.

Construction must wait until the Corps of Engineers was mustered and supplies of tools, tentage and cooking facilities could be brought to the site. A standing force of many hundreds would be marching from Woolwich presently, one of the first armies of this or any other century not to bear arms. For muskets they would have hammers, for swords you'd see ripsaws, for bayonets they'd carry chisels. And "Sergeant Major" Morris would have to thrash them into shape in double-quick time.

In the time since I'd been ordered to the endeavour, I had produced lists of all I thought would be needed, but certain it was that I had but the half of it under control. Wood was going to be a severe draw, for that was the greatest of my needs. Then there was the covering. I had calculated the area of canvas duck I would need, for although the structure was of wood in essence, the flat spaces between elements were best filled with sailcloth whitewashed to match. And whilst the decorative parts were being installed and fireworks placed, more duck would be needed to cover 'em against the climate. Then there were fittings, tools of all kinds, and many sundries; a formidable few pages all said and done.

I submitted my estimate lists to Andrew Wilkinson, the Storekeeper, on a visit to Whitehall at the end of the first working day. He was the first point of contact, though for certain the lists would quickly find their way to Woolwich where the professionals worked. It would have been better to submit 'em direct, but that ain't the way it's done. Wilkinson was a large, proud, finely dressed man, who I had encountered a few times before; large in sideways terms, I mean, as these chaps of desks and good living often are. He sat behind about half an acre of polished mahogany in a fine, lofty room all tricked out with books and baubles. I was bidden to sit, and I watched his mouth turn down as he read.

'Damnation! Were we at war, I'd not see such a draw upon our stock. At peace 'tis even more profligate. Where is all this wood coming from?'

'I know not, sir,' I replied, thinking somewhat rebellious that 'twas he not me who should be seeing to the procuring of it. Storekeeper?

'Well, it must be found somewhere. We'll have Montagu look into it. For the rest… yes, Woolwich can see to the bulk of it. I'll send it on.'

Though I knew it already, here was delegation made plain. Sure, the Duke of Montagu was charged with the organising, but precious little he'd know. He'd pass it on to Frederick, then down to Woolwich anyhow, would he not? Aye, the chain of command!

Wilkinson harrumphed and blew out his cheeks, but there was nothing he could say or do, of course. The stuff was needed, and it was by royal command. I'd swear he was thinking of wastage, when so much of our work is constructive and beneficial. Or belike he was thinking what a nuisance all this was and how it was keeping him from his clubs and his soirées.

I left his office and took myself off to the river, deep in thought. There would be a military camp pitched right there in the Green Park, and I imagined that royalty and His Majesty's court would be mighty put out about the disturbance before all this was done. Mustering of these forces was in the hands of Charles Frederick, although I hoped most sincerely that he and his Whitehall wigs had delegated the work to the professionals in the Board of Ordnance. He was better writing poetry or fiddling with old coins than having truck with quartermasters, but there's no accounting for politics. I just prayed that mustering would be expeditious because time was pressing, and I felt the king a-breathing down my neck.

This was like nothing I'd done before—indeed like nothing any of us had done before—so we were exploring new territory.

Chapter Eight

John, 2nd Duke of Montagu (1690 to 1749)
Master-General of His Majesty's Ordnance

In which building supplies are ensured, and the king becomes impatient

Wood, lumber, timber, deal, call it what you will, in God's name, I had got myself involved in it. Me, a titled gentleman, privy to the king, habitué and advisor to the court, holder of powerful offices, bartering and dealing like a common tradesman. It certainly did not set off that way. When Wilkinson told me that wood was wanting for the machine, I should have damned his eyes and told him that I had thought, as he was Storekeeper of the Ordnance, 'twas his job to find it. If Morris wanted wood, Andrew was the man. But I held my peace.

There the matter might have rested had I not recalled a conversation with William Hogarth, the Foundling Hospital governor. I am a governor myself, having signed Thomas Coram's second petition to the king in 1737, along with half the nobility and society. 'Twas a fashionable thing to do, true, but I still set aside some money for his cause, for I feel the need of those less lucky than I. Some time past, I recalled discussing certain shares Hogarth had purchased to his chagrin because they had somehow become worthless. Was there not a bankrupt sawmill in Limehouse?

My curiosity being piqued, I sent Hogarth a note asking in a roundabout way upon the sources of timber. If he held shares, he would get my drift. I smelt some advantage here, and my nose is ever acute. William Hogarth is wonderfully sensitive to the poor, the destitute and the sick, and he makes their fate, and the alleviating of it, a reforming passion. Nonetheless, he's become very wealthy in the expression of this passion in the making of paintings, prints and drawings, which have a lively sale value. I knew he invested in stocks, though after the collapse of the South Sea Scheme, I wondered at his continuing dealing in such fickle enterprises.[8]

We met of a forenoon, a day or so later, Hogarth and I, in a coffee house in Lamb's Conduit Street, not far from the hospital. Coffee houses are better places for important discussion, being much quieter than ale houses. That being said, it rather depends upon the time of day and who frequents a particular place. I'd never dream of meeting for serious talk in a place like the Bedford or Slaughters; if a rowdy crowd was in, y'd choke to death on smoke and lose your hearing ere you spoke a syllable. Before noon, away from the hurly-burly of Covent Garden and Leicester Fields, we had but the heady aroma of the roast, quietness save for the whirr of the grinder and a booth to ourselves. Our waiter provided the materials quite smartly and took himself off. I poured from our four-penny pot of coffee and watched Hogarth drop pebbles of Demerara sugar into it 'til it must have quite taken away the flavour of the beans. We picked up our cups without words between us and, for a few moments, sipped slowly lest we disturb the grounds.

'Fireworks?' he broke the silence with a laugh. 'You? Fireworks? 'Tis fine talk about the coffee houses, let me tell you. Montagu and fireworks! Hah!'

'I am doing my sovereign's bidding in this matter as Master-General of the Ordnance,' I said, a bit stuffy. 'Besides, Charles Frederick is charged with the organising of it.'

'Frederick! There's a mighty enthusiast for you. Know what I heard of Walpole 't other day? He said to me: "I wish you could see him making squibs, all bronzed over with a patina of gunpowder." Making squibs! Frederick!' And he barked with laughter.

'Charles doth rather take to this task with enthusiasm.' He laughed again, and we lapsed into silence over our coffee. I silently damned Charles for making a fool of himself.

Hogarth spoke first, for I had long remarked the curiosity growing in his face. 'You came not here to jest upon squibs and serpents. So, timber. What's your line? Have ye lowered your station to dabbling as well?'

'Yes, timber. We'll need lots of it for the machine.'

'Machine?'

''Tis the word used to describe the structure that displays the fireworks.'

'Ah.' He sipped. 'Lots of wood to be had if the price is right.'

'Where would one buy timber?' I asked, feeling not a little out of my sphere.

'Holland mostly.' He was perplexed at my line of enquiry. 'They mill it there mechanical; wind sawmills. Swedish stock. Can't beat Dutch prices. Twelve pound the ton.'

'Was it not you who told me of a troubled mill in Limehouse?' I saw comprehension and wariness cross his face, one on the coat tails of t' other.

'Aye, that I did. What of it?'

I paused to sip some more, then looked up from my cup. 'If the price was right, it could surely serve us. This mill…?'

It was his turn to pause and sip and mine to wait on the thoughts crossing his mind. He put his cup down and came to a decision.

'Charles Dingley's in Limehouse. Lies derelict, and the profit on my shares with it.'

'Can not this Dingley make repairs? Is he wanting of financial backing?'

''Tis not money he wants. He durst not repair for fear of the mob.'

'Fear of the mob! What mob, in Christ's name?'

'The pit sawyers are legion and mighty militant. There's many a mill smashed up by labourers who see their work taken off 'em. Wood mills ever have a hard time of it in England. Dingley wants none of it.'[9]

'If his mill were working, would it not make timber cheaper?'

'Course. Either mill what little we have here, or bring in rough logs from the Baltic. No Dutch middlemen. Half the price. Less than half, even. But what's your business with this?'

'So, milling here, you would recover the value of your shares…'

'Montagu, my friend,' he said to me, putting his cup down gently upon the board, ''tis a pity you can not work miracles, for that's quite what's needed.'

All this time, I was thinking mighty quick. If this mill could be repaired in time and rough timber found to feed it, I could well detach a squad of fusiliers from the Tower to protect it. The army was stood-down since the Peace, and those still on the payroll were at half pay, so it would be almost no inconvenience to deploy them. However, should the king hear of this scheme, he might think it amiss without a full account, so I would have to see to that quite smartly. Naturally, helping Will recover his lost investment was centre stage in my motivations, but there might surely be some slight gain for me through this small act of charity.

'How would it be,' I said as I poured more coffee, 'if I were to have the mill cordoned by fusiliers?'

The smile that spread across his face was a joy to behold, especially when a wry hint of craftiness impinged upon it. He gave one slow and mighty wink and tapped a finger on the side of his nose.

'And a little of the old...' he rubbed the same finger and a thumb together in that age-old gesture.

'Oh, I wouldn't dream of it.' Pause for a sip of coffee. 'What cut?'

'Ten per cent of everything?'

'Done.'

And we shook hands, which is all two gentlemen need.

I had audience with the king some days after my wood mill master stroke. By that time, I had apprised Frederick of my coup, instructing him to detail troops to Limehouse, and he had passed the word to Morris that building material would be forthcoming. Dingley had set the wheels in motion (oh, how apposite!) and work was being done to repair the mill and locate sources of bulk timber already at hand.

When I was shown into the library, King George was sketching designs with pencil upon foolscap, roughing out, it seemed to me, the inscriptions he wished to see on the machine. He had the central portion all sketched out and was filling in medallions with Latin texts. It was with great irony that I noted he'd written on the right side of the machine about the happy re-establishment of commerce. True, I supposed, except for timber from the Dutch.

'Montagu. I see no work being performed outside this window,' he said, casting down his pencil and waving at his view of the park. He sounded somewhat exercised. 'Time presses, man!'

'Yes, Your Highness, but all is in train. Mr Morris, the carpenter, hath surveyed the site and will return momentarily to begin work.'

'Then let him do so!'

'This grand design,' I interposed, 'will consume... would *have* consumed... more timber than was available to the Ordnance, but I have made arrangements for an adequate supply.'

'Details, details!' he cried. 'Be damned to the timber. I desire the work started *now!* And upon your head be it if I see no progress!'

'The carpenter Mr Morris hath staked the ground...'

'Staked! Staked! I can see the bloody stakes! I want not stakes. I want my temple!' He near as damn it stamped his foot.

It was clear that I'd not make my case for deploying the soldiers this day, so I decided to let it ride, thinking that if the king heard of it, he would now know its intent. In the fullness of time, I doubted not that he would be delighted at my expediency.

'Now, here, see,' he motioned towards his papers. 'All is sketched out, and it wants but rendering in fair copy. Bring a draughtsman from the Ordnance here on Friday in the forenoon. Have him bring paper, instruments. We will complete the design!'

'Yes, Your Majesty. At once, Your Majesty,' I replied, as obsequious as a servant ought to be.

'And *get working out there!*'

He dismissed me with a wave and turned back to his paper and pencils. My manhood was in the vice, and His Majesty had his hand upon the turn screw.

Chapter Nine

Charles Frederick (1709 to 1785)
Surveyor-General of the Ordnance

In which the Surveyor-General of the Ordnance convenes his staff and is assured that the great enterprise is in secure hands

I hastened down the stairs of my Berkeley Square house to take my breakfast. As I sat at my hot chocolate and bread, I thought to myself how unlike this firework was to anything I had done before. How could I have foreseen what this post would entail? Making fireworks and building temples was play, not work, surely? But withal there was the less satisfying administration. It was all well and good for Montagu to warn me off involvement in the department under my watch, but when it came to it, I found I had much work to do. On this day, I needs must convene a meeting with my two colleagues, the Storekeeper of the Ordnance, Andrew Wilkinson, and the Clerk of the Cheque, William Rawlinson Earle, to make sure that their people were mobilised.

I brushed the last crumbs of bread off the board, wiped a forefinger around the rim of the cup to get the last dregs, and rose to attend my toilet, sucking absently upon the digit and savouring the last hint of nutmeg in the mix I prefer. I washed carefully, dressed in my best, taking time to turn myself out well. I put on the small wig, the one with its short ponytail tied with a dark blue bow to match my waistcoat. I took a clean kerchief, for yesterday's bore the marks of my snuff habit. I fancy tight hose as I pride myself upon a good turn of leg. A final all-round in the mirror, and all was well.

It is not far to walk from Berkeley Square to Whitehall, and if the weather had not been moist, I'd have done so. Mayfair is a pleasant enough place, the new streets being largely wide and clean and the houses occupied by the sort of people one should mix with. It sorts my constitution well to stretch a leg, but this day the climate and my need for haste told otherwise, so I had my man call for a cabriolet. I'd not have a sedan chair, for their sickening motion plays badly with my humours while the stink of the bullies who lug 'em around would fell a dray horse.

I had sent word to Montagu of the hour we were to meet, but I had scarce entered my office when he strutted in, all cock-a-hoop with his tale of securing supplies of timber, but I hardly comprehended his words.

'Timber?' I asked, perplexed. 'Wood?'

'Yes, my dear Chas, *wood*. The king's grand design needs much of it, and that issue is now solved. I had thought such news would please.'

'Oh, yes. Yes, it does.' I supposed it did. I had frankly thought procuring of materials to be beneath me, let alone him. I am an aesthete, not a merchant. Why he was soiling his hands was beyond me and quite against his own admonitions.

'Now,' he banged his palms together, 'the king hath sent clear instruction that work should get underway instantly. We confer with your officials in the Ordnance.'

'Yes, I have contacted Wilkinson and Earle. 'Tis all arranged.'

With that we whisked down the stairs—he more energetic in this enterprise than me—and so out into Whitehall. We'd not normally walk any distance as the cobbles were ever slippery with filth, and one had perforce to scrape one's boots after even a short way. As we strode along, sweeping aside toe-rags, legless soldiers and other riff-raff of the street, he regaled me with all that needed to be done until my head began to swim.

'But, fear not,' he finished as we strode up to another office door. 'We need only meet and see that orders are given. That is our sole function in the endeavour. We delegate. Come.'

One would think that it was he, and not me, who had convened this meeting. A serving man ushered us into a long, wood-panelled room with thick Turkey carpeting and wide windows, which offered a view of Horse Guards. Bookshelves rose from floor to ceiling between the panelling, their serried tomes interrupted by spaces for fine china, knick-knacks and framed documents. It was a chamber I'd been in once or twice before in my brief tenure as surveyor-general. Andrew and William were seated beside the window in large, comfortable chairs, with an occasional table between them. They were finely dressed from head to toe for being seen, from well-set wigs to silver-buckled shoes upon their feet. A flagon of Madeira and four glasses—two of which were already in use—sat on a silver tray. They both stood as we entered. Earle signalled his man to draw up two more chairs, poured two glasses from the flagon, and offered them to us as we took our seats.

'Hey, John,' began Andrew Wilkinson as he resumed his seat, 'thought things were all quiet since Culloden, the Peace and whatnot, eh? Damn me if this late conceit of the king's hath set us all sixes on sevens.'

'Aye,' rejoined Earle, 'we were all stood-down at the Warren until this nonsense of George's. Fireworks, be damned!'

'True,' said Montagu, 'but needs must. Where do we stand?'

'I've authorised the release of whatever is needed from my stores at Woolwich,' said Wilkinson with a long swig at his glass. 'Our man Morris hath submitted his needs, and blasted extensive they are. I've given Woolwich a free hand there, and I've told 'em to be sharp about it.'

'Aye,' said Earle, 'and their readiness to the task is matched by my zeal in keeping the books. Burnt if we'll have sharp practice on my watch!'

'True, true,' repeated Montagu, tut-tutting. 'Shocking business if anyone were to make advantage amongst the bustle and confusion.'

'There will be no damned confusion on my watch! Nor bustle neither. The books will be scrutinised and not a farthing spent that's not accounted for. The gutter press is damnable for the lies they print!'

'On that head,' said Montagu, 'I carry a purse at Barclay's on the king's account for payments to the foreigners, but there will also be separate outlays where tradesmen take only coin. Such outlays are rightly payable by the Ordnance.'

'Then present me with a monthly accounting, and I'll send a banker's note for the sum to your purse at Barclay's. As long as the numbers tally, all will be well, eh?'

'Just so. And timber is well taken care of now we're milling at Limehouse.'

'Have to thank you for that, John,' put in Wilkinson. 'Stores would have been hard put else.'

'And the fusiliers served well?' Montagu asked.

'Oh, aye. They'd just to stand with their Tower muskets beside 'em to have the sawyers slink off.'

'Cowardly bastards! So, Dingley's receipt will be paid upon delivery of consignments?'

Wilkinson nodded and swigged. Montagu's face showed I know not what, but there was a twinkle in his eye.

'Morris tells me much sailcloth is wanted,' said Montagu, 'and, as it so happens, I might know a supplier who could help us.'

'No need, no need,' waved Wilkinson. 'I've sent to the Dockyard at Chatham according to Morris's estimates. All's in train.'

John Montagu nodded at this, whilst what I took to be a slight chagrin crossed his face, quickly replaced by an expression of benign neutrality.

'There will be need for much gunpowder of particular kinds,' I observed, entering the conversation at last. 'I have had much discussion upon this with Captain Desaguliers. What might be in hand with that?'

'The mill at Waltham Abbey is apprised,' said Wilkinson. 'I don't doubt but that sufficient will be available. Desaguliers hath that in hand. A problem, surely, to concern the Laboratory at a later date and not us at any time at all.'

'And what of mobilisation?' I asked, for it was forefront on my mind that the project be underway as the king was becoming impatient.

'Mobilisation?' asked Wilkinson as if it were a foreign word. 'That's all down to the Warren at Woolwich, of course. Nothing to do with us.'

'No, no,' agreed Earle. 'Nothing to do with us. Details.'

'A captain is assigned to muster the men,' continued Wilkinson. 'Morris hath made his requisitions; all in order. Details. Don't need to bother with details, damn me.'

'His Majesty,' observed Montagu, 'hath urged expedition in this matter. It might be well to deploy James Morris forthwith, and the man should bring whatever timber he can find and see to it that some form of work appears to be taking place.'

'Can't deploy the man 'til all's in order at the Warren,' rumbled Earle.

Wilkinson nodded. ''Tis a mighty ship that must start slow.'

''Tis not you,' replied Montagu with a wry smile and a swig at his glass, 'who must answer to His Majesty.'

'Yes,' I agreed, 'the screw is tightened from above.'

'From below, more like!' replied Montagu with a grimace, clutching his nether regions.

'Here, let me top you up, Chas.' Earle leaned forwards with the flagon. 'Running onto the shoals there.' I had drunk rather more quickly than the others.

We sat in silence for a short time, sipping our wine and watching an evolution of horsemen on the parade ground beyond the window. Though I could hardly credit it, it seemed that their part in the business of the king's fireworks was now concluded. And further, from all three in that room with me, the king's urgency could be sent to damnation.

Montagu broke the silence. 'What think you of this latest coup of Handel's?' he asked the company at large. 'Doth he cast the king as Solomon, think you, the gross flatterer?'[10]

'Nay,' replied Earl, 'he but sees which way the wind blows. He enjoys royal favour and so must keep his account topped up.'

Confirming my view that the business of the royal fireworks, the building of the machine, and all and sundry issues associated with it had been suitably dealt with from the board's point of view, the conversation had settled instead upon topics much more conducive to the gentlemanly consumption of wine in good company.

Thus was the mighty course of Britain demonstrably in capable hands.

Chapter Ten

His Majesty King George II (1683 to 1760)
King of Great Britain and Ireland

In which King George limns out the details of the machine

It was vital that my ideas for the great fireworks machine be laid down securely. Montagu had shown sketches to all those involved and had even sent copies overseas. I had him back to the library, bringing with him a draughtsman of the Ordnance. The library was the better place to work without constant interruption. I was to have Servandoni design and execute the elements of my idea, but the motifs and inscriptions would be all my own. No Frenchman could know what needed to be said on the subject by the King of England, and though it is seen published as his invention and design, all that appeared in words and figures upon the machine was of my devising. That day in late November, we rolled out my sketch and laid folio paper upon my large table beside it. I had by me a folder of sketches I had made of the individual design elements. The draughtsman set out his Keswick pencils, bread and instruments, and we got at it.[11] I had devised a classic Doric temple with flanking wings. It would stand on an elevated platform with walkways all round, the better to light the fireworks, with steps in three flights ascending to it. This was sketched quickly in plan and elevation, to be lined-in and inked when all was decided.

'Foremost amongst the elements,' I told Montagu, 'must be a central pedestal with the word 'peace' writ large and the date. Right here.' I indicated the place. 'And above this, there must be, of course, my name and title. Writ *very* large.'

The draughtsman worked quickly and well, and gradually, I saw the large sketch I had made, and those on my small scraps of paper, become graphic in this way: inscriptions upon the restoration of commerce under the best of kings (me), Liberty preparing her prince for war, the establishment of peace under my leadership and so forth. There were relief statues to be placed along the entire frontage, ten on one side, ten on the other, representing such virtues as honour, clemency and fortitude. Then, in the centre, a massive statue of the Goddess of Peace seated with Neptune on one flank and Mars on the other. And there would be paintings, revealed by hidden machinery during the progress of the showing. I'd been told of such things in Paris and St Petersburg, so we must have 'em here. Much more that I will not detail here was roughed out and filled in. I had the draughtsman back twice more, and it grew, that great paper plan, until by early December, we were done with sketching it out.

On a cold and raw day, when all thought of spring and the fireworks was a far and dim aspiration, Montagu came to me in the library with a great roll tucked under his arm. He untied the ribbons and spread the paper out upon the table, whacking glass paperweights onto its corners. As it unfurled, I was delighted to see the thing neatly rendered. It was massive, detailed and intricate. It quite took my breath away to see it in its final form, even though it had been of my own devising.

'Well,' I said to Montagu. 'What think you?'

He was quiet for some short time, and whilst he perhaps considered what words he should say, I studied his face. Writ largest was doubt. It seemed to me that what had taken my breath away momentarily had quite sapped his.

'It is…'

'What?'

'Quite… impressive in its size, scope and… and ambition.'

'Ambition? Do you doubt its feasibility? Do you doubt my judgement? Eh, eh?'

'No, no, Your Majesty,' he waffled quickly, 'but when one sees it…'

'One is overwhelmed by the awe of its conception, the ambition of its originator, the daring of its very existence! Is that not so?'

He nodded meekly. I wondered then whether I had given the old fellow more than he could get his chops around. Master-General of my Ordnance might have been a sinecure when first I gave it to him, but whilst this project was underway, John had to pull his weight. Delegate, delegate, that's the style. After all, I do it and do it very well.

'So, what of Servandoni and Ruggieri? What word?'

'We have letters post haste from both, Your Majesty, and I hope they will arrive severally within the week.'

'Good. Now,' he rivetted me with his eyes, 'what of the ground? Eh? It's laid out these last weeks.'

'Yes, Your Majesty. The site hath been surveyed and the location pegged, with tapes stretched between...'

'I can see the tapes, you addle pate! What I do *not* see is the machine! Construction commences... *when?*'

'As soon as our workingmen and officers are mustered from Woolwich,' he said. 'There are supplies to be gotten and...'

'Yes, yes, yes! Burden me not with details! Get working, man!' I paused, took a long, deep breath, and reined in my temper. 'What of these decorations and devices?' I whacked the paper with the back of my hand. 'I trust they will be in capable hands?'

'As soon as Chevalier Servandoni arrives, we can commence,' I replied. 'He hath been apprised of the plans and agrees with me that three craftsmen already here in England will support him.'

'And they are?'

'Andrea Casali, who is a famed sculptor, Andrea Soldi a most deft and rapid painter, and Andien de Cleremont who, I am told, is the best at the craft of rendering your decorative elements.'

'So be it. I trust Servandoni's arrival will be soon, for time presses. Keep me informed.' Montagu made to roll the paper, but I bade him stop. 'There are other copies?'

'Yes, Your Majesty, another is made, but perforce 'twill change once Chevalier Servandoni hath seen it and made his mark upon the progress of it.'

'He may make his mark,' I warned him, 'but he may not alter aught of the elements.'

'This is but a draught, but I will see to it that no great change is made.'

'So be it. Leave this copy with me then. Have more made, and give one to all engaged in this.'

I waved him out, leaving the drawing spread on the table so I could return to it every so often and gaze upon it.

CHAPTER ELEVEN

James Morris (c. 1700 to c. 1760)
Master Carpenter to the Office of the Ordnance

In which the building of the great machine begins, and King George makes an inspection

We had a proper military camp out there in the Green Park; 'twas quite the invasion. I had two Artificer Companies assigned by the Corps of Engineers, and more if I needed 'em. If you'd put together an army to march into Scotland and seen it bivouac, it would scarce have looked different, save in the place of cannon and limbers you'd see wains loaded with materials, tentage and cooking supplies. Workers there were aplenty, for the more hands we could muster, the quicker would go the work. The men ate and slept on site in the tent commons we had erected, and they were mustered by trumpet calls for every portion of the working day, just like conscripted men.

I would have no hand in the construction of the machine itself; my entire day was to be spent marshalling others to do as I bid, forming teams, and training untutored hands in simple tasks. It was a pyramid of authority. I drove them hard, knowing we had much to accomplish and precious little time to brook delay. The weather had been bone-hard cold, but into December, it moderated, which made work easier on the men but played hell with the ground. All too soon, we were working in a sea of mud churned up by horses' hooves and the wheels of wains and criss-crossed with the tracks of men going about their business. For sure, the Green Park was soon a brown one, and God knows what restoration work would be needed once 'twas back to its former use.

I worked under a huge tent, more a canopy really, with open sides so I could keep my eyes on the work yet still keep my plans and manifests dry. I had two trestle tables, one for the master drawing, which was now done in plan as well as elevation, and another for all my small sketches of the many decorative elements, such as columns, soffits, staircases and railings, and a host of other like details. Often my head became so lodged in these details that it became hard to see the whole picture. This frightened me more than a little, because at times like these, I would be overwhelmed by the enormity of the thing. Yes, I had confidence in myself, but it was taxing and sapping of my will. I kept all this to myself, for weakness perceived at the top strikes discord all down.

Once I'd surveyed the site and laid out the shape of the Temple of Peace, we began by setting the foundation posts in place. We buried a baulk of timber upright almost to the ground on the north, where the land sloped up. The hole went down probably four feet, and we sat the end of the timber on a base of gravel. We used six-inch round logs; no need to waste time by squaring 'em off. Then we sunk the southernmost baulk so it was level. When I say level, what I mean is, I used a horizontal sight stick on a plane table atop a tripod some distance off. I set the plane table 500 feet away on the Queen's Walk. I eyed through the holes in the sight stick to get the top of the first baulk in line. We call that first one the datum because we take all our measures off it. Once sighted on it, I swivelled the plane table sideways and had my men sink the southernmost baulk 'til its top lined up through the sight holes. Then we did the in-between ones all along, setting them in at ten-foot intervals, all level. Quick and easy. In this way, we got the foundation frame of the building roughed out really quick.

Before we could erect anything of the pavilions, we had to plank in the floor of the whole platform. We laid stringers of timber, six inches on the square, between our levelled uprights and pegged 'em in place. Wherever possible we used treenails because ironware is expensive and takes time to forge. Drilling a hole with an auger and banging in a wood peg takes a little longer than driving in a nail, but it's much cheaper, and the wood for the pegs was on hand. Once the stringers were set, we planked in the whole surface on top of them with two-by-twelves. I'll not bore with the details, but scarcely ten days had gone by before we were ready to raise the uprights of the building's corners.

All the while, as the structure was a-building, and I was working on the plans, I kept wondering how we were going to fit in with this Servandoni decorator. We would need to erect the medallions, plinths and other decorative devices, then set up platforms and scaffoldings for his workingmen to do their stuff. The timing and coordination of this would be terribly complicated, and time was always pressing upon my shoulders. I didn't see how there would be time for their work to be finished if they'd first to wait upon our part in making the structures.

I was down on my hands and knees one day, on the freshly planked surface of our huge platform, marking the placing of our uprights with black paint, when everything around me went quiet. I looked up from my work, a bit startled, and there in front of me was King George himself flanked by Princess Mary, the Duke of Montagu, Charles Frederick and sundry other court figures. In the instant, realisation dawned, and I set aside my paint pot and leapt to my feet, stammering out a greeting of some sort. 'Tis passing strange that when you first meet a great person, you expect him to be... great. But here was the king, not a step away from me, his eyes below mine in height and dressed in quite the ordinary walking-out clothes, although he did carry his sword sheathed at his side. Even with his small stature and the plain ordinariness of him, I was awed.

'Damn me if this isn't looking mighty well,' he said, stamping his boot upon the boards as if to test their solidity. 'And you are Mr Morris?'

I was deeply ashamed of my work clothes, for I had on stained breeches, a none-too-clean linen shirt and the floppy old tricorn hat I wear to keep my head warm. What with the sawdust on my knees from stooping and the paint spots on my hands, I wasn't what you might call presentable. I swept the old hat off my head and had made to bang the dust from my hose and offer apology, when he forestalled me.

'Honest dirt. Honest labour.' His Majesty waved aside my protestation. 'I care not a fig how you seem. 'Tis what you have accomplished thus far that interests me. Do you lack anything for your labour?'

I had never heard the king speak until now, so I was struck by his accented English. The accent you are raised with stays with you, I know; even so he had a fine command of our tongue, unlike his father before him.

'No, no, thank you, Your Majesty,' I replied, giving a deep bow. 'All is well supplied by Woolwich and Chatham.'

'That is excellent. We are impressed with the work so far, and as it grows, we will keep our eyes upon it from the palace yonder.'

'I am glad, Your Majesty, that our work here gives you satisfaction.' It's daunting the common things you are minded to say on the instant and the wise and thoughtful words that come after, which you only wish you'd said.

'Anything you need, anything at all, Montagu and Frederick here; they're your men. Work well.'

And with that, he dismissed me and turned, leading his entourage down the rough stair we had created for our work, and stepping into the mud of what was once the fine sward of the Green Park. Boots, shoes and hose became mired, and perforce the ladies' crinolines and petticoats swished through the mess 'til watching them pass, I was deeply ashamed.

That mud concerned me a great deal as the king and his entourage had to walk some 500 feet from the gravel of the Queen's Walk. It was not above a day later that Mr Frederick informed me that, at all costs, a way must be laid over the grass and mud so that future visits would not be so fraught. Though the king had been pleased with our work, Montagu had told Frederick that there had been sharp exchanges when the king returned to dry gravel and saw the state of his boots and the lower edges of his ladies' garments.

But how was I to accomplish this? Wood for 500 feet of walkway I could scarce spare, nor time and men to have it built. And it needs must be temporary, for once the machine was built, the sward around it would be restored to its pristine state. After much thought, I had the men make two runs of wood planks tied together with twisted ropes, much like a raft I had seen made by Crusoe, only these were but four feet wide and longer by twenty feet.[12] These two runs could be rolled up in bales and the first one run out ahead of the party. As they progressed, the second would be run out before them and the first rolled up behind and brought forward. Thus, for forty feet of planking and some rope, I had a cunning walkway.

Chapter Twelve

Giovanni Niccolò Servandoni (1695 to 1766)
Architect, Artist and Theatre Designer

In which the stage designer is summoned to London and is presented with a fait accompli

The summons from London was most *à propos*. When work on the façade of Saint-Sulpice in Paris was shut down for want of money in 1744, I took myself and my team off to Madrid first, then to Lisbon. I have never lacked for work, be it the design of theatre sets and machines for the opera at the Théâtre du Palais-Royal or the staging of firework spectacles in many cities of Europe. I go where the work is and where the staging of my machines and devices is most in demand. Drama, architecture, painting, opera, they are all one to me if they call deeply upon my skill and my *panache*. One of my finest works in the firework and music line was the extravaganza set off in 1739 from a pair of boats in the Seine, which was much applauded by the king and his court. It was the wide fame of this spectacle, unrivalled in the world at that time, that undoubtedly caused King George of England to seek my services. He wished *naturellement* to emulate the splendours of the French court and, stinging from the Peace of Aix-la-Chapelle, doubtless also wished to thrust a middle finger salute across the Channel.

The letter and banker's note from John Montagu followed me from my agent in Paris to my present place at the National Theatre in Lisbon. I was done with what I had intended to do there and was contemplating the possibility of returning to my old haunts in Paris, where there was word of staging Jean-Phillippe Rameau's *Zoroastre* at the Théâtre du Palais-Royal, with as grand and elaborate a stage machine as could be contrived. The London appointment, however, seemed to me more certain and offered considerable reward, if the fifty-guinea advance was anything to go by. Besides, I am quite fond of London. I'd worked there at the Royal Academy of Music until 1724, when Handel was staging

Italian opera. This was before my **Palais-Royal** sojourn and a return to my adopted home of France. Though born in Florence and christened Jean-Nicolas Servan, I much prefer to wield my Italian name, as many of us artists do. I would perforce do my work in English whilst there, though I doubted not that my rusty speech would need oiling.

So, London beckoned.

My man, Gaston, would accompany me, of course, as I would be quite lost without his ministrations to my clothing and *toilette*. There were also great chests of tools to take with us, many of which were long favourites, and special materials I must bring with me for every project I carry out, local suppliers being sometimes unreliable. Moving my *atelier* between cities on short notice is a complicated and expensive enterprise but one I do often. The chests of tools and materials alone weighed half a ton and would likely cost five *livres* to ship. Still, the bank note was generous enough. I have a team of local workingmen who operate the devices of my machinery, but these I had perforce to leave behind, hoping that suitable labourers would be available and could be schooled in the discipline, else I would need to send for them.

My calling takes me all over Europe, but I travel at any season with reluctance at best but more often with loathing. Late November is a terrible time to take to the sea and to the road, but the summons was urgent; the letter had been dated early that month. It seemed to have come remarkably quick until I realised that their foolish calendar was eleven days in advance of ours. With three weeks already wasted, I dashed off a reply, which I hoped would catch the next packet to London, explaining that I would make for Portsmouth without delay. I called together my local team, told them of my plans, and we began the labour of packing everything away securely. Perforce Gaston and I would take ship from Lisbon, weather the mouth of the Bay of Biscay as well as we might, and make landfall at Portsmouth. The fewer days on the sea, the better I would feel, so weathering east to round Kent and make the Thames estuary was not to be thought of. From the coast, we planned to take whatever coach was available and arrange for the transport of our tools, equipment and supplies by waggon or to London by sea.

Merchantmen there were aplenty in Lisbon Harbour, and passage to England was not hard to secure. On a blustery day, with a favourable wind, we rounded the Bélem Tower and hauled our prow to the north. I will not dwell long on the horrors and trials of that voyage, except to relate my certainty that we spent more time being blown south by west than we ever did in faring north by east. Sick and wretched, and wishing to God we had taken the longer route through Portugal, Spain and France by coach, we landed at Portsmouth not far off the middle of December. I made arrangements for my chests of tools and materials to be loaded aboard a coastal vessel, which would convey them to the Pool of London, whilst we would continue by post coach to the capital.

On arrival in Portsmouth, I was greeted from the ship by a messenger from London. The paper read that Montagu would await me at the coach stop in the capital and that he had engaged **Soldi, Casali and de Cleremont** to assist in the realisation of His Majesty's designs. This news sat well with me, for I had worked with them all before in England and found them quick and receptive to my wishes, but I did wonder what Montagu meant by "His Majesty's designs," for the realisation of designs was, of course, my task.

The coach road to London was foul, the weather was foul, and our tempers matched both the former. One steels oneself to travel by coach in the clement months; in winter it is done from sheer necessity. The discomfort of close contact with strange, unsavoury and verminous bodies, the jolting and swaying, are made quite unsupportable by the weather. The reek of the confined space is relieved only by opening the window, which results in bone-freezing damp and foul imprecations from the other passengers, who would clearly prefer to breathe in the warm fug of their own stink. And the inns upon the way, as travellers are held captive to them, are of the most unspeakable awfulness as to defy description. It says much for the lawless state of the English roads that our coachman sat upon a large chest of weapons, pistols and muskets all primed and shotted, and that his boy sat beside him with a brace of barkers across his lap. At one place upon the road—perhaps at Hindhead—there was exhibited a gibbet upon which hung the rotting remains of two of the less enterprising highwaymen, hardly a dent upon the vast population of their kind and clearly scarce deterrent to their thriving enterprise.

It was an immense relief to apprehend the buildings of London and to be greeted from the coach by John, 2nd Duke of Montagu, a tall, long-faced fellow with a twinkle in his eye and a quick wit. It was long since I had last seen him, but he had not changed greatly in my perception.

'It is good to meet you again, Giovanni,' he greeted me. 'I'll take you now to your lodging, we'll settle you in, then I will bring Casali, de Cleremont and Soldi to you, and we'll get to work.'

We were shown straightway to an inn on Curzon Street where there was warmth, dry bedding, and bread and meat that were almost edible. Gaston saw to my *bagages* whilst I ate and then found his place amongst the servants. The relief was short lived; business began immediately after I had eaten an evening meal. Montagu bustled into the inn ushering the three craftsmen before him, papers under his arm, a driven man and chafing at time already wasted. He led us quickly into a small withdrawing room where we all embraced and exchanged greetings. There was much bonhomie as we four were reunited, having crossed one with the other in intersecting circles for many years on works in England and the Continent. This was truly a meeting of great import and proportion; we knew each other's work, and had done much in England, but here for the first time, we were engaged together. All three were now living in England and fully employed executing the designs and aspirations of *les aristocrates*.

Wasting no time, John Montagu rolled out a large plan upon a table. 'Here now is the plan of His Royal Highness's desires,' he said without preamble. 'I have spoken much with him, and we have laid out the elements needed for the machine. Our Master Carpenter is already at work.'

Qu'est-ce que c'était! I was to use the design of another? What would the king of the *rosbifs* know of design, of architecture, of classical proportion?[13] Did they suppose to employ me as a mere artisan? I was here to design; to create. Here on paper was an extensive Doric temple, 410 feet long by 114 high, across the entire front of which were inscriptions, carvings, bas reliefs, allegorical pictures and figures, all immensely detailed and precisely laid out. I had been called upon in the past to design the machines myself—that is my calling—using mere suggestions put forth by the commissioners, but here was a plan cut and dried and all ready for the execution. Damn their insolence, these British barbarians. Where was *my* imprint in this?

'What do you say to this?' I snapped at Soldi and Casali, rapping the paper with my fingernails.

'Nothing we've not done before,' replied Soldi, 'although a great deal of work to have done in time.'

'*Si*,' put in Casali, 'but we work fast and well.'

Oh, they were so polite to their new employer, were they not? But I was having none of it.

'I was not brought here,' I told Montagu, 'to execute the designs of another!'

'You, sir, were brought here to serve my sovereign and to do his bidding.' Of a sudden, this witty fellow had become quite prickly.

'You sent me a scribbling on a piece of paper. What was I to think?'

'Since that first letter, much hath transpired,' he replied. 'In particular the lapse of a month and the urgent need for expedition.'

He stared straight into my face, and I into his, and we held it thus for many seconds. During this standoff, I ran the scenario through my mind and realised that it was a battle I would not win. We were here, our tools and materials were here… and the payment for our services would be generous indeed. And time was passing. Nevertheless, I determined that, if I could not exert influence on the choice of elements, I would at least ensure that my name was forever associated with it. I would have plans made, and I would see to it that William Jones, my favoured English draughtsman, would see to the creation of them.

I spoke first. 'Very well. That's how it must be. And hath your sovereign also designed the disposition of the fireworks? Because if he has, Signor Ruggieri will be as put out as I am.'

'The disposition of the fireworks is a matter to be discussed when Signor Ruggieri is here.'

'And at what time might that be?' The Ruggieri and I have always worked in close harmony as true artists must, and I feared interference into our efficient cooperation.

'I understand,' he replied in a very measured tone, 'that he is presently on his way and is expected momentarily. When he arrives, we will, of course, meet and discuss our plans.'

'What about the team of schooled workingmen who operate the machine? Who light the lampions that illuminate the artworks? The men who fire the display? Do we send for our men, or are hands of suitable skill available here? I doubt it most surely.' Montagu looked nonplussed at this, having clearly not considered the issue. It took him a moment to collect his thoughts.

'The Train of Artillery will be responsible,' he replied. 'It is early days yet. All will be dealt with in due course.' With this I was obliged to be satisfied, but it was an itch upon my soul.

'And commencement upon this building?' I smacked the paper with my fingernails again.

'Yes, indeed. We have surveyed the site and prepared the ground, and a team from the Corps of Engineers is already at work. On the morrow, you will meet Charles Frederick, the **Surveyor-General** of the Office of the Ordnance, and Master Carpenter James Morris, of whom I spoke.'

'*Eh bien*. Now, to this plan…'

We turned to the paper and discussed it in detail, examining every minute feature of it, and I made sure to be mighty critical. I made notes of the aspects I considered important in the execution of it and all the corrections I deemed proper to make. We concluded our meeting late in the evening, Montagu arranging to bring the three craftsmen early the next day, lead us to the site, and have us get down to business.

As I lay awake some time during the night in this strange yet familiar city, I mused at how close yet how far away were the desires, aspirations and dreams of the French and the English.

Chapter Thirteen

John, 2nd Duke of Montagu (1690 to 1749)
Master-General of His Majesty's Ordnance

In which the stage designers are introduced, and workshop facilities are found for them by nefarious means

On closer acquaintance, I had taken a disliking to this Giovanni Servandoni, Frenchman, Italian or whatever in Hades he called himself. Damnation, did he presume to gainsay King George II himself, the blasted whelk! He had not been so puffed up on my earlier acquaintance, and I wondered whether great fame had gone to the inflating of him. It had certainly increased his girth. He had no call to be so sniffy upon the king's design. Well, I thought I had shut him up fine, so when Charles Frederick and I went to meet him, I didn't expect any more airs and graces. He had a job to do, and the king's shilling was paying him. We came to the house on Curzon Street early in the forenoon following his arrival, and it struck me right away that our artistic guest still believed himself a bit above us. He had that air of looking down upon us from on high. Even though he was not a tall gentleman, he did have a tendency to look down his nose at the best of times, and a long and snooty one it was, set in a face that ran to more than the natural helping of chins. More than this, the man knew we were to conduct him direct to the building site, so was it quite so necessary to dress himself with a silken weskit and fine buckled shoes, a puffy-sleeved shirt with lace at the wrist and, especially, a sword? He was quite the beau and would cut a fine figure amongst the teacups and dainties at Bath Spa—saving his embonpoint—but would hardly be seemly amongst the mud and sawdust.

There was something else that came to my attention that made him more irksome to me. Whilst Frederick was reintroducing himself, having known Servandoni's work in England long since, I spoke briefly to the owner of the house in which they were lodged. I asked him if all was well. He told me there had been complaints: the food was not up to scratch, the beds were uncomfortable, the noise intolerable, and so on. Servandoni and his serving man wished to be moved immediately to better accommodation. Now, usually, I would see to it that the guests were promptly moved elsewhere with no questions, but this case was a mite difficult. I had heard of these rooms being available through a friend of the owner and had secured a lease until the end of April. As the rooms were to be paid out of the king's purse, the owner and I had signed for a sum that would appear on all bills and receipts. That this sum would differ from the one agreed between us on a handshake, and that the difference would be divided fifty-fifty in coin, was an agreement from which I was loath to withdraw. It was therefore necessary to employ my most charming and diplomatic face in assuring Servandoni that I would personally intervene on their behalf, and that conditions would be ameliorated on the instant. Harsh words between the owner and his housekeeping staff were later exchanged, and I was assured that all would be well… our little investment included.

We left the Curzon Street lodging and conducted our imported artist to the north gate of the park where Casali, Soldi and de Cleremont were to meet us. The four artists chattered as we walked, and I felt that, here at least, would be a concerted and well-directed team. Charles knew Andrea Casali from some years past.

'Signor Casali,' he said in greeting, 'the likeness you did of me yet hangs in my receiving room with pride of place.'

'And greeting the actuality,' replied Casali, 'I perceive no need for retouching the likeness, for the one mirrors the other.'

'Sir, you flatter me, and I thank you for it.'

We walked past the reservoir and across the grass to the machine. As they approached, I noted their awe as they beheld its size, and stopping some way off, they talked together in excitement. It was clear to me they had not seen its like before. We continued our walk, and I watched amused as Servandoni tip-toed through the mud like a maiden around a midden. His three assistants were much more stoic and made nothing of the mess. Frederick and I took them first to the row of tents where Morris had his carpenters and cabinetmakers working, creating all the details of the architectural façade; pilasters, mouldings, dados, capitals and whatnot. Whilst Soldi, in particular, was mighty interested, Servandoni looked around with his nose in the air and told us it would hardly do.

'We craftsmen are accustomed to working indoors,' he snooted, 'and it is certain that our paints will scarce dry, nor our plaister set, under these conditions.'

I know nothing of these things, so I sent a runner to find Jas Morris whilst we entertained them with a tour of the facilities. As Morris and his men were working here, I was tolerably certain that, even draughty and cool as it was, he wouldn't have any difficulty with his materials. Damned if I'd say so and reveal my ignorance, though. To my relief, Morris was found and came running when he was told who waited upon him. I performed the introductions.

'Cavalier Giovanni Niccolò Servandoni, please allow me to introduce Mr James Morris, Master Carpenter to the Office of the Ordnance.'

'Charmed to meet you.' He bowed. 'And here are my colleagues Monsieur de Cleremont, and Signori Casali and Soldi.' They bowed. 'This is a machine I have desired most urgently to work upon since first I heard of it. And I am sure my fame precedes me.'

'Aye, sir,' replied Morris with a candour I think only a man of his station could muster, 'I know of you. But, truth to tell, I know naught *about* you.'

He sniffed at this but seemed not minded to answer such impertinence from a mere beetle beneath his boot. 'These working places,' he declared, sweeping his hand around, 'will not suffice for our craft.'

'Oh, we manage very well with our stuff,' replied Jas, thinking to persuade him or at least to pull him down a peg, good cess to 'im. 'And it's not dissimilar, what we do.'

'To the contrary, our paints and plaisters and gessoes are of such sensitivity that cold and moisture will prevent them from behaving as we wish. You are merely whitewashing timber.' He turned to me and Frederick then, as being men nearer to his own level. 'You must find suitable indoor accommodations.'

'But, how will you work with us out here?' asked Morris. 'This is where building takes place. Can't move the machine indoors.'

'That is more than *evident*, thank you. What we do,' he said, explaining as if to a schoolboy, 'is to finish all pieces in a well-fitted *atelier*, then bring them to the site when they are ready to be installed.'

'So, just hoisting up and setting in place?' Servandoni nodded.

A look of comprehension passed across Morris's face, followed—I was not surprised to note—by one of relief and satisfaction. 'That's well then,' he said.

'Nearer the time of completion,' continued Servandoni, 'we will be here with the machine more frequently as we install all the devices and apparatus which animate it.'

At that time, I knew not what he was talking about, thinking that the Temple of Peace was but a static structure to hold fireworks. That it would be animated was news to me.

Morris's face fell a little at the thought of a closer working relationship in the future, but he masked it well. 'So,' he said, 'until then…'

'We have a copy of the plans,' interrupted the cavalier, 'which we will elaborate and improve upon. Then so soon as suitable accommodations are assured…' and he looked pointedly at me and Chas, 'preparatory work can commence. Mister Morris, you will supply the prepared frames for the painting of transparencies, and once the dados are built, we will install the sculptures, which we will first cast and paint in our *atelier*.'

'The… transparencies, monsieur?' enquired Morris with a face of mystification.

'Yes, transparencies. Thin linen is stretched upon frames. The figures are then painted upon it, and when in action, it is lit from behind with lampions.'

'These pictures are very large… How many lampions would one need, and how are they secured?'

'Many hundreds. They are held with brackets attached to laths of wood so as to shine through. I will provide you with drawings.'

'And there must be space in the back,' asked Morris, 'for them to be lit as you command?'

'We have teams of lamplighters, who scale the machine and light the wicks apace. Or…' and he looked pointedly at me and Chas, 'men will need to be trained to do this flawlessly and upon command.'

'This is a new craft not yet familiar to us here in England,' bubbled Frederick, 'and we are agog to see the execution of it.'

'Well,' replied Servandoni, 'given suitable workshop space, the transparencies *might* be brought to pass.' He then took me and Chas aside. 'Now, as to those suitable accommodations…'

It's odd how advantage presents itself. Once we'd walked the four of them off the site and assured them that work space would be found in good time—God damn Servandoni's foibles—I took Chas Frederick aside.

'See here,' I said with a hand on his forearm. 'Hitherto, the responsibility of finding accommodations is one that I have taken on. Far be it for me to presume to lift such a responsibility from you, but if you wish, I can pursue this issue further.'

I could see relief writ clear on his face, for it was doubtless nothing he knew how to deal with. He might have wits enough about him to locate guest houses, inns and the like, but work space was quite out of his purview. 'Twould well have been out of mine as well, did I not have connection with the Haymarket Theatre, and its proprietor, Samuel Foote. Foote is a most notorious rogue and blackguard, play actor, debtor, illegal stager of dramas and dastardly dealer in all he turns his hand to. He is forever running afoul of the law, the theatrical establishment and playwrights and actors at large. In short, he is everything that is abominable in the vulgar theatre and an altogether unsavoury fellow… and, of course, just the man I needed.

Foote had recently taken the lease of the Haymarket Theatre, perhaps the lowest ebb of that establishment's fortunes, and I was well aware he was not long out of the Marshalsea. In truth, he was only got out of debtor's prison by the favour of court intimates such as yours truly. I know not quite why we keep him afloat, but he is, of course, a man of theatrically persuasive powers and an enormous entertainer and wit. Perhaps his vices and virtues find a balance all told. Foote had two useful attributes for me; a work space in the lower crofts of the Haymarket and a constant thirst for ready money. He'd pissed away a fortune in inheritance before he was imprisoned, and he was pissing away another now. He owed me a debt of gratitude in helping to spring him with my attestations as to his solvency and good name. I had lied for him; now he would serve me.

I knew I would find Foote at the Bedford Coffee House, near the Covent Garden, his favourite haunt where he held court over a clutch of the finest theatrical and literary figures and not a few fops and fools and failed tragedians. I was there often myself with Garrick, Fielding,

Hogarth and the like, and we'd often play whist for a shilling a rubber. Some of the mad japes we hatched up over our coffee you would not believe. Foote is a Cornishman, and when not in high company, his far western roots show through in a directness of speech larded with barbs and witticisms. Even so, when in polite company, he will put on the apparel of his surroundings and behave with a comportment that is laughable if you have seen his other side. But whatever manners he may put on, he'll never conceal his lickerish visage with its drink-sodden nose, venous skin and baggy eyes. He is the wreckage of a handsome man.

'Well, my friend,' he began as soon as I had espied him through the tobacco smoke and weaved my way over to his booth, 'what brings you here except something you're wanting?'

'Something, my friend, that needs but two mouths and four ears in attendance.'

He waved away the two cronies who were rivetted to his every word, bade me sit, and pulled forward a cup. 'So, sounds a mite interesting.' He poured coffee, we sipped, and he waited.

'You well know that I am charged with His Majesty's fireworks.'

'Aye, but I hope he's not charged them up your arse,' he chortled, flecks of coffee-grained spittle gracing his lips. 'So?'

'I have need of work space at the Haymarket for the French and Italian designers.'

'French designers? Italians? Woo-hoo! So, woss wrong with the English, then?'

'Three of the four live here, and the fourth is brought especially from France for this endeavour.'

'So, woss in it for me?' His little eyes showed an interested light.

'Aside from discharge of an obligation, you mean?'

He bridled a bit. 'The discharge, I am thinking, is of gunpowder out of the seat of your britches!' He barked a laugh, broadcasting spittle, and sipped again at his coffee. 'Yes, yes, I am obliged to you. What of it? Cast off my chains! Aroint thee!'

'Attend me,' I answered, cutting through the theatre. 'I am the comptroller of the king's purse, and the king's fireworks need to rent a work space.'

At the mention of the king's purse, his expression became acute, as

I knew it would, like a gundog that points the grouse.

'Yes, of course, I have work space available in the undercroft. From now until April, I assume?'

'At what price?'

'Depends. Work spaces in such desirable districts as the Haymarket might be twenty guineas a month.'

'Might be?'

He looked knowingly at me. 'Well, there is a two-level payment system, y' know.'

'Oh, is that the double-entry book system where one figure is writ in ink in a ledger whilst t' other is but faery dust and moonbeams?'

'Akin to that, yes. Y' see, work spaces like mine could be as much as twice what I would charge.'

'It would be very proper, then, if the higher figure were to appear on the books.'

'Aye, that's what a landlord's ledger would show. Negligent to confuse issue.'

'Shocking, quite shocking.' We sat and sipped our coffee, and presently, he poured more. The coffee house buzzed and clattered around us, claps of harsh laughter and snatches of song overlying hubbub. Somebody began a sing-song recitation of a poem in a reedy voice to rhythmic applause.

'Fifty-fifty?' I asked, pitched under the din.

'That's normal in transactions such as this one. Banker's draught, of course.'

'And the mist and moonbeams?'

'Coin. Gentleman's agreement.'

And we shook hands, which is *usually* all two gentlemen need.

The day following, I brought Servandoni and the three craftsmen to the Haymarket Theatre by coach where we were greeted by John Potter, Foote's manager of the premises, and shown to the work rooms in the under-croft. This room was not much below the level of the street since the floor of the theatre was reached at the front by a flight of steps. Double doors at the back of the space opened out onto an alley at the rear, giving access to Suffolk Street.

'I know this place,' said Servandoni to Casali. 'I was here when great opera with spectacular devices was the rule. Now the performers stand in one place with no scenery behind them and sing in *English*.' He said "English" as if it signified the lowest level of barbarity.

'Aye, sir,' replied Potter as he waved an arm at the wide spaces and vaulted ceilings. 'In the old days, much more machinery was used in the spectacles than is now the case. 'Tis good that the space is used again.'

'It will serve adequately,' said the cavalier, and the three assistants nodded in agreement. 'I will require my chests of tools and materials, and so will these others.'

'Yours arrived by ship before even you did,' I told him.

'Scarcely surprising when one considers the condition of your roads.'

'I will have them sent from the dock directly,' I replied, biting back an enquiry as to how it was that the froggy roads were so very greatly superior.

'Good. We have the rough plan of the machine.' By this he meant the fine design the draughtsman of the Ordnance had made at the king's direction. 'We can begin setting out our work immediately.'

I was pleased to hear of their willingness to get started, for I had been so closely engaged in the creation of the drawing that I was fearful. 'Twas so intricate and involved that I feared, with any more delay, the work would not get done in time. It seemed to me a monstrous project, although I have no conception whatsoever of tools and materials and workingmen's duties. The sorting out of timber for carving the decorative devices, the acquisition of French plaister and other necessities, was between them and Jas Morris. I left 'em to 't.

Chapter Fourteen

Gaetano Ruggieri (1715 to 1776)
Pyrotechnician

In which a fireworks master is summoned to London and finds the assignment difficult to compass

My four brothers and I are now more French than the French. All five of us came from Bologna to Paris in 1730, invited by King Louis XV to organise his firework entertainments. Petronio, the oldest, made himself manager of our enterprise, combining our knowledge of fireworks learned in Italy with the arts of theatre, opera and ballet. We enjoyed great success and lasting respect with our spectacles in Les Jardins de Tivoli, and it was clear that here is where we would put down our roots. I believe the show in July of 1743 at the Theatre de la Comédie Italienne before the king was the absolute height of our craft. It was there that we first showed how we could send fire from a fixed structure to a turning wheel. A revolution in our art.

Though we Italians had invented and perfected much of this pyrotechnic art, it was sometimes difficult at first to practise this art in France; their artillerymen are mighty jealous of the secrets of their craft, and resent intrusion by mere "artists," especially those from foreign places. But in this, they fly against the modern trend that joins the ancient fire crafts with architecture, poetry, music and the re-creation of the knowledge and spectacles of the ancients. Though gunners may argue otherwise, and oft times even resort to violence, it is not enough anymore to lay gunpowder contrivances in patterns and fire them off with matches. This is not art, and it fails to satisfy the refined taste of the educated nobility and the higher members of society. In many ways, the French court hath set the standard of excellence in all manner of entertainments, and artisans like us are drawn to it from all over Europe. And fireworks are no exception.

So, Paris is our base, and that's where the Duke of Montagu's letter found us. Truth to tell, whilst Petronio was managing, Francesco, Pietro, Antonio and I played what might be seen as four second fiddles, and being the youngest of the brothers, I was the least favoured. Petronio showed me the letter and suggested that I might go. Underlying his "suggestion" was the clear truth that I was one brother too many. I agreed because I saw the invitation as quite beguiling, so he replied post haste. It helped, also, that of the brothers, I was by far the more fluent in English, having perhaps imagined such an opportunity when younger. To be working again with Giovanni Servandoni—as Montagu had implied—would be a joy, as he and my family had created such wonderful works for the Crown of France.

And these were new pastures; England, to our knowledge, had not yet embraced the new way of doing things. They were still entertained by mere artillerymen, else they would hardly have invited us. However, the sketch of the structure that Montagu had enclosed with his letter presented me with a sense of uncertainty. I could see beyond doubt where fireworks of various kinds could be placed upon the entire structure, but as to their number and composition, I was unsure. Until this was known, it would be impossible to plan in any detail. Montagu had written that the king required the display to be "...most extravagant. Lavish. Spectacular. Royal," so clearly much was expected.

Would I bring pyrotechnic materials with me, would I ship them later once the design was established? Mayhap I would use materials produced in England attached to the apparatus the artificers already possessed? And what of the highly trained teams that Servandoni and I employed, for making the devices, lighting the show and operating the machine? Would I send for them, or would men be trained in England? There was further uncertainty in my mind, for I could certainly borrow a team of men from my brothers, but Petronio would demand compensation for their temporary withdrawal. I assumed the English Crown would pay, but I had no certitude.

I hoped all this would become clear when Servandoni and I spoke with our hosts in London, but the more I thought on this, the more my sense of uncertainty bordered upon foreboding. Would we have a free hand to work as we must, or would their gunners resent our trespass? Surely, King George would not have tendered the invitation if there would be even the hint of discord. But even with all this, I would not let the sense of discomfort on the future dampen my desire to go, nor my enthusiasm in preparing to travel.

We were visited in Paris at that time by a colleague from Bologna, Giuseppe Sarti, who still practised in Italy but was wanting travel and further exposure to the latest in pyrotechnic craft. I thought to offer him the possibility of coming to London as my assistant, and he heartily agreed. He was also a man of more experience than me, so he would be a fine bulwark. We set out by coach carrying very few personal items with us; several changes of clothing and the necessities of the toilet. Even though I had decided to travel light, and to have whatever devices I required sent on to me, I did fill a small case with some few items I considered useful: a set of specialised tools, a few packages of powders, and some few yards of quickmatch, the fuse we used for our fireworks and which, I was sure, would be unheard of in England.

It was the middle of November when we set out from the coach stop near Notre Dame and trundled northwest to Le Havre by way of Rouen. We braced ourselves for the horror of the coach this late in the season. I had considered this route somewhat better than due north through Amiens to Calais; although this latter gives a shorter sea passage, the roads are twice as long and doubtless treacherous. We took ship from Le Havre to Portsmouth and then took a farther, and most miserable, coach ride to London; indeed, so miserable that it is better left undescribed, unless one wishes to be regaled upon the theme of mud, rain, fog and filth.

It was not until well into December that we arrived at Hyde Park Corner, having added the eleven days necessary to our reckoning of the English calendar. London seemed a damp and depressing place as we alighted from the coach, much as Paris is in the winter, and it got me wondering about the setting up and launching of our work in moist weather. Fireworks are ever at the mercy of the weather, and the precautions to keep all preparations dry are tedious, time-consuming and sometimes not effective. One prays with a will for good weather.

We were met by the Duke of Montagu as soon as we had alighted from the coach, and he eyed me up and down, noting my travel clothes and, I was sure, my black hair, brown eyes and southern complexion, not so much seen in the north. As I shook his hand and introduced him to Giuseppe, my misgivings on the nature of our future relationship returned. It was nothing that Montagu said but more what he did not say. Directly after we had made our introductions, I taxed him on the division of labour and the source of supplies, for this had been nagging me for the better part of our journey. I speak passable English, Giuseppe not so, and I perforce spoke for both of us.

'Yes, yes, all will be arranged,' he interrupted in a fussy and perhaps evasive way. 'Fear not.'

'Hath le Chevalier Servandoni yet arrived?'

'Yes, yes,' he replied. 'Just two days since. You will meet him on the morrow.'

'So sooner, the better,' I replied, 'as it would be well that we know where we stand from the outset.'

'Indeed, indeed. Here, for now, is the latest copy of the plans,' he said, unfolding a paper from his bag. 'It is yet preliminary but will provide you with some guidance.'

'No, no, you mistake me, sir. The disposition of the machine will come with study between me and Servandoni, but the division of responsibilities for the fireworks…'

'Tomorrow, tomorrow. Come, let me show you to your lodging for tonight. I am sure you must be weary from your travels and in need of rest and sustenance.'

That was all we could extract from the man that day, so perforce we followed in his wake to our lodging on Curzon Street, where we arranged our meagre belongings, and he agreed to meet us on the morrow. We dined quite well on chops and cabbage, and fearing their wine, we settled on ale, which was surprisingly well made. Later in the evening, we studied the plan he had thrust at me, and we began only then to realise the immensity of the project.

The Duke of Montagu brought Mr Charles Frederick to our lodging the following day after breakfast and introduced him to Giuseppe and me.

'Charles Frederick here is the **Surveyor-General** of the Ordnance,' said Montagu. 'The official who oversees your operations. I will place you in his capable hands. He will take you to Captain Desaguliers, the Chief Firemaster with whom you will work.'

'Even though I am **Surveyor-General**,' said Frederick, 'you will not see me much as my office is here in London.'

'The fireworks,' added Montagu, seeing puzzlement upon my face, 'are not made here in London but at Woolwich, which is some distance down the Thames. That is where you will work for the first part of your contract.'

It appeared that we would move to new lodgings shortly, so we were to return to our rooms and pack our belongings in preparation. They would be conveyed to us before the end of the day. There was much confusion in our minds, thinking that arrival in London would clarify, not confuse.

'What of the meeting with le Chevalier Servandoni?' I asked.

'We shall meet him at the machine in the Green Park,' said Frederick. 'You will also meet James Morris, Master Carpenter to the Office of the Ordnance. They will be awaiting us. Come. See to your valises, and we will depart.'

We repacked our personal belongings and put them in the hands of a servant who would see to their despatch. We threw our capes around our shoulders, for there was rain in the air, not enough to be wetting but sufficient to dampen and render us chilled. London was not greeting us well, and although April and the hope of clement weather were long away, moisture was always a consideration to us. Our practice lives and dies at the whim of the climes. We came down from Piccadilly, past the reservoir, and got our first glimpse of the great temple almost end on. Coming around to the front, we were impressed by its size. I had to confess that none of the structures I had worked on for the King of France could boast such mass and solidity. We worked largely with facades where there was much framing, propping from the rear and sailcloth to fool the eye, but here were the makings of a true building in its three dimensions.

The platform that ran the whole length of the structure would be surmounted, we were told, by a great central temple with two smaller temples at each end. Walls were roughed in to a fair height, and whilst we watched, workingmen were setting curved pieces of wood in place for a central arch, working high above our heads on scaffolds. There must have been a hundred men on the site—perhaps more—and the buzz and to-do were terrific. The area of the park around the site was a chaos of tents, waggons, stacks of lumber and workbenches. I have long experience with just this sort of endeavour, but never before had I seen such ambition, such a grand vision. I could only marvel at the organisation that all this would entail.

'*Fantastico,*' said Giuseppe beside me. '*Questi Inglesi sono pazzi!*'

'Quite correct,' said Mr Frederick with a smile. 'Indeed, we English are mad, but don't tell the king.'

I laughed and told Giuseppe what Frederick had said. His face reddened at first, but he soon saw the sparkle in our host's eye. 'We have learned much Italian through relentless exposure to your opera.' He smiled, though I suspect it was a jest. 'Go up the stairs. I will find Mr Morris and meet you directly.'

We climbed the three flights of stairs to the platform, trying all the while to stay out of the way of dangling ropes, hurrying men and swinging baulks of timber. And there at the top, and looking down upon us, stood Giovanni Servandoni and his craftsmen. I hurried up the steps, embraced him, and then held both shoulders at arm's length as we smiled into each other's eyes.

'*Ainsi, mon ami,*' he cried in our native French, 'what a place for us to meet again! Who would have dreamed when we last met…?'

'Where have you been since?'

'Oh, Madrid, Lisbon… where the work takes me. *Et toi?*'

'Tivoli, Tivoli, where else? Paris and the king are very generous, but…'

Giovanni smiled knowingly. 'But? Petronio, eh?'

I nodded. 'Ye-e-s. With my brother, one lacks the room… the space to express oneself.'

He banged me on the back and hugged me again. 'So, here we are! And who is your comrade?'

I introduced Giuseppe Sarti, and Giovanni, in turn, introduced his craftsmen de Cleremont, Casali and Soldi, two of whom I'd met before.

'But, tell me,' and here Giovanni looked around and lowered his voice, 'what do you make of our hosts?'

I lowered my voice, too. 'My nose tells me that there are politics playing that we know nothing of.'

'Just so. The bastards have quite designed this machine without a by-your-leave from me. A *fait accompli*, my friend, shoved under my nose. Be sure that your fireworks are not presented to you also as a *fait accompli*. In fact, make your lists before they do, and make them generous. See the size of this machine?'

'Oh, yes. Generous is what their king hath demanded.'

'Then generous it must be. So, thousands of rockets, just like in Paris, hey?' He have me a quick poke with his elbow. 'Hsst, here I think comes Morris!'

A solid, muscular man of middle-age strode up the stairs to us, with Frederick huffing a few steps below him. He was dressed like the other workingmen in plain-spun work clothes with a much battered and worn hat upon his head, but he carried himself with authority.

'James Morris,' panted Frederick introducing us, 'here are Gaetano Ruggieri... and Giuseppe Sarti... our firemasters.'

'Pleased to meet you, gentlemen,' said Morris, sweeping off the battered tile. 'I hope we'll have a structure ere long fit to grace your fireworks.'

'Now we see it, we understand the scale,' I replied. 'It is wonderful and will tax our skills to the utmost.'

There was little more time for conversation as Frederick had some business for Morris's urgent attention, so we took our leave of him and descended to the ground to await Frederick there.

'We return now to our exile,' said Servandoni. 'We work in the undercroft of a theatre through want of suitable accommodation here.'

'Really? We are being taken directly to this place Woolwich, where the fireworks are to be made.'

'Divide and conquer, think you?' He raised his eyebrows. 'Or mere expediency?'

'Let us give them the benefit of the doubt,' I replied, 'and see what comes about nearer the time of completion. We will surely be together then.'

'What of the teams?' I asked him. 'What of our trained men?'

'We'll get them here in enough time to show them the way of the machinery and the lighting sequence. Mid-March would be fine. You'd not want to train the gunners here. I fear the use of their artillerymen; that way lies disaster.'

'A mix of ours and theirs might be even worse...'

With that we parted, and presently, Charles Frederick joined us for a return walk across the park to where a carriage awaited us. It seemed strange to me that such a vast project could be undertaken by scattering the executors piecemeal across the city. I taxed him upon it.

'Servandoni and I must be in touch,' I began, 'for the choice of elements and their disposition is ever one of close discussion. How can this possibly be effected?'

'It is necessary so soon?' he asked.

'Indeed, it is!'

'Then we shall put runners with a boat at your disposal so that by written notes, you may appraise each other of your respective work. Will that suffice?'

I nodded, thinking to myself that if such "efficiencies" were the rule in this enterprise, we'd be hard put to see it through.

'For now, I think it must, but let us await the practice of it ere we judge.'

A carriage ride took us to a stair beside the River Thames where we stepped into a boat to carry us downriver to Woolwich. The earlier weather had eased, and the sun was making an effort to part the clouds. The journey would be quicker than usual, I was told, because the tide was on the ebb, but this did mean that passing under the arches of London Bridge was not without peril. Our boatmen knew what they were about, though, swinging the bow of the boat central to an arch and then shooting the craft swiftly upon the falling water. Once through and in sight of the Tower, the Pool of London opened before us. In all my travels, I have seen much, but I had never witnessed at close quarters the docks of a very large city since a visit to Genoa in my youth. There were fully hundreds of ships of all shapes and sizes moored on both sides, rendering the passage for even small boats restricted, and what waterway there was, was equally crowded with small craft. Not all ships could be unloaded at the docks, so cargoes needs must be swung into small boats, which flitted back and forth to the wharves. 'Twas a chaotic condition. Our steersman had continually to avoid other boats, and often the oarsmen would need to pull up, showering us with drops from their raised blades.

There was much harsh language on the river that day, and, though my English is passable, what came to my ears was incomprehensible... except in intent. The smell that assailed us as we closed upon the Pool was both exotic and disgusting. How can one put into words a miasma of tar and tobacco, fresh wood and rum, sugar, tea, spices and wine, all overlaid with rottenness, bilge, seaweed and corruption? A new world opened to our noses. As Frederick heard me and Giuseppe talking of all we saw, he changed to Italian, which he carried off quite well.

'There is much debate in Parliament,' he told me, 'over the crowding of the docks. More space is wanted, but the dock owners are loath to spend the money.'

'Is it not to their advantage? Surely, cost outweighs delay.'

'Not for them. It affects the merchants, and it is they who are agitating for better facilities. They must write off much in spoilage and great loss through theft. It must come to a breaking point soon.'

As he spoke, we passed close under the stern of a three-masted Dutch merchantman as planks of sawn timber were being swung outboard on a derrick. I thought of the piles of prepared lumber I had seen in the Green Park and remarked upon their cost.

'John Montagu tells me,' he said, 'that we have saved a great deal by using our own wood, and also by bringing in whole logs from the Baltic, which we have sawn locally.'

'I admire the efficiency of your organisation.'

'Ah, well, 'tis through our faith in Britannia that we employ English materials and industry.'

He seemed hardly aware of the irony in bringing me and Giuseppe and Giovanni's team from overseas, whilst here we were on the way to visit their own expert. I said naught, but he did remark on my raised eyebrow. To smooth things over, I told him I was intrigued by how far the Arsenal was from London. We learned that the site at Woolwich had been used for a century or two as a proving ground for cannon and became by degrees a storage place and then a full Arsenal for all the Crown's needs of both the army and the navy.

Once landed, we were taken swiftly to a building in a place called the Warren and shown to an office. A young man rose from behind a desk with a smile, and thinking naturally that he must be an assistant or flunky, I looked beyond him for his master.

'Welcome, gentlemen,' he said. 'Captain Thomas Desaguliers at your service.'

I could not have been more surprised that this stripling of not more than five- or six-and-twenty was the man who had been made royal firemaster. What experience could he possess? What technique had he under his control at that tender age? The anxiety I had felt for so long at the nature of our cooperation began to wane as I realised that the balance of power and expertise must surely fall our way. After we bowed to each other, our eyes met, and my impression changed. I saw in his eyes an unsuspected will; a steady, penetrating intelligence that belied his youth. And also, I thought, an intransigence and a challenge. Though these were but quick and passing fancies, it came to me that all would not be as one-sided as I had at first imagined.

Chapter Fifteen

Captain Thomas Desaguliers (1721 to 1780)
Chief Firemaster of His Majesty's Royal Laboratory

In which pyrotechnicians meet at Woolwich, the ground rules of cooperation are spelt out and a sore lack of capacity is noted

Here, I thought, was a collision between natural philosophy and artifice. I am not a contemplative man, and it is not in my nature to wax philosophical, but as the two Italians were introduced to me, I did feel a turning point. We were two worlds, each rotating about its own axis, and each unto itself complete. Here were the entertainers from their warm, flamboyant world spreading an ephemeral joy through artifice, and here were the natural philosophers who used the same contrivances to explore deeper into the nature of the world. Whilst one would launch a rocket and enthuse over its colour, its swift passage and the nature of its display, the other would measure its height, its velocity and its potential to be harnessed for knowledge. We at the Laboratory lent our gunpowder craft sparingly for entertainment, concentrating much more upon its potential in the pursuit of advances in warfare. The king, though he knew it not, was driving a wedge between our two worlds, and I suspected that after the Peace celebration, things would never be the same again.

Charles Frederick ushered Gaetano Ruggieri and Giuseppe Sarti into my office. It was rather comical, as it always is with strangers, to watch their faces as their eyes dart and flit around the little office seeking Captain Desaguliers and then settle after a pause upon this unlicked cub, with dawning comprehension poorly masked. On my part, it was a pleasure to meet a firemaster of the family I had heard so much of. Introductions were made, and I led them to the drawing laid out on my table.

'Please be seated, gentlemen. Now, the order of business,' I began, 'must start with the number and nature of the fireworks, for as we are to make them here, we want much time for the task. Firstly, then, may I ask you gentlemen your general views upon this?'

'Signor Sarti speaks only a little English,' said Ruggieri, 'so allow me to speak for him. We have discussed this much over our travels and are in accord.'

'Good. I, in turn, am fluent in French and know a little Italian, as doth Mr Frederick, so we will manage well.'

'Firstly, then,' he replied, 'your king hath instructed us that this exhibition must rival, or even exceed, anything done before.' And here he removed a much-crumpled letter from his handbag, unfolded it and read: "…we desire the greatest, the best, the most extravagant. Lavish. Spectacular. Royal." His very words.'

Frederick nodded at this, recalling Montagu's gushing words with relish, whilst my bowels turned to water.

'Now,' continued Ruggieri, 'what stock do you presently hold?'

'Very little,' I replied, 'for we make stock to order as the occasion demands. This will be the case now.'

'So? And what of powder?'

'The mill is informed that there will be a demand, but its production is largely of powder for muskets and cannon, of which we have great stocks. Useable for mortars and aerial explosions certainly, but for rockets, gerbs, fountains and so forth, the fillings will have to be made special.'

'And the same for effect powders and modifiers?'

'Just so. The Waltham Abbey mill hath the capability, I doubt not, but time will be of essence.' I brought forth a sheet of paper from the drawer and picked up my pen to begin a list of items. 'So, before we proceed on that front, however, let us decide upon the scale. Numbers and kinds.'

'Yes, numbers and kinds, indeed,' said Ruggieri. 'Let us begin with rockets. In view of our past experiences in Paris and elsewhere, and in view of your sovereign's desire to excel and exceed, I would estimate ten thousand.'

'Ten *thousand!*' I cried. 'We… we could not produce 10,000 rockets in ten years!'

This was fantastic. I had no idea 'til now of the scope of this project. In my ignorance, I had assumed flights of a dozen or so rockets and a sufficient number of other fireworks to excite delight, and all conducted by my men on the ground. Of course, I was foolish; had I not seen the designs of other great spectacles on the Continent, and had I not worried upon the scale of it? Did I think the great Temple of Peace would be adorned with a few squibs? This was outside anything the Laboratory had before encountered, and I was foolish to be so caught off guard.

'Ah...' He paused for a great deal of time whilst my mind whirled. 'And the rockets are but the start of the list; there are thousands of other devices, gerbs, fountains, wheels... This news confirms my worst fears.'

'Your worst fears?' asked Frederick quickly, lending me time to regain my composure. 'What worst fears?'

'I had feared that, because nothing on this scale had been attempted before in this land, you would be woefully ill-equipped to bring it off.'

'But the scale, so-called, is of your devising,' I answered, my fear now swinging into choler. 'We are here to agree upon numbers. Let us now do so, and make it reasonable and possible.'

'What is reasonable and possible to you would be inadequate to me and doubtless also to your king.'

'His Majesty expects much...' began Frederick and then snapped his mouth shut when he saw the thunder in my face. 'That is, some compromise might...'

'No. No compromise.' I was adamant. 'The Royal Laboratory is setting this display, and it is from the Royal Laboratory that the fireworks must come!'

Ruggieri folded his arms across his chest and raised his chin, and only then did I begin to realise what a fix I was in. I could not have the role of the Ordnance minimised, but neither could I rise to the challenge in supplying the need.

'We will not,' he said, 'lower our craft to suit your standards, and neither will Giovanni Servandoni. *Especially* Giovanni Servandoni.'

'And the king...' Frederick tried again.

'*Alora*... I can send for what we need from our supplies in Paris...'

'No, no, no!' I cried. 'It is not to be thought of.'

But in a trice, my anger melted, and a great wave of despair flowed over me. Was I to drown myself in a midden of my own digging?

'Then you are twixt...' said Ruggieri.

'Yes, yes, I know! Scylla and Charybdis. You do not have to tell me, sir!'

As I looked at Ruggieri with his folded arms and Sarti, who had gleaned plenty enough of what had been passed betwixt us, I could read the thoughts behind their eyes: "This little boy playing with the men; what knows he?" They were right, in their way; the impasse would have to break, and I was the weakest strand.

'Tell me,' said Ruggieri after a long silence, 'what facilities have you? May we perhaps visit?'

I took this as a signal, kindly meant, to allow room for contemplation and perhaps capitulation as well. I showed them the necessary cupboard in the hall, and once they had performed their ablutions, I led them across Laboratory Square to the Old Barn where cartridges and similar filled-paper gunpowder products were produced. It is a large, high room with workbenches arranged in rows upon which the assembly takes place.

'Your boots please, gentlemen.' Before they could pass the door, I examined the soles of their footwear to ensure they had no iron nails. 'Pockets and bags, please?' They opened them without demur, for they knew the consequences that followed upon the slightest spark. 'No iron or steel, no tobacco tools. Good. We may enter.'

It was not a time of high production, so few were working there. In this room alone, a work team of forty souls would not be unusual, and the benches could accommodate many more. I had been in my post not yet a year, so I had never seen the Laboratory at wartime strength, though I had benefitted mightily from its craft on the field of battle! I took the visitors straightway to the end of the room where rockets were being made under my direction.

'We have much to learn from rockets. We are experimenting with powder constituents, and the ratio of the throttle the better to predict their height and range. We make measurements with a theodolite and apply triangulation.'[14] As I spoke, a workingman was drawing upon a rope wound round a pasteboard case, pulling it tight so the case was constricted at its end. 'We have dowels of three sizes for the throttles, and the rocket is made in every other way identical. Thus, we can gauge the effectiveness of but one factor, eliminating the others.'

'And you would do the same by changing the powder,' said

Ruggieri. 'Perhaps adding more or less charcoal to adjust the rate of deflagration?'

'Just so.'

'Why?' He waved his hand about. 'Why all this?'

'We seek to know the nature of the weapons under our charge. One amongst us hath lately won a medal for his sterling work upon the trajectory of cannon balls.[15] It is by science that we maintain our military superiority.'

'Rockets? Military superiority?' he barked. 'Rockets can not surely be weapons.'

'Not now, indeed, but they could be. There may well be a role for the rocket in warfare, but we'll not know if we fail to enquire.'[16]

My words flew quite over his head. In my flight of science, I had quite forgot that he was an artist, a designer of spectacle. Mathematical computations were nothing to him. Triangulation? Rockets in warfare? Bah!

'But what you see here,' I explained, 'this is but experimental work. For firework production on royal command, this whole room would needs be filled with workers.'

'Even so,' he replied with his chin in the air, 'not a chance of making enough. We must send from France.'

I bit back a hasty response and took a deep breath. 'May I allow you to look around the room whilst I confer with my superior?' I asked, nodding in Charles Frederick's direction.

Whilst Ruggieri and Sarti walked amongst the benches, observing and enquiring, I took Frederick aside.

'What would you have us do?' I asked.

'Have *you* do?' he replied. 'It is a cleft stick, for to satisfy the sovereign's demands, we needs must employ the signori. Therefore, we needs must have them send for supplies…'

'But we *can not*.'

'Why can we not? There seems, Captain, to be nothing in the way of it but your pride.'

'Rather the pride of the Royal Ordnance! The Crown can not be seen to bow down to the French in this. Popular talk is already against the bringing of foreigners to provide our entertainments, let alone materials that we ourselves should supply. To do so for a royal occasion would be ten times worse than a damned Italian opera. The king would do well to…'

'Do you presume to instruct your king?'

'No, no, of course not, but can you not see what grist this would be for the pamphleteers and writers of obnoxious critique?'

'And your solution is?'

I simply shook my head.

I had no solution then, although the germ of an idea had begun to grow in my mind. We had expertise enough, powder enough and all other needs enough, but what we lacked were space and hands. Vast space; hundreds of hands. I would not yet communicate my thoughts to Frederick, and particularly not to the Italians, but there was some cheer in my mind as we joined our guests and continued the tour of the Warren. There was much to see and much to discuss in our various methods, so similar in most ways but curiously different in others. I determined to talk much longer with both Ruggieri and Sarti about fuses because there I had much to learn. Through that whole day, I thought we might bore the ballocks off old Frederick, but he was engaged with us and gave rapt attention. Yes, he was a damned meddling nuisance, but I had to admit that the fireworks could not have a greater champion.

I bade the three of them good day at three hours past noon so that Frederick could take them to their lodging. We agreed to meet on the morrow and strive to arrive at a determination of the numbers and sorts of fireworks. I was tolerably certain that Ruggieri thought he had me beat, and that he would oblige us to send for materials from France. In this, I think, he underestimated me, for the scheme forming in my mind was solidifying the while.

The problem was one of volume. The afternoon had taught me that, to a great extent, the kind of fireworks they used were comparable to ours in fundamental nature. There was nothing about the simple ones that was not easily done by us, and of the more complex kinds, I knew were as adaptable and crafty as needed. Certainly, the construction of the wheels and large set pieces was something we had never done before, so they would perforce need the hands of experts. The fabrication and use of fuses were matters of mystery to me, and there I was avid to learn all I could, for the methods of firing such enormous structures in sequence beguiled me.

No, 'twas a matter of volume only; a matter of finding enough skilled hands for the fabrication.

And there the Laboratory would fall far short.

Chapter Sixteen

Gaetano Ruggieri (1715 to 1776)
Pyrotechnician

In which the disposition of the fireworks is decided, the reader gains some small education on their sorts and types, but discord breaks forth

My second impression of this Captain Desaguliers was the better one. A young man short on experience perhaps, but when it came to it, I saw no hesitation in him. At first horrified by the numbers we considered normal, he quickly became the calm, knowledgeable host. There must be, I thought, more flexibility and resourcefulness in him than I had at first gathered. Though I was sure that, on the morrow, he would try to beat me down on numbers, it would not be the one-sided affair I had at first thought. There was mettle and a steadfast quality in him. In the end, though, he must surely give way, for neither Giovanni Servandoni nor I would compromise our craft or our reputations. And King George II wanted the best; that was why we were here.

After a fine supper of soup and a lamb chop, Giuseppe and I sat down with a bottle of quite unfriendly claret, unrolled the sketch of the machine, and made extensive lists. The nature of the fireworks made here was not dissimilar from ours in essence, though the making of the great wheels, both fixed and turning, was something I was sure they had not attempted on our scale. There were no problems with naming of things for I found, to my surprise, that the English had adopted some of the words from the French. The meeting at the Laboratory had made it quite clear to me that we must, if anything, rather increase our numbers, the better to appear to be beaten down to the final figure.

Clear, also, was the need to meet with Giovanni as soon as possible. It was not necessary to be at his side whilst the decorative elements were being produced, but a clear decision on firework disposition would not wait too long. I had already used one of Frederick's "runners" but only to let Giovanni know that this route was open to us. We felt acutely the pressure of passing time.

Charles Frederick collected us in his carriage from our accommodation in the town of Woolwich, showed us again to the Warren, and bade us farewell as he had other tasks to see to in London. He would send a cabriolet for us at the end of the day. Desaguliers was all ready for us in his office with the plan rolled out upon the table and pencils and paper at hand.

'There are three elements to the display, as you know,' I began. 'The first two, the duration and the rhythm, play into the third, which is the nature of the materials and, subsequently, their number.'

'We have staged firework exhibitions before,' he replied shortly, 'so let us get at it. How long will the show last, think you?'

Here was an abrupt and rather forceful beginning to what must be a long relationship, but I saw no animosity in him, merely expedition and anxiety to have the full extent of the project before him. My thoughts of the night before upon his mettle were proving accurate.

'Three hours should suffice, hence our estimate of the number of rockets.'

'Twilight here might commence at seven in the evening,' he thought, 'so I am sure the show will begin around eight o' the clock.'

'Especially as music is wanting for an overture, which is a sad neglect.'

'Are we to begin our planning *today*, or would you rather I send for ruled paper, that you might compose the overture first?'

'I do beg your pardon, Captain. I misspoke. Let us, indeed, turn our energies to the fireworks.'

Desaguliers pulled forward a sheet of paper and a pencil and drew a swift line from one end to the other. This he divided quickly into three with slashes of the pencil. 'So, three hours. Your opening must surely be a flight of rockets. And they must be large. The number and size?'

Here was a decisive, almost zealous, fellow. I pulled out the sheaf of lists from my bag and spread them out fanwise. 'It wants large honorary rockets. I'd say a hundred.'

He wrote that in quickly. 'What size of rocket do you employ? In England, we go by pounds, the largest of which is six pounds.'

'Our measures are quite different. Are your six pounds the size of the ones you showed us yesterday?'

'Yes, we have six, four, two and one.'

'Then, six let it be. One hundred of them... no, to be sure, one hundred and twenty.' He quickly wrote the weight down, but left the number at 100, and looked me in the eye.

'One hundred and twenty, one hundred,' he said with a roll of his hand. 'Come, sir, none in the crowd will tell the difference.' My little test failed; he was not to be outscored.

'One hundred it is. Then, whilst they are playing out, there must be flights of smaller rockets and a play of air *ballons*. Are you familiar with air *ballons*?'

'Good God, yes. Mortars. Four-and-a-half, five-and-a-half, eight and ten. Inches, that is. How many of each? Let's get 'em down.'

And so it went all day: 'Gerbs, but one hundred... *pots de brin*,[17] firing together...? *tourbillons?* Yes, of course, we have a wheelwright... Easy, we can make gerbs by the thousands... no, those would be *caduceus* or *girandole*... do you not have pumps...?' I was hard put betimes to keep up with him. The young man was all businesslike and forthright and would brook no nonsense. There was argument, there were differences, but to a large extent, what I specified was more or less what he wrote down. We went through my lists with great labour, often consulting with Signor Sarti in our language, which the captain managed quite well. The list grew, his timeline became impossibly dense, and so he took larger paper and sketched it out again in grand scale. I was impressed by his deft writing, his swift grasp of points where we differed but, above all, by an obliging yet uncompromising nature. At the sound of the noon gun, we paused for lunch and to relieve ourselves, then worked well into the afternoon. Upmost on my mind was the fellow who yesterday showed great horror at 10,000 rockets and who today took it all in his stride.

'Now, we have a good idea,' Desaguliers cried, flinging his pencil down. 'Some 10,000 rockets, and perhaps twice that number of other items, including 136 suns and wheels. 'Tis phenomenal!'

'Are you capable? Is the Laboratory capable?'

'Of course, but I'd not be the one who writes the order of firing, nor the sequence. That I do not envy you. We have done this before, you know,' he added, 'but not, I will confess, on such a scale.'

'Later, we must draw up the roster for fuse men, and that must be in concert with Servandoni. So now you have the plan and the numbers of fireworks. The next step, and quickly, is to decide what you make here under my direction and what we send for from France.'

'You are sending for nothing from France, signor.'

'Nothing? But only yesterday…' I was flat-footed by the man's turnabout.

'Dobbiamo portarli dalla Francia!' said Sarti. *'Forse anche dall'Italia?'*

'No, none from France; none from Italy,' he replied evenly and slowly. 'This is an English celebration, and every single ounce of gunpowder burnt in it will be English.'

'But you have not the capacity! You know this!'

'We have private makers in London who can fulfill the need.'

'No, no, no! There will be no control of quality. How can we be assured they will answer?'

'I will see to it that they do,' he replied, and there was some steel in him.

'That might be *your* quality. Is it mine?'

'They are one and the same. You have seen the Laboratory, you have examined the work, and you know the quality of it.'

'This is dangerous! It is far better that we send from France.' I could not imagine the consequences of ill-matched items, of no control over quality, with no idea of performance. It was not workable. 'I insist upon it.'

'I insist that all will be taken care of here.' He pointed a finger at the floor.

I did not dare have the quality of my work compromised; I had broken from my brother Petronio in Paris and had made this visit to explore new ground. I could not, would not, allow it to fail on account of a stiff-necked Englishman, who was at his nurse's breast whilst I was already lighting spectacles for the crowned heads of Europe.

'Can you not see the dangers that might arise?'

'Can you not trust my judgement?'

There was the nub of it; no, I could not. He had told me himself that the Train of Artillery had never staged such a spectacle; he was struck by the numbers required and had not the experience.

'No, I can not,' I said. 'Why are you steadfast that nothing comes from Europe?'

'Our king hath brought you and Cavalier Servandoni here to stage a spectacle of English prowess, of English might,' he replied, 'but he little understands how his position and his throne are undermined by so doing. If it were broadcast about that more than half the fire thrown forth was French, the people would laugh him to scorn.'

'I need no lecture in the politics of this country! Your sovereign hath commanded this. Am I to suppose you go against the will of your king?'

He held my eyes; in his, I beheld a great certainty of purpose that belonged to a man twice his age and, even then, of a passing rarity.

'Yes, I believe I do.'

Chapter Seventeen

John, 2nd Duke of Montagu (1690 to 1749)
Master-General of His Majesty's Ordnance

In which sufficient supply of fireworks is assured, and the duke once more finds the means to line his pocket

Charles Frederick came to my office all a-fuss with his problems of the supply of fireworks. In a nutshell, Ruggieri and Sarti had worked with Desaguliers in drawing up a list of necessary items, but there were insufficient hands and work spaces to supply the demand. And now Ruggieri and Desaguliers were at loggerheads about it, one demanding to send from France, the other insistent on English products throughout. As usual, I damned Frederick for bringing problems below my station—and indeed his—to my office. But it seemed on further discussion that there were ramifications of a political and legal nature.

'We are put in a bind,' said Charles, 'for he is adamant that we use only English fireworks.'

'I agree with that. So we should! (Oh, do sit down.) I can imagine the flood of ribald pamphlets from the gutter that we must rely upon France and Italy for royal entertainments. 'Tis bad enough already, and this would make it much worse.'

'Just so. Perhaps His Majesty reads too much of the rubbish broadcast in the streets, but I know it doth exercise him. But Ruggieri will not cooperate.'

'Will he not, by God! Thinks he to give us the same shines as the cavalier?'

'He doth indeed,' said Charles. 'I have talked with both of them and have, at least, asked them to do nothing more 'til the supply is decided.'

'So, we have a truce, then?'

'For now. But in this case, in order to supply the need, we must go to private firework makers.'

'Hmm. If we must, we must,' I replied, for the more British through and through we made this thing, I thought, the better it would seem in popularity. 'Let Tom Desaguliers see to it. The Ordnance contracts to private merchants as a routine. See Earl, tell him where it stands, and please... don't vex me with it.'

'Ah, but the issue lies in the fact that to do so is illegal.'

'*What?* How so, illegal?'

'They may not make fireworks or set them off—the private makers—and to do so is to break the law.'

'Ah, yes!' I recalled Desaguliers hinting as much. 'Tom mentioned this, and I asked of the entertainments at Vauxhall, Ranelagh Gardens, Cuper's...'

'All illegal. He tells me that there is a statute on the books that expressly forbids the making of squibs, rockets or any other gunpowder devices save by the Royal Laboratory. His very words. I have done some research. The statute dates back to the time of King William and hath never been repealed.' He pulled a paper from his bag and handed it to me. 'But, 'tis honoured more in the breach...'

'...than the observance, yes, yes. So, to have a contract with these scofflaws is to be in with 'em? My, my, what a pickle. Though you have a way forrad or you'd not be bothering me.'

'Tom wants to visit a Mr Benjamin Brock, who hath a workshop in Whitechapel. He asks me if I would accompany him. He wishes to offer this Brock a contract in exchange for immunity from the law, but he hath not the authority.'

'And he knows this Brock?'

'Knows *of* him but hath had no truck with him, being outside the law.'

'Then I give you the authority.'

'And the king...' replied Charles with a wary look to his eye.

'Need not know. He despises details, and this is one such. Albeit, a large and rancid one. I so charge you. Yes, go with Desaguliers on my parole.'

Charles sighed with relief and stood up to leave.

'Wait. Wait a moment.' I had the germ of a scheme that I thought might do me well. 'It could be, on consideration, better if I were to do this. Though I trust you implicitly, Charles, it should be me who takes on the responsibility. Better I take upon me this onus than pass it to you.

We all three will visit.'

He seemed quite relieved at that, so we made plans to meet on the morrow with Tom Desaguliers and find our way to Whitechapel.

We collected Tom with Frederick's carriage at a dock near the Custom House, whence he had come from Woolwich. Our coachman pulled up close by the Ald Gate and called down that he durst go no farther. I thanked God for this, for the shaking over the cobbles was playing hell with my bladder. The streets had become narrower, the man said, so he'd not be able to turn the coach, and in such tight and unsavoury places, it might be in peril from miscreants. And we'd hardly call three sedans into the warren of close and stinking lanes, could we but find them. Thus, we must walk, cat-called for our finery by urchins and ever dancing a trio to avoid turds and I know not what.

'We should have dressed down,' I remarked as Chas failed to negotiate a pile of dung. 'What was I thinking?'

'Good God,' he cried, shaking his boot. 'Every corner is a shitting place!'

'And more yet for pissing,' I remarked, wishing I'd the nerve.

'Better so,' remarked Desaguliers, who had grown into confidence whilst leading us into this midden, 'for I am certain that Brock boasts no necessary cupboard in his premises.'

'I'd as lief hold it then,' said I. 'You've a pisspot in the carriage, have you not?'

'Aye, I have,' Charles replied, though anon he had no qualms at dropping his fall-front against a wall. A number of turns deeper into the maze of streets, we found Brock's premises in Baker's Row; a large and rambling row of houses along one side of a narrow, rutted lane. There was no sign on the outside to indicate what went on behind the doors and shuttered windows, so there was little hint that the activity therein was against the law. But in this part of London, very little of order, law, morality or government had ever penetrated, and there was little need to do so now. Seekers of clandestine depravity could walk in these narrow ways quite unfettered from the law that operated farther west. Perhaps Tom had been this way before, but for Frederick and me, it was a scene only before glimpsed in one of Hogarth's prints.

Before we knocked at Brock's door, I enjoined my colleagues: 'I will deal with Brock alone lest he be cowed by our presence together. So do you, on my word, make a show of examining other of the premises.'

The door was opened at my knock by a young stripling, who in an instant tried to close it upon our boots. It took a deal of shoving by Tom to clear this little guardian from the door. We entered a room bare of furnishing save for a bureau and stool against the wall. Our commotion brought a young man down a stair at the rear of the room. He was no more than two-and-twenty and dressed in working clothes, but I took him for an authority and likely the proprietor.

'Gentlemen, welcome. How may I help you?' His look of curiosity began to turn to fear, for I could see him realising that an official visit of some legal nature might be underway.

Tom took a step forward. 'I am Captain Thomas Desaguliers, Chief Firemaster at His Majesty's Laboratory. I present John, 2nd Duke of Montagu, and Mr Charles Frederick, Surveyor-General of His Majesty's Ordnance.'

They bowed, and he replied in a small voice, 'B... Benjamin Brock, at your service.'

'We have important things to discuss,' I said to this Brock, taking control of the meeting from Tom. 'And 'twere best we speak straight.' I made myself ominous.

'I... I am at your service, as... as I said.'

'D' ye make fireworks here on the premises?' I asked.

'Yes... yes, we do.' The man looked thoroughly frightened.

'We thought as much. Captain Desaguliers, would you please oblige me by taking Mr Frederick upon an inspection? Mr Brock...?'

'Inspection?' Brock answered, knowing that a trap was being sprung. 'Why... yes. Yes, of course...' He leaned up the stair. 'Anthony! Come!'

An aged assistant wearing a frayed smock descended the stairs. 'Take these two gentlemen to numbers three and four, and show them the workplaces. Check their boots, bags and pockets.'

When we were alone, I looked Brock in the eye. He quailed but stood his ground.

'Now, look 'e here. Did you know that making of fireworks is expressly forbidden by the laws of this land? Well?'

'I... we speak of it... us firework makers.'

'Speak of it be damned! Is the law but *bespoke* in this part of London?'

'We have ever conducted our practice...'

'Conducted your practice in ignorance, then?' I asked. 'Or, more likely, known but willful suppressed?'

'My father... He died but a year ago. I am new to this, but he never told me of particular laws...'

'Well, laws there are. *Particular* laws. And have been these fifty and more years.' I withdrew Frederick's paper from my pocket. ' "By the 9th and 10th of William, Chapter 7, it is enacted: That if any person shall make or cause to be made, or sell, give, utter, or offer, or expose to sale any squibs, rockets, serpents, or other fire-works..." Need I go on, or do you get the gist?'

He shook then with fear, failing to mask it in any wise. I let him stew a little.

'To judge by the extent of what is carried forth in these premises, I would think a long spell in the house of correction might well be warranted. Fines and confiscation as a routine.'

Seeing his crestfallen face made me relent, for I am not a cruel man. 'But the laws are... flexible. And can be made more so. Why? Because we have need of you.'

'Need of *me*?' His surprise and curiosity were writ large upon his face, though not yet betraying a whit of growing comfort with his position.

'Captain Desaguliers hath charge of the king's fireworks and must supply the designers of the spectacle from the Laboratory at Woolwich. But there exist not enough work spaces or hands to accomplish the task.'

'Are they not bringing materials from France and Italy?'

'Never!' I replied with force. 'This is English through and through. So, we would contract with you to supply what materials can not be made at Woolwich.'

'Me!? Us? A contract for the royal fireworks!' Delight replaced concern on his face as a sunray chases shadow.

'Yes, indeed. The Royal Arsenal will provide you with powder from the mill at Waltham, thus controlling quality. Captain Desaguliers will then provide you with lists of all that will be needed, and as you fabricate the pieces, you must send your receipts to me, and I will reimburse you each month in coin.'

'I can not thank you enough, Your Grace.'

'Oh, but you can.'

'Any service I can provide, please ask it.'

'Well, then. Touching upon the figures you provide as your work progresses… You must send every month to me, and me alone, a reckoning, and one should include a small surcharge.'

'How small might such a surcharge be?' he asked warily, suspecting a trap.

'A figure of perhaps five-and-twenty per cent might suffice.'

'And, let me guess, 'tis the other five-and-seventy per cent of the receipt that comes to me in coin?' He was a sharp player, this one, and knew his way around. 'Quite the thimblerig, Your Grace.'

'Heaven forfend! 'Tis but a service charge that I levy to protect you from the wrath of the Crown.'

Now he looked very cannily into my eyes and nodded slowly. 'And were I to be asked about this?'

'You would be silent, for it is 'twixt you, me and that wall. You look to your part, and I insulate you from William, Chapter 7, et cetera and a spell as His Majesty's guest.'

'But doth this contract not expose us firework makers to the law, where before we would have gone unremarked?'

'So it might, save that you will not bruit it about, and whilst upon this business, you will be kept immune.'

'And thereafter?'

'I will see to it that your protection continues,' I placed a hand on his wrist, 'and I am a man of my word.'[18]

'As, too, am I.'

'*Quid pro quo*, hmm?'

'*Quid pro* just so,' he nodded and smiled, and we shook hands as gentlemen do, with me raising him to one such in this endeavour.

We made our way back to our carriage at the Ald Gate, with me pissing a wavering trickle into the pot as soon as we had boarded. Good God, no matter how bad this got, they'd never cut me for the stone.[19] We discussed this forenoon's proceedings whilst swaying across the now-benign cobbles. Brock had extensive premises where men, women and children worked at benches, and Tom reported that much of what they were making was in all ways familiar to him. He further reported that there were other premises in Whitechapel and that piecework in people's houses also took place as demand required. A Mr Pain ran a similar spread of workhouses, and he thought that Brock could parcel out piecework to him, with perhaps only a small surcharge. That all of this was conducted outside the law—or under the nose thereof—and that reputable places of public entertainment employed these artisans regularly was a surprise indeed.

'Are you sure of all this, Captain?' I asked him whilst we jolted along somewhere around the Tower.

'I have seen their displays. Their workshops fulfill my expectations. I know what they are capable of.'

'And now you must convince Ruggieri.'

'As soon as Brock is well started, sir, I will take him there. He will be convinced.'

'And if he is not?' asked Charles.

'That, sir, would be a diplomatic problem, not a technical one.'

'And thus, outside your sphere?' he said with a twist to his lip. I laughed aloud, which I perhaps should not have.

That's where the situation stood. We proceeded south and west, dropping the captain off near the Custom House. We agreed that it was a good piece of business we had done that day and congratulated ourselves that once again, Britannia's resources had been called into the endeavour.

Chapter Eighteen

Gaetano Ruggieri (1715 to 1776)
Pyrotechnician

In which the Italian designers visit a London firework laboratory with great pessimism, an agreement is forged, but further discord ensues

Here was duplicity; they had lured Servandoni to London with great promises and had presented him with a *fatto compiuto*, relegating him to a mere hired artisan, and here was I lured with similar promise and faced with the refusal of my tried and tested supplies. It was unimaginable to me a month ago that Sarti and I would be drawn into visiting a firework laboratory deep in the slums of London to cast our eyes over materials we would not have graced our attention with. I had no confidence in the quality of the materials that Desaguliers insisted upon, and no amount of discussion with him and Charles Frederick would convince me otherwise. So, in order to lay the dispute to rest once and for all, I allowed myself and Giuseppe to be conducted to this establishment in Whitechapel. I will say this: I went there with a conviction in my heart that I would find it amiss, and I was prepared to stand my ground.

It was a dive of narrow streets that would put le Fief d'Alby of Paris to shame, although I must confess that I knew that area by repute only and had never ventured to set foot anywhere near there. We were grateful to Desaguliers, who had advised us that clothing, and particularly boots, should be of solid working quality, the better to remain unremarked by the denizens, and the better to suffer the shit they would pick up. A mist of rain did its duty in rendering the foul backroads adhesive.

Desaguliers introduced us to this Brock person in a low-roofed dive of a dwelling, and again I was in the presence of a mere youth. Where in God's name, I thought, were the people of age and experience; was the whole firework industry here in the hands of striplings?

'I am pleased to meet you, Signor Ruggieri,' said Brock, returning my bow, 'for the reputation of your family is known to me. And Signor Sarti, it is a pleasure as well.'

'As you know, Mr Brock,' said Desaguliers, 'the Signori are keen to examine your methods and to assure themselves that your work will be consistent with mine at the Laboratory.'

'Well put, Captain,' I exclaimed, 'but better to say we trust you not an inch and are here to verify our suspicions. Let us examine your workshops without further ado.'

As soon as these words were out of my mouth, I regretted their brusque nature, but on the other hand, I would prefer to hold these people at a distance, lest they fail to satisfy us. I hated to be in this fix, but the success of the spectacle hung upon it, and my reputation and that of Giuseppe as well. Brock coloured at these words, and I think it was with effort that he held his peace. Desaguliers's lips tightened, but he said naught.

The workroom in the building we were taken to rather surprised me, for it was large and well lit. They were as strict as we for inspection before we were allowed in, and I noticed that, like ours, all the tools were made of brass or copper, with not a piece of steel anywhere. Some few workers were busy filling and ramming cases, and one was rolling pasteboard upon a dowel. In looking round at the stacks of pasteboard and barrels of powder, the tools and pots of paste on the benches, I saw nothing that was of lower standard than in my own workplace. Against a wall at the back, a rack held a dozen or two of finished gerbs, and another rack contained what looked like drivers.

'How many are employed here?' I asked Brock, for there were few workers for such a large space.

'At present very few, for we have no great celebration to prepare for. When the season begins, we'll likely get orders from Vauxhall, Mulberry, Marylebone and others perhaps.'

'What is afoot now?'

'We're making stock. In the winter season, we lay up the most needed items. Gerbs, crackers, pumps and fountains we consume by the hundreds. We also sell them individually,' and here he glanced at Desaguliers for affirmation, for this trade in particular was most frowned upon by their law. The captain shrugged slightly and nodded his head, apparently all the approbation needed to flout the law.

'How many hands when busy?'

'Here,' he swept his hand around the room, 'perhaps twenty, but in the other places, why... we might have three or four score. We piece out.'

'Let us examine some of your work,' I said, waving at the pile of gerbs in one of the racks against the far wall. 'Bring two pieces, one from the top of the pile and the other from below.'

He smiled widely at this, seeing my ploy quite clearly. The two items he handed me were to all appearances identical, but I pulled back the covering paper from their tops, and with my ivory toothpick, I probed the powder therein. An experienced hand can gain much information on the consistency of the packing this way and thus the control of quality between batches. I felt no difference. I handed them to Sarti, who weighed them in his hands, examining minutely the artisanship and nodding approval.

'Let us look at a pair of drivers,' I said, handing the gerbs back. 'I assume that's what those are in the other rack yonder.'

'They are indeed. Again, stock for use in the season.'

'So, you do wheels?' Drivers are used at the periphery of a wheel to make it turn by the force of their deflagration, and they must be made well and identical one with another. If these people made and launched wheels, their work must be of a good standard.

'Certainly,' he replied, stepping over to the rack, selecting two and passing them first to Giuseppe.

'What size wheel?'

'Well, the size largely depends upon the depth of the client's purse...'

Giuseppe passed the two drivers to me. *'Non è affatto male,'* he said. 'Not bad.'

'These?' I asked. 'What size wheel would you drive with these. How many?'

'Biggest we ever did was ten feet. Eight of these. Must say, it needed a push to get it started.'

'Who makes your woodwork?'

'We employ a wheelwright when needed,' he replied. 'We have

paid especial attention to free running.'

It was not a simple proposition to make a wheel to spin freely, and although they would never have the complexity of ours, I began to be impressed. Against my inclination, my will and even my prejudice, I was beginning to come around to the possibility of employing these people. But I was not happy yet.

'You tell us you piece out. What assurance is there that your pieceworkers meet your quality, let alone ours?'

'Alfred!' called Brock to a worker across the room. 'Go you to Crawford Passage. Tell Jacob I want three of what's on the bench, and bring 'em here quick.'

Whilst we waited, we looked again at the work spaces, picked up and put down many of their tools, and could find nothing amiss. We'd not long to wait before the man Alfred returned with three candles, or at least that's what I took them for.

'What do these contain?' I asked Brock.

'These are pumps, sir. They pump out six bright stars. Hence the name.'[20]

'Ah. That accounts for their length and narrowness. We don't use these things, though we know of them.'

'Pumps are a large feature of our shows,' said Desaguliers. 'I was surprised before to find you didn't favour them.'

'These are too small for our grand designs because they will not shoot their stars so high, and I find that when made bigger they perform but poorly. Withal, they are very tedious to put together. But let us look again at quality.'

We examined the work minutely as before, looking very hard for flaws, and again found nothing wanting.

After leaving Brock's establishment—for want of a better description of rambling streets of crowded houses built for dwelling—I thought to face Desaguliers with my conclusions. Indeed, it was only at the dock after the swaying, rattling coach had crashed over the East End cobbles, that my thoughts fully formed. A wherry awaited the captain and me to take us down to Woolwich. Amidst the masts and yards and hulls of the Pool, I finally found my voice.

'I would speak to you in Italian,' I began, 'for my colleague Signor

Sarti must be fully informed of my thoughts and intentions.'

'That will suit well,' he replied in my first language, and so we continued.

'We have found the quality of fireworks made both here and in Woolwich to be adequate for our needs.' He had the good grace to keep his face clear of expression, though within he might well have been triumphant. 'And we also believe you capable of supplying sufficient numbers.'

'I am pleased on both accounts,' he said with no inflection, 'and I will proceed with the ordering of powder, the procurement of materials and the enlistment of workingmen.'

I merely nodded at that, keeping my thoughts to myself for a few minutes whilst we continued away from the Pool in silence, with just the swish of the sweeps and their creak in the tholes.

'You must know,' I said after a while, 'that when I was invited to this country, I had little notion of what I would find here. England hath been closed to us in these pursuits, so for me this was a bold step. I see competence, I see ambition… but…'

'I think I have assured you in all particulars that the Laboratory is competent to stage this spectacle at your direction…'

'That is it!' I interrupted. 'At *my* direction!'

'I am perplexed, sir,' he said, turning on his seat to face me. 'You will direct us in laying the pieces for the show, in the setting of the fuses, in the order of firing. In short, the operation of the whole.'

'Yes, Servandoni and I will direct this, but can you assure me that your men will… *can* work with ours in this?'

'Your men, sir? I do not follow you in this.'

'Servandoni and I have teams of trained men. It is a concerto; it is a ballet; it is a symphony; and each part must work harmoniously with each other part for the space of three hours. Our teams ensure this.'

'Yes, I knew Servandoni had a team to operate the machine, of course. But my men will fire the show. That is why you must instruct me in this choreography of yours. So I may command my men.'

'No, I must command the whole. And my men must oversee.'

'This can not be,' he replied, changing to English. 'The men of the Train of Artillery are English soldiers. By no means can such servants of the Crown be commanded by other than their own officers, let alone a foreigner.'

'What?' I cried. 'How far doth this confusion spread! Surely, your king employed us for exactly this?'

'Certain he did. He expressly commanded that the Board of Ordnance would put on this spectacle with the Train of Artillery under the command of Charles Frederick and the Chief Firemaster, and that you and Cavalier Servandoni would be employed to organise the décoration and the execution of it.'

'*Mio Dio!* Doth that not include firing the show?'

'As I say, it can not. I'm to sit with you and prepare a plan to communicate to my gunners. The Train of Artillery fires the show, as we have ever done.'

I could not, would not, accept this. These blasted artillerymen had never, ever been exposed to the art of fireworks. They were damned gunners, and it was clear they knew naught of our art and were ill-equipped to execute it. Everything I had feared on my journey here was coming home.

'This is dangerous!' I told him, then reverted to Italian for the sake of Giuseppe. 'You have not the experience, nor the skill, nor the time in which to learn either. We were brought by your king to stage this spectacle, and that is what we are bound to do.'

'I am sorry,' he replied. 'I may have spoken too directly. This matter is beyond the rank of a mere captain. I must defer to higher authority on this. I think we must consult with Mr Frederick. We are to meet a few days hence in the Green Park.'

With that we remained silent for the remainder of the boat ride—an uncertain and pregnant silence that rebuilt walls which had been fast falling away—only to bid each other adieu at the dock and return to our dwellings. As soon as I was in my room, I dashed off a long and detailed note of all that had transpired, called a runner to the house, and had him take it as hastily as he might to Curzon Street. Servandoni would read it on the morrow, if not sooner.

Chapter Nineteen

Charles Frederick (1709 to 1785)
Surveyor-General of the Ordnance

In which Mr Frederick is admonished for his neglect, and all parties convene to plan the order of the spectacle, although differences arise amongst nations

On a cold day in mid-December, I left Lucy abed, performed my ablutions swiftly, and came down stairs for breakfast. My sister-in-law Frances Boscawen accosted me on the stair. She was up from Cornwall to visit us and was taking an uncommon interest in Lucy's welfare.

'What, off to the Green Park so early?' she asked, a defiant turn to one corner of her lip.

'You know I am,' I said, 'for if I am not there, things may go amiss.'

'Nobody can never not be done without!'

I looked long at her, digesting this circuitous construction. 'Whilst I'm not indispensable, Frances, if I leave others to proceed, I spend more time repairing their errors when I return than if I had been there all along.'

'But you are there from first light to dusk, and when you crawl home, Lucy finds you so spent as to be no fit company.'

I sighed, for I knew she spoke truth. The great spectacle was consuming my life's essence and yet also filling me with a great and competing joy. I had had, perforce, to set up an office of sorts in a lean-to shack on the site, and there I was from the early hours 'til the light was gone. I had got a man to lug in a brazier and charcoal, and with cocoanut matting underfoot and a warm fug in the air, it was as hospitable as such makeshifts can be. But 'twas not home… And, yes, Lucy was neglected, and so was all the society life that circled about her and Berkeley Square.

What was I to do?

'It is some scant months 'til the spectacle unfolds,' I said. 'Lucy is patient. She must be; she knows she must be.'

'Whether or no, you are married not three years and making her a widow.'

This charge angered me, for I am not by nature willfully neglectful, nor am I senseless to those around me. I let my choler subside, for I am not one to wear my heart upon my sleeve for daws to peck at. And she was acting the daw.

'Lucy knew full well what she took on ere we were married, as you know full well what *you* took on when you married a sea captain.'

She harrumphed at this and would have spoken further had I not intervened.

'And the tract of civilised land 'twixt this house and the Green Park can scarce compare with the stretches of ocean between Truro, Cape Finisterre and Pondicherry!'[21]

I left her to think over her precipitate thoughts, whilst also resolving to be my best with Lucy and see to her more assiduously. Though niddling and intrusive, Frances had her point.

Now came the time when art, spectacle and gunpowder were melded. Ruggieri and Sarti were working with Desaguliers on the fireworks, and Morris and Servandoni had the building and decoration of the machine in hand. Now was the time for all to meet at the Green Park and plot a concerted way forward. I called all five of them together. I had set aside a long table and six chairs in my lean-to shack. Then I had a coffee shop in Half Moon Street send a man with cups and an urn and had him return betimes to see to the refilling of it. There had been friction amongst the people, and I believe coffee to be an excellent lubricant of the humours.

I rolled out a copy of the king's drawing onto the table, with my amanuensis by me to take notes and prepare fair copy. I had written out an order of the meeting, for I wanted discussion to be well controlled and to the point. The order was laid out on four heads: building, decoration, fireworks and the performance of the work on the day.

'Gentlemen,' I began once they were all seated, 'it is a pleasure to see us together for the first time. I do apologise for the separation you have been obliged to undergo in this first week of our endeavour. Geography and convenience have not served us well…'

'Have served us very poorly indeed,' observed the cavalier.

'But have resulted,' I continued pointedly, 'in warm, commodious workplaces where our tasks may be conducted in comfort. Ahem. The first order of business, the machine. Mr Morris, would you report for us, please?'

'As you can see outside yon tent flap,' said Morris, 'work is going apace. Platform all done and walls coming on nicely. There's a deal of decorative woodwork in the plan, so I may need to muster more cabinetmakers from Woolwich.'

'Do so. Other considerations?'

'No, sir. All progresses well.' He paused for a moment and smiled. 'But we want for better weather.'

'That I sadly can not provide, but 'tis a mercy it hath somewhat moderated this last week.'

'Yes, it has, sir. Aside from that, all is well.'

'Good. We will look over the machine after the meeting. As to the decorations; Cavalier Servandoni?'

'We have found the sketches of the sculptural and painted elements quite inadequate, but I will employ the necessary skilled draughtsman to render working drawings as they should be. It will be necessary to make changes to some of the motifs…'

'Changes?'

'Yes. Several of the classical allusions are quite inappropriate…'

'King George would not wish his designs changed in the slightest, or the descriptive text upon the panels, either. Let us speak no more of this.'

'But we must…'

'No. Do you question His Majesty's judgement?'

'His choice of motifs is wanting…'

'The choice of motif will stand. But, Cavalier Servandoni, you have *carte blanche* with your interpretation thereof, as the renowned artist you are.' Flattery, employed judiciously, works charms where forthrightness incurs stubbornness. 'Report please upon your work.'

'We have begun work on the inscriptions,' he replied sulkily, 'which are simply painted upon flat panels. The sculptures will follow.'

'And all is well with the transparencies?'

'Mr Morris sends the frames to us. We are accustomed to wood of a better quality, but I doubt not that the merchants of your island have difficultly in procuring material of suitable quality.'

'And when are these transparencies to be set in place?' I asked as politely and carefully as I could, for below the table, I was twisting knots in the hem of my day coat.

'When the structure is at a sufficient state to receive them.' A long look across the table at Morris, returned in trumps I was gratified to see.

'Good. Other considerations?'

'There will be need for much lamp oil. Whale oil is best.'

'I'd as lief not use it,' said I from experience at home when our clockworks were oiled. ''Tis vile and stinks so. And it is costly.'

'It also provides the best light, and I'll have no other. And if there be a vile contest of stinks, the brimstone will out-duel the oil, no question.'

'Thank you, Cavalier Servandoni. So be it; you will calculate the amount and I will have the Storekeeper of the Ordnance procure it. All else is well?' He nodded.

'Now, the production of fireworks. Captain Desaguliers?'

'We would first discuss the order of the firing, for we have a problem...'

'Production first, please.' I was not to be deflected from my agenda, even though I detected an unease in the way the firework men eyed each other.

'The Signori Ruggieri and Sarti,' continued the captain, 'have satisfied themselves that the Laboratory at Woolwich is capable of producing the varieties and quality required.' A nod from Ruggieri. 'And we have together visited the premises of Mr Brock in order to ensure that his quantities and standards will be adequate to the task.'

'And what of the installation?'

Gaetano Ruggieri answered this question with a nod from the captain. 'We must consult with Mr Morris on the design and fitting of the brackets, sockets and fixtures for the fireworks. The wheels must be on axles, the rockets in racks or boxes and the fixts securely placed.'

'Fixts?' I asked.

'Yes, sir. Those which play off in one place are called fixts.'

'And these fittings?'

'They will be installed once the structure is near complete.' An inclination of the head from Morris. 'One critically important operation is this,' and he stabbed the grand girandole on the drawing with his finger.

'What of it?' I asked.

'It is for the grand finale,' said Ruggieri. 'This great structure in the shape of the sun will be illuminated with hundreds of *pots de brin* to pick out VIVAT REX in glorious fire.'

'I can see the drawing,' I replied. 'What of it?'

'Your sovereign had designed this—or, at least indicated its existence in his drawing—but Morris agrees with me that it can not be erected if the cartouche of the Lion and Unicorn remains. It is one or the other.'

'The king must be consulted on this,' I replied, 'but continue with the assumption that the girandole will be made.'

'Surely,' interrupted Servandoni, directing his attention to Ruggieri, 'you are not questioning the wisdom of the English king? For I am not permitted to do so!'

'That hath no relevance!' I replied. He had angered me. 'It is not a matter of decoration but of choice of motif.'

'It is a matter that your sovereign hath shown himself fallible.'

'That will be enough!' He was testing my tolerance, whilst knowing full well there was naught I could do to rein him in.

'Besides,' he continued, 'that great cartouche would be impossibly heavy, and I doubt if it is feasible for your builders to erect it.'

'Now, wait just a minute…' said Morris with choler rising in his face, but I waved for silence.

'This is for the king to rule upon, so I hereby table it.' I hammered the table with my coffee cup for silence. 'Any other issues with production of the fireworks? No? Good. Now, as to the order of firing upon the day. You have a problem, Captain?'

'Yes, indeed we do,' said Ruggieri without my leave, 'and one upon which I and Captain Desaguliers disagree. It is for you to mediate.'

'Captain?'

'Sir, the Train of Artillery must be commanded by its own officers.'

'But, of course, it must. Wherein lies the problem?'

'I have been brought here,' said Ruggieri, 'to organise and stage the king's fireworks. It is a vast undertaking which can not be let go. I command the order and the execution. It must be so.'

'I have told you,' put in Desaguliers, 'that our gunners will not—*can not*—be ordered by another. This is clear! Charles Frederick agrees,' he said, waving his empty cup in my direction. 'English soldiers, English commanders. Is that not so, sir?'

'But we have teams of fuse men and scene changers,' interrupted Servandoni, banging his cup down and scattering grounds. 'They are highly trained, they have been with us for years, and they will not be left out!'

'You may have your scene changers!' cried Tom. 'But Ruggieri must *train* my gunners, *not* command them, for it is they who will light the show.'

'Gentlemen, gentlemen,' I said, 'I am sure we may find some middle ground…'

'There is no middle ground,' replied Ruggieri with a wave of agreement from Servandoni. 'There are but two avenues: either we bring our men from France, or we return thither, and not one *sou* of what you have paid will you ever see!'

Good God almighty, how in heaven's name did this land in my lap? And where was John Montagu when I needed him? This could break the entire enterprise; it would be impossible for the Ordnance to stage the fireworks without Ruggieri (though damn me if we couldn't do without the cavalier). But the signor and the cavalier were Castor and Pollux; if one abandoned, so would 't other. And damnation on Thomas for being so stiff-necked. But, 'twas true, as I thought on 't, he was right, and I was unfair; we could not break the chain of command. The soldiers would not stand for it—though precious little they could do outside of dumb insolence or mutiny—but the commanding officers, they would never tolerate it. And, looming above all of this, and perhaps withering it into insignificance, was the great English public. Here was Mr London Town, fresh smarting from the Peace of Aix-la-Chapelle, which was none of his damned business anyhow, now watching the spectacle of an Italian Frenchman giving orders to English soldiers. I was loath to criticise my regent, but what in God's name was he thinking when he invited these damned foreigners? Did John and I not discuss this very eventuality? Oh, what a pickle!

'Wait, wait, wait!' I hammered with my fist on the table. 'We will cease discussion of this matter…'

'*Il faut en discuter maintenant!*' shouted Servandoni, all bristling and jowls a-wobble.

'No!' I banged the board again. 'We will not discuss it now. You, Cavalier Servandoni, will have your team with you, of course. They will be sent for when they are needed.'

'Mine, I know of. It is of *his* we speak.' He shot a finger at Ruggieri.

'I know full well of whom we speak! It is upon the matter of Signor Ruggieri's men that a decision must be made, but it will not be now. I will table this discussion until we may meet with higher authority.' I waited to ensure no more eruptions from the table, though sulphurous steam was issuing from French and Italian caldera. 'To continue with the order of business…'

I brought the meeting back into order somehow, but I was all atremble from the tenor of it, for I despise discord. Once concluded, we visited the Temple of Peace in the making, and I sent a boy to Whitehall with a message to Montagu that we should meet with Desaguliers and Ruggieri, and no other, as soon as might be. I instructed the boy to bring a reply directly.

'Whilst it would be forward to question my sovereign's polity…' I was seated that afternoon with Montagu in his office, a short time before Ruggieri and the captain were to attend.

'And wisely so, as your position—indeed, your career—hangs upon it.'

After this pronouncement, I held my peace, not quite sure where the bounds lay 'twixt duty and treason and what side of the same fence John might be on.

'Say it!' he said, waving his hand around. 'These four walls.'

'Well… it seems to me that when calling in these Frenchmen, the implications might not have been quite thought through.'

'Very diplomatic of you but damned wishy-washy. Not thought through at all! Royal whim. No thought for the army, no thought for the chain of command but, most derelict of all, no thought for popular opinion. Spending British guineas on Continental entertainment, and employing frogs and maccaronis to order English soldiers to pull it off? Folly!'

I bethought me of that first encounter with John on this very subject, when I had raised the issue of friction between our foreigners and their English counterparts and seen him wave it off. He saw this very scene unfolding back then, but was loath to tackle it head on. Now the pie was rubbed in his face, like it or no.

'Still, we must negotiate ourselves through this present mess,' I continued. 'But how? The enterprise can not collapse nor be scaled back, for then how would the king look?'

'Aye, Charles, and how would *we* look? Within these four walls, bugger the king.' He sighed. 'Fully half of government is spent in protecting the Crown from itself. The other half is engaged in the mere running of the country.'

'But what of this contretemps? Blasted faction!'

'True, but 'twill not glide away. We must stamp out this fire lest it spread.'

'How?' I asked. 'For it seems to me insoluble.'

'Insoluble? I never heard of a fire that *was* soluble...'

I sighed. 'I mixed inadvertently the two elements...'

'Sorry, I make light of it.' He nodded and smiled. 'To solve the issue, we divide.'

'Divide? Are we not divided already? Divide in what way?'

'Ruggieri must have his men, or he will leave.' He counted upon his fingers. 'If he does, the show fails. Desaguliers must be in command of his men. If not, the show fails. So, we assign one part of the structure to the French, and the other to the English.'

'Can this be workable?'

'Charles, attend me,' Montagu tut-tutted. 'It must be workable, for there is no other avenue. Surely, if the Peace of Aix-la-Chapelle could be cobbled together by some species of diplomatic legerdemain and inglorious arse sucking, then anything at all under God's blue vault is equally possible... But here, I think, are our guests.'

Montagu's secretary knocked upon the door, ushered Ruggieri and Desaguliers into the room, and brought chairs forward. John waved the secretary to a side table and bade him take notes.

'Gentlemen,' began Montagu once they were seated, 'I am apprised of the problem, which was first raised to me as a political issue.'

'I have heard enough about your damned English politics already,' said Ruggieri. 'I was brought here to arrange this spectacle, and if I can not do so, I see no place for me here.'

'It is not our politics alone, Signor. Would King Louis of France not bat an eyelash if an Englishman were to offer the same presumption with his army?'

'Perhaps so,' he conceded, 'except that he would not have been placed in such a fix to begin with.'

'That is beside the point,' I said, 'for we are in it for whatever reason.'

'Your sovereign…'

'It is not to do with English politics,' interrupted Montagu. 'It is not to do with French politics; but it is to do with every man's politics. We believe this to be more of a functional issue than a political one, do we not, Mr Frederick?'

I nodded, agreeing with him on this but deuced if I knew where his thinking was taking us.

'Tell me, Captain, hath such a spectacle as this ever been done before in this land?'

'No, sir,' replied Desaguliers slowly. 'I think you know never.'

'And would the Laboratory find it possible, without the assistance of Signor Ruggieri, to pull it off?'

Desaguliers was silent for some time. 'Again, we would be hard put except it were scaled back.'

'And that would not be to the king's liking. Indeed, it is unthinkable.'

'So, what's to do then?' asked both Ruggieri and Desaguliers almost comically in chorus.

'You see,' said Montagu to Ruggieri, 'it is not the substance of the thing but the perception of the thing. It is how your involvement is seen that is the nub of it. And you, of all people, would know substance from artifice, the real from an illusion of it. That is your craft.'

'What of it then?' He was as mystified as me. 'Do you play with me, sir?'

'No, I do not. Here, then, is our proposal. You, Signor Ruggieri, will identify the most critical parts of the firework show, and you will employ your men to see to these on the day. I hereby grant you leave to bring them here as soon as you wish, and the Crown will undertake to cover their expenses. You, Captain Desaguliers, will sit down with Signor Ruggieri and take deep and extensive instruction from him in the firing of the remaining parts. The French will fire part of the show, the English will fire part of the show, and in the heat and noise of the moment, no one will remark the difference. Can you work with each other in this way?'

The room was quiet for a considerable time as Ruggieri and Desaguliers eyed each other with assessing expressions. There had been much animosity between them over this: on the Italian's part because his plans had been turned topsy-turvy and on the captain's part because he saw no way to accommodate the military with the private. More than this, the captain's youth played badly against Ruggieri's experience, and in his heart, I am sure the former felt unsure of himself. Who would not when working with one of the greatest exponents of his craft in Europe and so at odds with the old English methods and approaches?

Ruggieri was the first to break the silence. 'I see no problem with this. I can send for my men directly. But,' and he glanced at Desaguliers, 'there will be much to teach in a very short time.'

'You know not how much I know already,' rejoined Desaguliers, 'so how do you presume that I have much to learn?'

'Pardon my presumption,' he replied quietly. 'We must sit with each other and discuss the extent of our knowledge—both of us—the better to see where we stand.'

I could see the thoughts working behind Desaguliers's eyes and knew that he must agree, but did I also see a hint of... almost excitement? 'I am willing if you are willing, for I see no other way forward.'

'Then let us shake a hand on that,' I said to them, 'and strive to make agreement.'

They rose from either side of the table where they had been seated and shook hands, very tentative. Mistrust and probity lay in the eyes of both, and I knew not whether John Montagu had achieved but a truce, rather than a true ceasefire.

'Are they not chalk and cheese?' he remarked once they had left the room. 'The natural philosopher, the artist; the soldier, the entertainer. Chalk and cheese save when it comes to their damnable squibs and crackers!'

'Though, how will this arrangement play out with the sovereign?' I wondered.

'Won't matter a nun's fart to him as long as the spectacle unfolds. Less he knows the better, and I'll not tell! Mores the point, the satirists, pamphleteers, vendors of discord, ink stained grubbers... John Bull wishes no more truck with the Continent, and they'll see to it that the view's broadcast.'

'Can we not keep it from them?'

'Aye, as like have Pandora change her mind.' He shrugged his shoulders and sighed. 'Come, coffee and a pipe.'

Chapter Twenty

His Majesty King George II (1683 to 1760)
King of Great Britain and Ireland

In which King George meets the designers of his firework display

My devoted and constant servant John Montagu fussed into my reception room with Charles Frederick and a great gaggle of gentlemen in tow, all of them tricked out quite finely to present themselves to the sovereign and hear his will. Now they had become settled in London, it was time for King George II to meet them all and give them their marching orders. They had by now been awed by the vast outline of my Temple of Peace, and now they were to be awed by me. What I needed most from them was the number and kind of the firework effects they would give me. These effects must be equal to the machine that displayed them, and they must be greater in number, variety and impression than anything seen before in this realm or any other. This I had made clear.

'Your Majesty,' intoned Montagu, 'allow me to present…' and each, in turn, came forward at the call of his name and bowed mightily. I spoke a few words of welcome to each, then bade them come and sit around my table where I had the plan laid out.

'Now,' I began, 'I have brought you gentlemen here on the charge of my purse in order to bring off this endeavour. Now that there is peace throughout our realms, we may bring this celebration to fruition in a spirit of harmony and good order. I need not tell you that nothing in England like this hath been put on before, and that is the reason why you are all here.'

I am not without perspicacity, and Montagu had hinted to me ere this meeting was called that harmony was wanting in certain quarters. I looked carefully around the table but saw nothing untoward in their faces (except of course awe, I pride myself, in being in the presence of

His Majesty, the King of Great Britain, etcetera, etcetera).

'The machine progresses well,' I continued. 'We have visited Mr Morris and assured ourselves that he will be finished to our satisfaction. Now, as to the decorations. Cavalier Servandoni?'

Montagu had apprised me in particular that all was not well with this gentleman; he had been of the opinion that he was to devise the entire decoration and that I would merely approve his choice. This is the way 'tis done in Paris for King Louis XV, it is apparent, and he was surprised that I had gone along so far in my designing of it. We are not France.

'We are established in a workshop of sorts and are fully engaged in executing Your Majesty's designs. Needless to say, it is my task to make but sketches into works of art, for there is much upon the plan that needs improvement.'

'Improvement where? I assume in detail, not in substance?'

'Changes may need to be made in the disposition and choice of the elements…'

'There will no changes made in the *choice* of what I have laid out. None. In filling out the sculptures and rendering the images, most certainly. But not in the subjects I have chosen.'

'Tis passing amazing how one man can so contain his ire that not one wisp of steam escapes from his ears. 'Tis a prodigious accomplishment, of which I suspect his vaunted opinion of himself makes the deployment necessary and often.

'But, Your Majesty…'

'No buts, the plan is clear. I am pleased that you are fully engaged in executing my designs.' I could descry the monumental battle in his face, though not one syllable durst he speak. 'Now, as to the disposition and number of the fireworks. Signori Ruggieri and Sarti?'

Ruggieri spoke for both the Italians. 'We employ, Your Highness, an alternating pattern of air effects—mortars and rockets—with ground effects such as wheels and fixed pieces. Thus, rhythm and harmony are established. We commence, of course, with flights of rockets…'

'The details, thank you, Signor Ruggieri, may wait. I am more concerned with the *quantity* of the fireworks. Their number.'

'Indeed, Your Majesty, we…' a wave of the hand to Sarti, who remained silent throughout and, Desaguliers '…have concocted lists of all that will be required. In brief, we plan for around 10,000 rockets, thirty-six suns and wheels, and perhaps 20,000 other sorts of fixt fireworks.'

'Ten *thousand* rockets? This is excellent!' It o'er-topped my expectations. 'But tell me, this must surely exceed anything you have done for King Louis XV of France?'

'Most certainly, Your Majesty. We feel it will be unique in all the world.'

'Most excellent.' I near as damn me rubbed my hands together.

'There is one small issue, Your Majesty,' said Frederick. 'On the drawing, there is a large cartouche of the Lion and the Unicorn, and above it a great girandole; the sun figure with VIVAT REX writ large upon it.'

'What of it?'

'My artificers are of the opinion that, if you wished to have the girandole, 'twould not be possible to erect it with the cartouche in place. 'Tis one or t' other.'

'But the Lion and the Unicorn are essential!' Damned if I'd not have the royal crest.

'So, we dispense with the sun figure? The girandole?'

'No, no, no! It also is indispensable.' There was a long pause as all sat around the table, none wishing to gainsay his monarch. I thought of that great sun girandole and all those fires, and the spectacle its ignition would create, and then thought of the cartouche lost in shadow beneath it. 'Well, then, what form of firework will the girandole be?'

Ruggieri spoke up first. 'There will be 6,000 rockets headed with stars, rains and serpents which will burst forth, whilst VIVAT REX is outlined in cascading fire.'

'Six thousand! And cascading fire? Can you do this?'

'We can and will, Your Majesty.'

'Then damn the cartouche.' I turned to Servandoni. 'Make it much smaller. Paint it on a flat board, and hang it below.' He nodded, and I sensed a look of relief in his eye, for 'twould be a monstrous thing to carve and erect.

I turned to young Tom Desaguliers. 'Thomas, it is good to see you. We remember your father most fondly. [22] What of the firing?'

'Thank you for your kind words, Your Majesty. All is in train. We have laid out a plan for the order and sequence, and we are engaged with Cavalier Servandoni in planning the order of actions upon the machine.'

'Well and good. These actions are to be close meshed with the firework?'

'Exactly so,' he replied, forgetting my honorific. 'The teams of artillerymen assigned to the lighting must be meshed with those in control of the rigging of the machinery.'

'Cavalier Servandoni, what actions do you plan?'

'There are sixteen transparencies painted in *grisaille*, which represent…'

'Aye, I devised 'em m'self. I know what they represent, damn it.'

'Just so, Your Majesty.' He paused and gathered himself, almost hissing like one of Newcomen's satanic engines. 'As the firework plays off, these transparencies are lit from behind. Then, at the conclusion they are withdrawn by machinery to be replaced with the same in full colour.'

'Yes, a full colour transformation. I knew you would be up to such a cunning scheme.'

'Quite so, Your Majesty. Just as you *hinted* in your sketch. And the ground before the machine is lit with hundreds of *pots de brin*…'

'A species of firework, Your Majesty,' put in Frederick sentientiously, for which I damned his intrusion.

'…which are fired so as to mesh with the presentation.'

'I leave the order of it in your good hands and those of our firework artificers.'

'Thank you for your kindness, Your Majesty,' replied Servandoni, just slightly on the safe side of vinegar.

'Now, Captain, what of the Laboratory? Have you the making of the fireworks in hand?'

'Yes, Your Majesty, all is in good order…'

'You hesitate, sir?'

'It will be a magnificent spectacle, Your Majesty, and one that…'

'Cut to the meat, Captain!' though I smiled.

I caught his quick glance over to Montagu and a corresponding nod. 'There is not sufficient resource within the Laboratory, so it is necessary to bring other hands into the fabrication by contract.'

'Do you not do this often at Woolwich?'

Montagu intervened at this point. 'We do indeed. I cite but the examples of the supply of timber, the order for powder from Waltham, the shortage of pasteboard, whale oil for thousands of lampions, isinglass and cotton thread, the...'

'Silence! Tax me not with details! *I despise details!*' Though Montagu is a good and faithful servant, he fails—and perhaps always will fail—to spare me the humdrum. Whale oil; good God! 'Are the fireworks being made, and will sufficient be ready upon the day? That is the question, and all of it!'

'Yes, Your Majesty,' they replied in chorus.

'And will the lighting and the actions of the machine be all in accord?'

'Yes, Your Majesty,' they replied in chorus but with slight glances between 'em.

'Any other business?' I asked, fool that I am. Should have simply dismissed 'em, for Montagu spoke up.

'There is the matter of music...'

'There will be none. It wants not the distraction of music.'

'But, Your Majesty, a musical overture to a firework is the very fashionable thing now.'

'Be damned to it! And be damned to you!'

He opened his mouth to reply, glanced quickly around the table, and decided mayhap that it would do him no good to press this suit further.

'All done?' They nodded. 'Good. Then go you all about your various tasks. It hath been a great pleasure to greet Cavalier Servandoni and the Signori Ruggieri and Sarti. Work well, and you will all be rewarded with our satisfaction at your accomplishments. A very good day to you all, and may I wish you all a very happy Christmas, though I trust you will not take long out of your tasks in which to celebrate it.'

I waved 'em all out of the room and had my man pour a generous glass of wine. Whilst my plan for celebration of the Peace was an excellent one—and the culmination of it would also be of excellence, I doubted not—the part betwixt the two ends, where one had to rely upon underlings to carry out the task, was fraught with irritations.

Chapter Twenty-One

John, 2nd Duke of Montagu (1690 to 1749)
Master-General of His Majesty's Ordnance

In which the Christmas season is celebrated, a brief excursion taken from any talk of the king's fireworks, and guests are both japed and challenged

I bethought myself what a fine thing 'twould be if I had the participants in the king's grand endeavour around to my country house on Blackheath for a celebration of the Christmas season. I kept better stocks of food and drink there than in London, the house was fully staffed and more amenable to guests, and my wife, Mary, was down from Boughton House in Northamptonshire for the Christmas season. The house is not above ten miles from London, so a carriage ride of a couple of hours would not be too great an inconvenience. Blackheath is close to Woolwich, too, for those of the party who lived and worked there. I chose the eve of Christmas so that, once well wined and feasted, they could either take themselves home severally or stay the night and return to London for Christmas Day.

There were two good reasons for wishing to entertain them; well, three if you include my fondness for food and drink and good company. In the first case—and in all truth—I was sick and damned well tired of nothing but fireworks. My life had been kidnapped by the bloody project; me, who is the first to climb aboard a sinecure when such a bauble is dangled before me. Sure as mutton, the king knew the extent to which I would become embroiled, and he must have been laughing himself silly over it. All well and good to counsel Chas to delegate, but one can only follow that path if one hath no vested interest in the thing. Beyond royal displeasure, which I might possibly weather, there were other inducements of a fiduciary and financial nature that kept me to the task.

My second motive for a festive break was that I wished to find some way of inducing harmony amongst the players because it was quite evidently wanting. We'd hardly make a success of this thing if we stood against each other like warring factions. 'Twas high time to lay signature to the Peace of Blackheath-la-Montagu.

And that third motivation of mine, my fondness for the kitchen and the cellar, would be happily satisfied in fine style. My cellar and kitchen in town were always excellent, but Blackheath was far superior. I had my staff lay in a fine goose, a brace of quail, fillets of plaice and ham for a soup of pease. Mincemeat and apples they had in plenty, and vegetables preserved from the autumn, so nothing was wanting there. I had them send a boy off for the freshest of Wallfleet oysters, for meat is nothing without such a sauce. And we had suet and flour and plums enough for a fine pudding, which we would grace with a brandy custard. Aye, we would welcome the baby Jesus into this vale of tears in fine style. We rarely decorate the place, as we are more often at Boughton over Christmas, but this year my forced presence in London warranted some festive flummery; holy and mistletoe along the picture frames and I know not what. By the time our guests were to arrive at four in the afternoon, the house looked very well and welcomed visitors to its front hall with an enticing aroma.

Christmas is a time for jollity, and there is nothing that amuses one's guests more than a harmless bit of fun. I was ever one for the handicraft joke, which goes beyond the wielding of words and uses devices to achieve its ends. There is an endless list of simple household items that can be pranked to make 'em work in surprising ways. Or not work. Mary looks askance at this practice, oft times chiding me for these excesses, but no harm is ever done through laughing and good humour. I recall the time fondly when I had my gardener at Boughton change the direction of one of the fountains so that, when a concealed *fontainier* was turned on, the guests were sprinkled! Merely sprinkled I say, though some reported the incident quite differently. But I have no truck with Quaker-faced sourpusses, so let them say what they might. A mere sprinkling, 'twas.

I had sent a carriage to Curzon Street for the French and Italian craftsmen, and they were first to arrive. The second carriage from Woolwich arrived not long after with the two firework men, doffing their cloaks and gloves and bringing with them a cloud of cold and a whirl of snow. I had no sooner shut the front door, and seen all our foreigners into the drawing room, than Chas Frederick and Jas Morris arrived almost together, each with his lady wife upon his arm. I felt it important to have Morris along with his wife. I valued immensely his workmanship, devotion and solid British character. He was a fine foil to our French and Italian artisans, and I was sure I could count upon him to hold up his end at table. I have to say, I would have scarce recognised him in the street as I had only ever seen him in his working clothes. Here before me, wigged and powdered and dressed, was a transformation.

I had Lady Mary escort Lucy Frederick and Elizabeth Morris to the drawing room. Tom Desaguliers was last to arrive, alone as he always is; although smiling and wishing me well for the season, there was ever a distance betwixt us, try though I might to find a way through. Perhaps my trying was, itself, counter to my intention, and served only further to drive a wedge? A curious, austere and inscrutable young man I thought him then. But, had I known then what I later learned, I feel I would have seen him in a different light. I knew not that his wife was heavy with their third child, was unwell with the burden and would otherwise have attended him tonight.

I had not long taken delivery of a tierce of fine Amontillado from my merchant in Spain, so with glasses of it in our hands, we started off the festivities right well. I have this curious drinking glass, an identical match for the other eleven, save that it hath a small hole drilled in its rim, just below the edge. When one hands out the drink, one must be careful to offer the glass to the chosen guest so that he takes it with the hole closest to himself. Thus, when he tips the glass up to toast, the wine dribbles out and makes a God-awful mess.

'Good will and cheer to the season!' I cried and raised my glass.

'*Salut*, good health, *santé*, cheers,' rang out all round as the rest raised their glasses and drank.

Frederick was the first to fall prey to the evening's japes. I had chosen him because I knew he would see me as the perpetrator and join in the merriment, and so it transpired. His first surprise at applying more Amontillado to his chin and cravat than he did to his tongue caused laughter all around, including his own. Presently, the bell sounded, and we joined the ladies in the drawing room, but before we went through to the dining room to take our places at table, I called for a brief pause. I had decided upon a very perilous social experiment, but I do so love to take gambles, and I rarely lose a wager.

'Ladies and gentlemen,' I began, 'before we sit to dine, I would like to tell you a story. It is a salutary tale for Christmas, for this is the time of goodwill to all men, be they of other countries or other creeds, or from far places, for we are all one in God's eyes. When I served the first King George as governor in the West Indies, I knew that the worth and usefulness of the islands under my charge was founded upon the labour of slaves. Since then, I have come to the view that no man is free until every man is free. To that end, Lady Mary and I have seen to the education and welfare of several of our Negro brethren. Please welcome Ignatius Sancho, who hath lived here in Greenwich since the age of four years and is welcome in this house in freedom.'

Our protégé, Ignatius, stood forward from the door where I had asked him to wait and bowed deeply. He was a fine-looking fellow, some thirty or so years old, and of stalwart and loyal disposition. He was well turned out for presentation, wigged and with his best suit of clothes. I ever felt that Ignatius, and our other charge Francis, were embodiments of the sons Mary and I had lost in infancy.

'Ignatius is a writer, a poet and a musician.[23] Before we sit for dinner, I would like you to hear him play one of his own compositions.'

I waved him over to the harpsichord and bade him sit, whilst our group formed a loose circle about him. I could see that they were all intrigued by this crossing of their bounds, some more than a little discomforted. But if they felt discomfort now, it was as yet nothing to what I had in store. Ignatius played us a menuet of some minutes, with such delicacy and refinement that I knew in my heart I would win the next round. Music crosses over and brings concord.

'Though he is carved in ebony,' I cried, 'Ignatius is made in God's image. Come with me, all of you, into the dining room.'

It is a beautiful thing to see a well-laid table, with the silverware just so, the napkins neatly folded, the glass and china sparkling, and all blessed with the gentle light and scent of well-placed beeswax candles. A multitude of dishes had been laid on; there was the goose, the quail and the fish, the great tureen of ham and pease soup, and many other delicacies awaiting us. Red and white wine, Madeira, port, and I know not what else stood in waiting carafes.

As they gathered around the table, I paused them again.

'See,' I said, waving at the table, 'fourteen places are laid, yet we are but thirteen. Unlucky so. Tonight, the composer and poet Ignatius Sancho will dine with us to bring our number to fourteen.' Lady Mary smiled widely, privy to this little subterfuge, but her eyes moved quickly about the company.

Silence, 'tis said, speaks with a voice of thunder. All those around that table were stuck upon the butterfly pins of their society, their station and their place. After my announcement, 'twas as if some person had reached up and stayed the hand o' the clockwork of the world. Even the candles appeared to hold their waver. Not a mere performing curiosity to incur light applause before dinner; a living, breathing man with mind and appetite. One amongst us. Thus, we stood.

Warming my heart, and rewarding all my expectations, Jas Morris spoke first.

'Come, Mr Sancho, sit between Elizabeth and me. We would know as much as you can tell us of your life.'

Guests breathed out, chatter broke forth, chairs were pulled out, and much seating and getting comfortable occupied the moments before I called again for silence. We bowed our heads and held hands around.

'Give us grateful hearts, oh Heavenly Father, for all thy mercies, and make us mindful of the needs of others not so privileged as to sit with us at this table. Through Jesus Christ our Lord. Amen.'

'Amen.'

Now, with a great hurdle jumped, and a bold experiment validated, 'twas time for more lightness and cheer. I made a wager with myself that Frederick would not again be the victim of another jape, but as we were now fourteen around the table, the odds were long. The handicraft joke I had planned needed a thick soup so the victim could not see the bottom of the bowl, and I had arranged it so the tureen was nearest my place. I had a trick up my sleeve...

'Here,' I cried, 'who's for a bowl of soup? 'Tis a thick broth of pease and ham.' I seized bowls, filled them with the ladle, and passed them along. They picked up their spoons...

'*Mon dieu!*' came a cry along the table as de Cleremont discovered the frog at the bottom of his bowl. Oh, how perfect it was that one of the Frenchmen should have taken the tricked bowl, but thankfully not Servandoni for I was sure he would take it ill.

'Fear not,' I laughed, 'for 'tis but made of green sealing wax.'

The gentlemen laughed loudest—even de Cleremont—for they were already primed, and the ladies followed when they saw that it was but a jest. The laugh of the victim renders parole for the rest to join.

'Fie, Charles,' said my wife in mock earnest, 'your japes are beyond the pale. I always tell you this: you will drive more away than you will ever endear.'

The laughter of all was an antidote to her words, and this signalled the opening of conversations around the table whilst people helped themselves from the plenitude of dishes and tipped much drink down their throats. I caught snatches of conversation: '…named me Sancho after the character in Cervantes…', '…*ici il pleut continuellement*…', '…three times what it was worth…', '…*magari trovarli in Italia*…', '…only freed once Lady Montagu had…', '…ebony? Don't see much of that…' and so on. All signs that things were running well, oiled by drink and victuals. And not a blessèd word about fireworks.

Next came my jape with the fish. Before we entered the dining room, I had had my people bring in one salver with a cover upon it. This I passed to Andrea Soldi, recommending a rare treasure of the sea to him. Alas, when the cover was lifted and the dish revealed, he had but the skeleton of the fish, the bare bones of his meal!

'Usually,' I cried to the table at large, 'I make no bones about the food, but today I make no fish about it!'

More and more, the party was attuned to laughter, only Tom Desaguliers being reluctant to drag forth a smile, though he was well enough content to be with us. So, the meal went its way with fine food, fine wine and fine company.

Presently, the dishes were taken off, a fresh table cloth brought out, and then the meal concluded with the triumphal entry of the pudding and sundry sweetmeats and fruits. More wines were brought out, glasses replenished and all went swimmingly well. An excellent evening was had, and all guests chose to wend their way home, late though the hour had become. There were no more Christmas Eve japes after the fish. Lady Mary was right; sufficient unto the day… No one was discommoded, no hurt was given nor received, and each laughed with the other.

But I think the greatest jape I pulled off that Christmas Eve was to have such gentry, denizens of the Royal Court and London society, sit down to dinner with a black man.

CHAPTER TWENTY-TWO

Captain Thomas Desaguliers (1721 to 1780)
Chief Firemaster of His Majesty's Royal Laboratory

In which the pyrotechnicians make a New Year's pact and determine the disposition of their troops

'I wish you a Happy New Year,' said Gaetano Ruggieri as he entered my office in the Warren on the first day of January. 'In France we make a covenant by kissing under a sprig of *gui*.' He smiled weakly. 'But I will not presume so far.'

'For that I am grateful.' I smiled too, but no more openly than he. I had woes enough at home and had foolishly allowed myself to carry them here. 'For us, New Year begins on Lady Day, the twenty-fifth of March. And we kiss under our mistletoe only at Christmas.' I laughed lightly. Since our handshake with Montagu and Frederick, we had danced a menuet of uncertainty about one another; a truce only.

'Of course, your mad calendar.' He paused some long moments. 'We... we are brought together under curious circumstances...'

I waited to see how much further his thoughts would take him, reluctant to interfere lest he turn away. We must work together from here on, we must set aside the anger that had coloured our previous intercourse, we must find common ground. All this I could feel coming up in him yet not easy of expression. I decided to reply to him in French; it was the first tongue of my father's Huguenot household—Latin ran a close third—and I was perfectly fluent.

'*Des circonstances curieuses certainement...*' It opened a way forward as I hoped it would, though he remained still distant, detached.

'Working together... different means, different ends... we are worlds apart.'

'Well, we can thank God that Montagu's found a way for us to work side by side.' I had thought ill of Montagu ere he intervened to resolve our differences, but since then, I was seeing a side of him that made me think differently. I was almost reluctant to admit, even to myself, that I had begun to *like* him.

'Hath Montagu done so? Can we work thus?' He was not meeting my eye. 'By what magic do we lay aside the harsh speech, the angry words? On the say-so of a politician? Is it so easy to go forward?'

'Well, I'll not kiss you under a sprig of *gui*,' I replied, perhaps more lightly than the circumstance warranted, 'but I do feel we can mend things if we try.'

He waved a hand, angry in dismissal. 'Do not be frivolous with me!'

'Please.' I held my palms up. 'Continue.'

He breathed in deeply. 'It begins with trust. Yes, you have shown yourself capable—beyond my expectations for one so young—but you must know that this enterprise of ours *can not* fail!'

'Of course, it can not. The king hath set great store by it; much hangs upon it. By God, my career hangs upon 't.'

'Hangs upon *you*. You have much to learn. Do you have an idea of how much you have to learn, or are you yet cock-a-hoop that you can pull it off?'

'Have I not shown you,' I replied evenly, 'that when the time comes, I rise to challenges?'

'Aye, so you have, so you have.'

'What then? Shall you trust me to rise more or no?'

'I must, must I not?' He took a deep breath. 'For me, selfishly, it must not fail.' He paused, turned about, and gazed out of the window, seeing naught. As he turned to face me, I could see him coming to a resolution. 'We so often use allusions from past times in common speech, do we not? Well, I have burnt my bridges. When I told the Duke of Montagu that I would return to France if my demands were not met, it was quite untrue.'

'You could not go back?'

'Never. There is nothing for me there. Servandoni? Yes, I work with Servandoni here, but when he returns, he works with my brothers. And Sarti; he plans to return to Bologna. But for me… I came here to find a new… challenge… This is hard for me to say… When you raised the problem of command, when you stood against me and dashed the possibility of this work here, I was cut free to drift. I had nowhere to go. Nowhere. And that is why this enterprise hinges not upon me—for I know my craft and my capabilities more than you can imagine—but upon you, who have so much to learn that you know not how much!'

I looked now into Ruggieri's face, and in that moment, I saw myself as he saw me. I am young; I am not yet fully acquainted with the way of the men I work with, nor have I wanted to be. I keep this life and my home life ever distinct; the one does not in any way cross into the other. It is only through complete concentration on the work at hand that any worthwhile result is forthcoming. Hitherto, then, I have kept myself alone here, have worked diligently upon my researches, and have eschewed the company of those around me. Until now: in this relationship with Ruggieri I had stood my ground and faced a man ten years older, with ten times my experience, from a foreign and unknown milieu, and I had done so in defence. My barrier against the souls around me had risen on command, but it was clear to me now that no man can be an island unto himself alone. Standing there, face to face with the great Gaetano Ruggieri, I took a step I hitherto knew not I lacked.

I have often pondered the nature and power of language and have thought that the words a man wields are but the smallest visible peak of a vast mountain of understanding; or misunderstanding. Below the words we speak to each other is a world of thought that never becomes expressed; can not by its very nature be expressed. Now, it is a very strange thing that Ruggieri and I had hitherto conversed in English, and though his command of my tongue was good, I became convinced that had I spoken from the outset in French, we might never have come to such a pass. Our speech in French this day moved mountains.

The time for healing was now.

'I will learn from you as much as you can give. And I will learn it gladly. Shall we begin now? From this very instant?'

He stepped forward and took my hand, as an Englishman would do. Then—and this I ascribe to the power of language—he seized my shoulders with both hands, and we clasped and kissed upon both cheeks, as only Frenchmen would do.

'We lack only a sprig of *gui*,' I remarked, and we laughed together.

We arranged our work at the Arsenal on two fronts. On the one hand, there was the production, which was going full ahead with Giuseppe

Sarti at the helm. As the pieces were made, they were stockpiled in brick buildings around the Warren specifically designed for the storage of powder and cartridges. Not one piece of wood was used in their construction, nor one particle of iron or steel in their fittings. Nearer the time, these pieces would be taken to the Green Park with extreme care and stored in a brick building that the Corps of Engineers was raising inside the north pavilion of the machine. Brock's production from Whitechapel was sent directly to the Green Park but supervised by Sarti, who was charged with control of quality. He proved quite capable of working with Benjamin Brock, and he told us his English was improving. He would come away from London, I doubted not, with a most curious inflection to his speech!

On our part, with Gaetano Ruggieri instructing me upon the making and setting of fuses, and the planning of the order of firing, I was well engaged. I had my team of gunners by me, and we exercised the order of firing again and again, 'til we could do it even after death. We had Charles Frederick to Woolwich several times to go over the firing plans, and greatly excited he was to be so involved. The man's nose for gunpowder was prodigious, though his continual questioning did become irksome. He did win one small battle: he insisted—with a little encouragement from me, truth to tell—that we would have some pumps. He was smitten with the idea of shooting many stars from one case, and so Ruggieri allowed Brock to supply a few and position them in front of the machine, to be fired by my men at certain points in the display. Gaetano insisted, though, that they not appear on the official disposition.

And touching on that "official disposition," Ruggieri and Sarti worked hard in the evenings, draughting a description of all the firework effects, and had copies sent by our runners to Servandoni so he could add detail of the decorative elements. This compilation put me in mind of the descriptions I had seen of Empress Elizabeth's coronation in St Petersburg, although those were finely set out and printed.

By his title, Mr Frederick was commander of the Train of Artillery, but in truth the post is titular. The commands for firing of the machine would be issued by those who knew what they were doing, so we enjoined him—in the most diplomatic terms—to sit by and watch the spectacle unfold. Thus, below him, for our sensitive political reasons, we perforce made two divisions: my team of gunners would answer to me, as was our routine when firing a show, whilst Ruggieri's team would answer to him. In our scheming of the order of firing, we had divided the spectacle into distinct parts. I minded not that the most complex and difficult operations were in his hands, for his people would needs scale the rear of the machine on rope ladders to ignite many of the high effects. My men would work closer to the ground on lightings more familiar to them.

'There is one thing,' I told him whilst we were working over the division of forces. 'The matrosses and gun captains are proud... and ignorant. For certain there will be discontent amongst them at your French crew.'

He smiled. '*Vraiment*, the head-to-head of you and me but lacking the will or the understanding to set it aside.'

'Exactly. There is much anti-French sentiment amongst the people.' I became brisk. 'But an Italian needs not another lecture on French and English politics from me.'

'Enough said. Sufficient to be aware of it. But some of us frogs and maccaronis are quite tolerable...'

There was a world of difference between the way the Ordnance fired our firework shows and the ways of Ruggieri and the artists, and it was all in the ignition. If your mortars, your rockets and your candles are on the ground or set on low racks, the men may light them with portfires; these are slowmatches that are a length of hempen cord treated with saltpetre so it smoulders slowly. When reaching up to wheels or setting off rockets, it is best to attach the slowmatch to a linstock, a length of wood or metal with a hook on the end, the better to be safe. Even a complicated show with many pieces may be lit this way, provided your men have a set pattern and react swiftly and readily to commands. This was our way at the Ordnance, and the men of the Train of Artillery were well drilled in it. Many was the show in Hyde Park we had lit this way.

The new way, as I was now obliged to view it, was a world more involved. The fire had to be conveyed to many pieces at once, at great speed, and often high off the ground. For this was applied the art of fuses and the quickmatch. Certainly, we were already familiar with delaying fire by the use of fuse, but our craft was beyond rudimentary by comparison. Of course, I knew this. One of my first speculations upon hearing that Ruggieri would be employed was upon exactly this head; I remembered wondering how they arranged their displays, how their timing was effected, and what systems of fusing and ignition they might employ.

Now, I would be privy to their secrets.

Chapter Twenty-Three

Gaetano Ruggieri (1715 to 1776)
Pyrotechnician

In which the master pyrotechnician instructs the pupil on the secrets of quickmatch and its application, and the pupil is awed and surprised

'Look at it out there now!' I waved my hand at the Laboratory window slashed with rain and at the plane trees shaking their limbs in defiance. I turned from the window to face Thomas. 'Moist weather is the bane of our lives. I know why, in God's name, this show *must* take place in April, but could a more changeable season, insusceptible of prediction, have been chosen?'

Spite of these words, I was happier now than I had ever been since arriving in this dreadful country. Certainly, the slashing rain was horrible, and perhaps boded not well even though it was only the middle of January, and the politics here rivalled the worst of French court intrigue, but the sunshine in my soul outdid it all. I've ever hated discord—that's why I'd so happily left France—so to encounter it here upon my arrival was daunting indeed. But our New Year's pact held well, and I had become more of an intimate to this strange and distant young man than I think any other had. And he, too, had learned a great deal whilst we stood face to face, saw where the land lay, and pinned ourselves to the task.

"Tis months away yet, so try not to fret over it,' Thomas replied. 'I have known glorious Aprils.'

'And I have seen Aprils where if the shit of dogs fell out of the sky, there would be improvement.' But I spoke in jest, for I could not let myself be downhearted.

'Well, yes,' he said, peering through the smeared glass. 'Many's the fine spectacle delayed or ruined by the gods of the clouds. I am perhaps fortunate that none I have staged was ever quite washed out, though we have toiled in rain on occasion.'

'So, too, have I, but that's our lot. We'd not be in this business if we couldn't manage.'

'But, for a spectacle such as this, many days are needed in setting it all up, multiplying the probability of rain. I have ordered as much fine oilcloth as I think we'll need.'

Once a firework was installed, we used a square of thin oilcloth to cover it against the weather. This took much time and was costly, as oilcloth of the fineness we needed was in short supply and not cheap. It is useless to use tarpaulin, for it is too heavy, thus sitting upon the touchpapers and damaging them, and besides, it would need to be lifted off before the lighting. Thin oilcloth could be left where it was; once the firework was lit, it would be blown away.

'Good. Let us pray for one of your best Aprils,' I laughed. 'Or dance a mumbo-jumbo in Whitehall to appease the gods, as they do in Afric climes!'

'Save that they dance to bring on rain, not stave it off.'

'Oh, ovviamente...'

On that day November past, when Thomas had first seen the number of rockets that Giuseppe and I proposed, he had quailed. It was then that my misgivings came fully home to me; how could this young man and his famed Laboratory be capable enough for us to pull this off? Then, on following days, as we had sat down and worked through the lists of fireworks, he became all business. He rose to the task at hand, encompassed the enormous quantities, and organised the procurement. Still he lacked one piece of comprehension; still he failed to grasp the true enormity of what he was called upon to do. Yes, he knew the numbers; yes, we had discussed placement and disposition on the machine; yes, we had assigned sections of the display amongst ourselves. And the fireworks were piling up in their brick warehouses. Yet it was only when we began to discuss fuses that, I believe, he came truly face to face with it all. Why was this? Why would some small detail of how to light a firework become a sudden ray of revelation?

It is a headlong collision. In England, the gunners fire their shows with a slowmatch—a length of hempen rope steeped in saltpetre—and they run from one piece to another, lighting as they would their cannon.

Such hath always been their practice. In France and Italy, when setting off fireworks on a machine, such as those we had developed over the years, it is impossible to have men fire the pieces together in this way. As but one example, in the very first section of our disposition for the king's April spectacle, we planned a fixed sun motif, two stars, a compound piece of points and rays, and four large double wheels. The only way to light these in the correct order—which is the effect we strive for—is to have them connected by what we call quickmatch. Each of the fireworks on these pieces must be connected to each other by a fuse that will burn in an instant. With this first section of the show, there would be perhaps thirty such leads, as we call them, with another twenty following straight after. All this I began to explain as I got down to the business of showing Thomas our methods.

'Well,' Thomas told me, 'we can join fireworks one to another with straws of differing lengths. We take a wide, clean straw of rye and fill it with fine slow powder. It must be tamped down and packed well so as to burn evenly.'

'We did this many years ago, but it would hardly serve for present purposes.'

'No, of course not,' he laughed. 'Indeed, I am somewhat shamed to describe the crude methods we use for fusing, but we have gone no further in our development at the Laboratory for want of application.'

'Well, here is a small length of the quickmatch we use.' We had sat ourselves on stools each side of a trestle table, and I laid out two feet of the fuse I favoured. I had about me on the table the tools I would need in showing him how it was done. 'I brought a small amount with me for fear you might not have similar.'

'Aye, we know how to make it, of course,' said Thomas, taking it between his fingers, 'but we lack skill in the craft for want of practical application.'

Quickmatch looks for all the world like a straw made of paper, scarce the thickness of a pipe stem.

'How do you make this?' Thomas asked me.

'Here's what we do. There is the outer, which you see here, and the inner. The outer is made by rolling thin news-paper into a tight tube around a fine wooden dowel well rubbed with beeswax. We go one turn about the dowel with a small overlap. The paper is brushed with a paste of flour and water as it is being rolled, just the same as for firework cases. Then, when dried, we slide it off and use the dowel for another.'

'So, you are making a straw, but we would take one from nature.'

'Just so, but ours are as long as we wish to make them. Now the inner. We take three parts of saltpetre to two parts of isinglass and dissolve them in a little very hot water and spirits of wine.'

'Isinglass?' he asked.

'A size made from fish bladders.'

'Oh, aye, sturgeon glue.'

'Just so. We boil the liquor away until the mixture becomes thick, then take a length of twisted cotton thread—and this may be as long as you need—and soak it well. Then we remove the pan and, whilst still warm, take it quickly to another room away from the fire, and pour in mealed gunpowder to give a paste. Then—and this is the part that takes great skill—we wind the thread upon a loom, running it the while through a handful of the wet powder.'

I took a pencil and paper and quickly sketched the loom; a simple frame of two horizontal dowels that could be rotated with a handle so as to wind the quickmatch up from the bowl through the hand.

'The isinglass?' Tom asked. 'It allows the gunpower to stick?'

'*Precisamente*. One can also use skin glue, or that made from hooves and bones, but isinglass and others made from fish are finer. Then we dust the wet fuse with dry mealed powder until it takes no more, then set it to air on the loom.'

'And finally, when dry,' said Thomas, 'cut to length, and pass into the paper straw. And you add more paper straws as needed for length.'

'*Si*, as long as needed. This straw is two feet long, which is about as much as can be managed on the dowel. They can be joined one to another with a turn of pasted paper as they are slid on the fuse. We then coat the whole in tallow. The paper is to protect the quickmatch and, with the tallow, render it proof from moisture.'

'Do they not become unwieldy at great length?'

'Certainly, they do. They need to be tied in place, and I think their length is proportional to their reliability.'

'How fast doth this burn?'

'It goes in a trice. It must be quick so that our pieces are lit all together.'

'I mean, at what speed?' Thomas had that keenness in his eyes.

'I have never made a measure. Why would I?'

'It would be excellent to know how quick it goes and what might be the influence on the velocity of different grain sizes of mealed powder. We could set up measured lengths of it and time its deflagration on the second minute of a watch.'

'Ah, ever the natural philosopher. You and your damned rockets again! We have not the time nor the materials to waste upon such speculation.'

'I know, but in the fullness of time...'

'Set aside your predisposition to natural philosophy. We have work to do.'

I pulled forward the great chart we had made listing all the components of the display that Thomas, Giuseppe and I had agreed upon.

'Now then, rockets first. Ten thousand, six hundred and fifty of 'em. These we set in holes in wooden rails with a groove along the top. One quickmatch to start each rack.'

'Oh, aye, we do the same.' He nodded. 'The efflux from one rocket sets fire to the next, and so on. We have some racks for flights of twenty, but I'll have the woodworkers make a start on more.'

'Hmm. Twenty? We'll need racks for hundreds, and our list shows sixty-six such flights.' Thomas scribbled some notes.

'Including the grand girandole?' he asked, pencil poised.

'No, that one alone will consume 6,000 rockets headed with stars, rains and serpents, and I want them all in one flight.'

'*All in one flight?*' he asked, disbelief upon his face. 'Six thousand!'

'Yes, and 'twill be phenomenal. That's what we told the king, did we not?'

'Aye, but he knew not that all would erupt at once.'

'Then even greater will be the sovereign joy. We shall have them in boxes of 100 each, each box fused to the other with quickmatch leads.'

'Boxes? I don't comprehend you.'

'Simple. A box of wood with its top drilled with holes. A pattern of ten holes by ten, with a rocket dropped into each. When any rocket is lit, its deflagration in the confined space of the box sets off the rest.'

'One hundred all at once!' Delight was writ on his face.

'Yes, yes, but all sixty boxes *at once!* Six thousand!'

Delight was replaced with awe. I watched him as he framed this in his mind's eye. But ever as I laid on more and more of the detail, he flinched not and held himself to the task.

'And the boxes will be upon the roof, which your men must scale to fire them?'

'Just so. Now,' I continued, 'the other fireworks. We have twenty-one thousand, nine hundred and fifty-four.' Again, I watched his face and his manner.

'"Tis a daunting list when one sees it all laid out thus,' he remarked. 'But it is a matter of mere numbers...'

'Yes, indeed,' I replied, 'and a quickmatch for every one.'

'Of course. Every single piece...' I could see his mind working, grasping at the scale of the thing. 'And each match connected to the next. Light one end, and in an instant, your entire piece is lit all at once.'

'Yes. A set piece, such as a sun or a wheel, might have twenty or thirty such leads, as we call them.'

'How are these connections... leads made?'

'You bend the fuse upon itself and make a slit at the point of the curve to allow the fire to flash through. Here, let me show you.' I bent the match over tightly and exposed the inner cord with my knife. 'Hand me a small fountain. Now, you open up the top paper, add a small spoon of fine mealed powder, and push the fuse into the fountain like so. Now, I tie it and the paper together with linen thread. Then I measure out the length of lead needed for the next firework, bend the quickmatch once again, slit the bend and continue. Once your length of match is used up, you splice the next length to it side by side, insert it into the top of the next firework, and so forth. It is careful work, and it must be done just so. Imagine if one lead were to fail; then all those following would not be lit.'

'Good God in heaven!' he cried. It was as if the glory of God had thrust aside clouds and, of a sudden, shone down upon him. 'That's 20- ... nay, 22,000 such leads! 'Tis impossible!'

'Save that we do this all the time,' says I, all sing-song like and with a smirk upon my face. Then, I decided to play my trump. It was naughty of me to hold back my *pièce de résistance* from him, for I had already made a crack in his cocksure opinion of himself. Now was the time to demolish the wall. 'Tell me, Captain Desaguliers, how much quickmatch think you we need?'

He shook his head. 'I know not... I would have to calculate. Given time, I could...' And he picked up a pencil as if to start.

'Let me save you the trouble.' I held silence, watching his face and relishing the tension and anticipation therein. 'Over two-and-one-half miles of quickmatch.'

Thunderstruck is such a shallow word, so inadequate to the task. *Stupefatto* is no more useful. The man was wordless in wonder, in awe... and in fear, I warrant.

'*Oh, si*,' I continued to rub it in. 'Stretched out straight, it would lie from here nigh to the Royal Observatory upon its hill at Greenwich!'

'But we can not... We don't have the... two-and-one-half *miles*?'

'And we must begin the production soon,' I said into a long silence. 'We'll need to build several looms and procure supplies. And you need men who will be capable quickly to master this craft.'

'Aye. But... you may not command them...' he said uncertainly, raising again the spectre of our strange relationship.

'*Mio Dio*, must I dance a menuet about you lest you play the porcupine?'

'You can instruct me, then,' he replied swiftly, 'and I will pass on the craft.'

'Then the blind shall lead the blind, and both shall fall into the... what is the water by the road? Ditch!'

'What then?' he cried. ''Tis the only way!'

'No, no. It is too uncertain. Did I not say how critical are the quickmatch and leads? And even I am not the best at it.'

'Well, then,' said Thomas, 'would it not be far better if we bring in your people now? Surely, you must have those amongst your team who can do this?'

My relief was immense, for this was the resolution I had striven for. I had frightened the captain loose-bowelled upon the enormity of the task, but he was coming around nicely. Men skilled in this art are few, and the thought of passing the craft along, through him, to unskilled gunners gave me great pause.

'I can gladly send for Henri and Michel,' I told him, 'and I am sure my brother can spare them. He will require recompense for their time, of course, and the others of my team who will follow nearer to the date.'

'I will send a runner to Mr Frederick forthwith; write me a letter for him, and he will take measures regarding passage of your men.' Thomas rubbed his hands briskly and jumped up from his stool. The man's bounce was phenomenal. 'So much to do! The building of the looms will be in the hands of the Master Carpenter, and there you must advise him. Then I must put in a requisition to the Ordnance Storekeeper, Mr Wilkinson, but what he will make of miles of cotton thread, news-paper, and… what? Perhaps half a hundredweight of isinglass. I dread to imagine.'

Thereafter, we were all busyness. The Laboratory at Woolwich never saw such activity since this nation was at war with France, but all now was directed towards peace and, in irony, again cemented by the burning of gunpowder.

Chapter Twenty-Four

John, 2nd Duke of Montagu (1690 to 1749)
Master-General of His Majesty's Ordnance

In which the duke is hoist with his own petard, but wreaks disproportionate vengeance

The villain! The whoreson! I piss upon him with scorn and contempt![24] That bastard robber filthy turncoat! We shook hands like gentlemen. Oh, vile!

Here's how the foul Foote's devious duplicity played out: I had taken Servandoni and his crew to the Haymarket, introduced them to Potter, the manager, and made sure all was satisfactory for them and all their tools and equipment set up for work. Since then, the Christmas season had come upon us, and I had found myself busy upon other projects, mercifully not related to these damnable fireworks. At the time of the artisans' establishment in the workplace, I had gone straight to Barclay's and seen to it that a banker's draught for the rental was sent to Foote without delay. I expected him to send a boy back to my office directly with a note saying it had been delivered, but nothing. The next day I sent a note back saying that we should meet. No reply. I waited over the Christmas season; give me my due, I waited several weeks. When no note came from Foote by the opening of January, I took myself down to the Haymarket in hopes I might find him in his lair.

'Montagu! What a surprise,' said he as I marched into his squalid backstage office. 'I don't doubt you're come to check on your workingmen.'

'You know damned well what I'm here for!'

He raised his eyebrows in mock incomprehension, the serpent.

'The money,' I said with as much restraint as I was able. 'The money.'

'Oh, of course, I had quite forgot to send a receipt for the banker's draught.'

'Don't bandy words with me, you blackguard! We *shook hands.*'

'Ah, now I recall…' how I held off from throttling his fat neck, I know not '…we shook hands upon concluding the rental agreement.'

'We shook hands as *gentlemen*,' I spat out, 'upon the subject of my cut of the proceeds.'

'As to that, 'tis your word against mine, though I'm no *gentleman*.'

'What? What? You'd cheat me, who sprang you out of the Marshalsea! Who vouched for your *Dish of Chocolate*, the shittiest play ever staged![25] You cur! Give me my money!'

He looked me right in the face then. '*Your* money? You never had the money. You had but the promise of it.'

'I sent you a banker's draught…'

'From the king's purse, not yours. Besides, 'tis all spent. I have great debts to cover, as you would know only too well.'

'You…you…' Me, speechless? 'Twas not to be countenanced.

'Oh, come along, Montagu,' he sneered. 'What need have you of such small money?'

'That is not to the point! By God, I'll…' In truth, I knew not what I would do.

'What *can* you do?' he voiced my thoughts. 'Would you denounce me? Hardly. Would you attack me? Dare you?'

'I can withdraw my designers and their workingmen from your damned premises. I paid you double what the place is worth.'

'The *king* paid double…'

'I'll pull 'em out and have you return the payment!'

'And explain their withdrawal how?'

The scoundrel had me by the ballock hairs, and he knew it. I could not displace Servandoni without incurring terrible delay and not a little fury. I could not explain the sudden change of plan. And I could make no mention of this swine's duplicity to a living soul. I could do nothing—*nothing*—except stew in embarrassment and high dudgeon.

No, 'twas not the money, 'tis never the money, 'tis always the joy of the chase. I stormed out, swearing by Abraham's tackle that I would avenge myself on him.

Chance favours those who seek her. Only a week or so later, I was at cards in the Bedford at Covent Garden with the Duke of Portland and the Earl of Chesterfield. The Fieldings were there as well and some others; Woodward, I recall, and Leone. We had a box, as most did, so we could be private in our cards and converse yet still enjoy the hubbub overall. Most took coffee as their poison of choice, but some liked wine with their whist, and all had tobacco. Certain, we enjoyed our games, but none but the sharps amongst us paid much attention to the fall of the cards. We were with each other for the talk, the scuttlebutt, the rumour, and what was a shilling or two one way or 't other? The talk that night came around to the credulity of the populace, as we had remarked some vile pamphlet trumpeting a clyster of tobacco smoke to cure a distemper of the bowels.

'Why, the evidence is all about us,' cried Chesterfield. 'As if a puff of good Virginia up your arse would cure anything at all!' He eyed the mouthpiece of his pipe with distaste. 'People will believe anything if it's writ in ink.'

'Aye,' replied Henry Fielding. 'Some have even taken my pure fiction for truth, gainsay them how I will.'

'True,' replied his brother, 'for 't other day some cove was asking on the whereabouts of Tom Jones and did he live nigh here!'

'But in japery, surely,' said Chesterfield, 'the book not yet bought out?'

'No, no. This is the point of the thing. He was in earnest.'

'Aye,' added Henry, 'he's seen a draught and thought it a real thing!'

Amidst all their roars of laughter, a horrible, wicked plan began to grow in my mind. A jape to end all japes and a condign lesson to one who would play me for the dunce. The toad Foote was at the Bedford that night, as he often was, holding forth across the room to a gaggle of cronies, so I made sure my back was to him.

'On that head, I'll wager,' I said slowly, 'that if somebody were to noise it about *in print* that he could do the most impossible thing in the world, he would find fools enough in London to fill a playhouse who would think him earnest.'

'You would wager?' asked Portland. 'Upon what exactly would you wager?'

I picked up a flagon from the table. 'If I were to tell people that I could climb into this bottle, and be seen within it upon the stage of a theatre, I wager I could put a bum on every seat.'

'Never, never!' they all cried together. 'Outrageous!'

'How much?' I asked them. They saw I was in earnest. 'How much would you wager—any of you—that this could not be done?'

'What, climbing into the bottle?' asked Leone, slightly flown from the earlier, replete state of the flagon in question.

'No, no! That I could gull fools upon the feasibility of it. And lift their coin.'

'That people would come to a theatre for such an evident jape?' asked Chesterfield.

'Yes, just so. That they would be intrigued and curious enough to buy tickets.'

'I'll give you five guineas you'll not do it. 'Twould be seen right off as a hoax.'

'I'll lay you five, too,' shouted Portland.

'Me too. And me,' cried the rest, until I had the makings of a very fine purse should I pull this one off. But the money would be nothing to… I glanced over at the table across the room where the foul Foote was holding court and could scarce contain my glee.

'So,' said the ever-practical Fielding. 'Where shall this hoax be done, and how shall it become known?'

'The best theatre for the purpose,' I replied, again eyeing the fat, venous face over my shoulder, 'would be the Haymarket, would it not?'

At this, they all roared and clapped and made such a bedlam and halloo that I perforce hushed them lest Foote should look our way. 'Twas clear the idea of stealing one on him delighted them.

'I will take on the task of publicising,' said Fielding, rubbing his hands, 'for I have excellent contacts amongst copy writers, news-papers and printers.'

'So, you'll get up the making of a playbill?' I asked.

'Aye, and pamphlets, broadsides, news-paper notices. We'll have it in the *London Magazine*, of course, and we'll do the *Gentleman's Magazine* as well. Get both sides.'

'That Tory rag!' shouted Portland. 'I'd as lief wipe my arse on it!'

'Well, I'd not wipe mine on 't,' retorted Fielding, 'for fear my bum would come away the shittier.'

'Aye, and find their scurrilous words writ backwards on 't!'

'Hey, Fielding,' said another amidst the laughter, 'my five guineas are at stake, and if ye do the job too well, I risk losing 'em.'

'But, don't pull up your horse on the account of a couple of guineas,' I cried. "Tis the joy of the chase, not the money.'

'But look here, Fielding,' said one of the fellows, 'you're a magistrate, damn it. D' ye not find it unseemly to play such pranks?'

'No law is broken, no person incommoded,' he replied. "Tis but a harmless jape. Besides, I have grave doubts that 'twill come to anything.'

'But should it, then persons would be incommoded.'

'Aye, lighter in pocket and redder of face. And more fool them.'

We took tobacco and stoked up our pipes directly. I got pen and paper from the landlord, and for the next half hour or so, we worked upon the text of the announcement, which Fielding would then get set into print.

'The theatre must be reserved before this bill is finalised,' said Chesterfield, streaming smoke. 'A date must be set.'

'One of us must visit John Potter,' I said. 'He's Foote's manager.'

'Will Foote not become suspicious,' asked Portland, 'and wish to know more of the entertainment offered at his very own theatre?'

'Not him,' scoffed Henry Fielding. 'He cares not a fig what goes on there unless he is front of stage, acting the lead in one of his own damnable plays.'

'It should be you to book the day,' Chesterfield said, pointing the stem of his pipe at me, 'for 'tis your jape.'

'No, I can not. He… I think he might… he might know me from… somewhere. Let it be John. John Fielding. Will you do it, John?'

'Aye, I suppose I can. I am unknown to him and he to me.'

'But first,' I said, holding up a hand, 'an oath of secrecy. Should this scheme come off, those gull'd by it must not know its origin. Do I have your assurance?'

We all passed our hands over the table, and each man in our box shook the hand of each other, whilst I watched over to assure myself that all was done well.

John went the day following and made a booking with Potter, also enjoining him to say naught of these arrangements to Foote. This was simple as the master had left London the eve before. It was agreed that, were he to keep silent and allow the event to proceed, he would keep the takings. So it was that the Haymarket Theatre was booked for a January night and the playbill printed and circulated. The news-papers took it up and printed many variations, most of which we had never been party to. Here is how it appeared in one form in a news-paper:

> At the New Theatre in the Haymarket, on Monday next, the 16th instant, to be seen, a person who performs the several most surprising things following, viz. first, he takes a common walking-cane from any of the spectators, and thereon plays the music of every instrument now in use, and likewise sings to surprising perfection. Secondly, he presents you with a common wine bottle, which any of the spectators may first examine; this bottle is placed on a table in the middle of the stage, and he (without any equivocation) goes into it in sight of all the spectators, and sings in it; during his stay in the bottle any person may handle it, and see plainly that it doth not exceed a common tavern bottle.
>
> Those on the stage or in the boxes may come in masked habits (if agreeable to them); and the performer (if desired) will inform them who they are.
>
> These performances have been seen by most of the crowned Heads of Asia, Africa, and Europe, and never appeared public anywhere but one: but will wait on any at their Houses, and perform as above for five Pounds each time. A proper guard is appointed to prevent disorder.[26]

We had set the prices at seven-and-sixpence for the stage, boxes at five shillings each, the pit for three and the cheapest, up in the gallery, for two. We argued a little over the cost, some reasoning it was too high, but we agreed that the spectacle would be more seriously taken if the price were steep. And that is how the great hoax of the Bottle Conjuror came about. It was widely advertised and talked of until the whole town, it seemed, knew of it. Some amongst my conspirators were already counting their guineas lost, so great was the public knowledge. I could not have dreamed how well 'twould unfold.

Beyond my wildest dreams, in fact, and well into nightmare.

CHAPTER TWENTY-FIVE

Charles Frederick (1709 to 1785)
Surveyor-General of the Ordnance

In which the hoax of the Bottle Conjuror is witnessed, to the embarrassment of all parties present

The duties of Surveyor-General continued onerous despite what Montagu had counselled. Why, he himself spent an inordinate amount of time on the fireworks project: he selflessly devoted time to assuring a source of timber, he arranged accommodation for our artistic guests from France and Italy, and he even went out of his way to secure the work space in the Haymarket Theatre. And what might have come to pass had he not secured the production of fireworks with Mr Brock? All well and good to counsel me to step back and leave it all to my underlings, when he presents such an example. For me there were numerous processes of a political and administrative nature associated with the fireworks, and I took them all on gladly for, truth to tell, this project had won my heart. I did wonder at first if the sinecure I had been sold was more work than it should have been, or whether there was still some delegation that I should be seeing to, but as I become more embroiled, the fireworks became my life. I would stay in my Green Park "office" all day, return home to Berkeley Square spent from the travail, and yet still need the evening to entertain, for one's social and society duties must never yield to fatigue. Nor should husbandly devotion.

It was in this o'er busy frame—not long after the Christmas season—that I read in the news-paper of an entertainment at the Haymarket Theatre of an extraordinary nature. I resolved to put aside my cares and escort Lucy there, for it would give her more attention than I had of late afforded her. The advertisement promised a singular conjuring trick, and I discovered that tongues were wagging in society circles, and quite a stir was being made of it.

I mentioned my interest in this unique offering at the Haymarket to John Montagu when he chanced to visit the Green Park on yet another matter of the fireworks. I had only just showed him the announcement in the *London Magazine* when the poor fellow had some sort of coughing attack. I had not known him to be of a susceptible nature, though I knew the season treated him poorly, but after a glass of port, he quite regained his complexion. He remained thereafter somewhat distant as I mentioned the names of those of my acquaintance who said they would attend. He paled a little, I thought, at the mention of the Duke of Cumberland. When I asked if he would attend, he said he rather would not but was not more forthcoming.

There were hundreds of people crowded into the Haymarket, up Charles II Street and as far as Pall Mall. Carriages were every which away, with grooms swearing, servants elbowing, and such a crush of crinolines and fineries that 'twas a wonder none were injured in the press. We were fortunate to arrive long before the hour, for it was clear that not all would get in. A hubbub a little way down Haymarket from us resolved itself into a wedge of bully boys forcing a way through with the Duke of Cumberland and his entourage in their midst. Presently, the doors were flung back, and Cumberland and his party forced in first, gaining the best seats at the stage for seven shillings and sixpence. Our man had accompanied us from our coach and so judiciously used his elbows that he secured us a five-shilling box. We seated ourselves and lit the candles in the sconces, as did others all around us, for that was all the light there was in the place. Once we were done, there were sufficient candles to light several poor families for a twelvemonth. The room filled rapidly, the remaining theatregoers forcing into the pit and the galleries, parting with their two and three shillings as they forced into their places. There were cries and shrieks as men were jostled or squeezed, and ladies grossly incommoded by the press.

Before us on the stage was a wooden table with a green baize cloth and upon it a quart bottle. No other accoutrements or devices were seen. There was no shade of movement from the curtain behind, nor was there music or other entertainment to distract and mollify the audience. Thus, we stood or sat, becoming increasingly impatient to witness the spectacle. Once the hour of seven o' the clock came, the anticipation rose further. Then as the hour passed, the crowd became restive. Fellows were calling catch phrases and coarse witticisms, and a portion in the pit began a rhythmic stamping. The shouting continued louder and louder, jostling began in the pit and the cheap seats of the gallery, whilst those in the boxes began to hurl insults. 'Twas clear that control would soon be lost. As the shouting reached a crescendo, a man appeared from behind the curtain, vainly attempting to call for order and shouting that if the Bottle Conjuror failed to appear, he would refund their tickets. The bellowing redoubled, and he scuttled away.

Objects were now being flung upon the stage, and then the Duke of Cumberland swept a candle from its sconce and hurled it onto the platform. There was a brief flare as something on the floor caught fire, and the crowd panicked. The ladies and most of the better gentlemen pushed swiftly for the doors, whilst other men leapt upon the stage, stamping out the flames, then tearing the table leg from leg and smashing the bottle. The crush in the doorway was fearful, and I observed one lady entirely stripped of her crinoline and clutching the rags of it around her *dishabille*. Hats were lost, wigs were torn off and flung, and some who pushed forcibly to the doors did so without their cloaks. As we forced our way out of our box from the rear, we witnessed the commencement of destruction in the pit below us. Seats were smashed and thrown out of the doors, the very panelling of the walls was torn away, and the curtain ripped from its rails. One fellow charged with his shoulder at the panelling of one of the boxes, only to have it tear away and send him plunging face first to the floor.

By the time we debouched into the street, with our man clearing the way before us, the rioters had piled seats, panelling and even floorboards onto an enormous pyre in the middle of the Haymarket and set it ablaze. The theatre curtain followed out of the door and was hoisted up upon a pole and waved to and fro above the blaze. As the riot roared out into the adjoining streets, bystanders who knew nothing of the circumstances became involved, fights erupted whilst loafers and chancers did the rounds of purse-snatching and watch-stripping. As we thankfully entered our coach, parked some way distant, we saw a phalanx of foot guards running towards the commotion.

Lucy was mercifully unharmed, though so discomposed as to be subject to fainting and the application of salts all the way home. I had tried by this outing to repair my inattention to my dear wife, but instead was admonished as soon as we came in our door, that she would rather sit at home, a near-widow, than be subjected to such nonsense. And please to be very cautious about suggesting further excursions, thank you very much.

I heard tell that the owner of the theatre, Mr Samuel Foote, would have been torn limb from limb had he been discovered, but his whereabouts were unknown. He later protested his obvious innocence in a jape that so clearly disadvantaged him. It was never discovered who had perpetrated the deed, but certainly 'twas a shame that Mr Foote was so innocently taken a victim. Thus ended the hoax of the Bottle Conjuror, and many was the red face the day and the week following, mine included.[27] Cumberland was not to hear the last of it, for there appeared in a news-paper the following notice:

> Found entangled in a slit in a lady's demolished smock petticoat, a gilt-handled sword of martial temper and length, not much the worse of wearing, with the Spey curiously engraven on one side, and the Scheuldt on the other; supposed to be taken from the fat sides of a certain great general in his hasty retreat from the Battle of Bottle Noddles, in the Haymarket. Whoever hath lost it may inquire for it at the sign of the Bird and Singing Land, in Rotten-row.[28]

Someone told me that the Duke of Cumberland had sworn to hunt down the perpetrator of the prank and see him hanged, but I thought this unlikely, for it would be so bruited about by any trial or exposure as to open the entire episode again to public ridicule.

Sleeping dogs…

Chapter Twenty-six

James Morris (c. 1700 to c. 1760)
Master Carpenter to the Office of the Ordnance

In which death comes to pass, the building of the great machine goes apace, and the duke mollifies friction amongst French and English allies

Work continued apace throughout a miserable January. Miserable as the weather was—for we had to be out in it whatever—'twas for me made more melancholy by the rapid decline of my father. I needs must be beside him in Woolwich, and I needs must see to the building of the machine, so I was drawn in two conflicting ways and naught to be done to alleviate. The prospect of the Thames seen from a boat became engraven upon my inner eye 'til I could know every reach of it in a dark room. My dear father passed away at the end of the month. He had lingered long, but I took solace in knowing that he'd seen my sketches of the machine and smiled upon the enterprise and my great part in it. Working thereafter into February, I was assailed with a guilt for the sense of relief his passing gave, though he'd lingered o'er long in this world, and I knew in my heart that his passing had been a merciful release.

Now, whenever I stood back along the Queen's Walk and saw the thing in its entirety, I was awed at what we had accomplished, my part in it, and the thought of my father perhaps looking it all over and nodding his head. Never again in my career would I be called upon to oversee such a vast undertaking, and 'twas just a shame that he was not on this earth to see it. The weather had begun to turn in February; although still rainy, it could be counted upon to be warmer. We had had the devil's own task keeping things dry after a fashion whilst we worked in rain and sleet, and there had been much call for canvas duck to make temporary coverings. And the higher our scaffolding got, the more precarious became the work. So far, but three men had fallen from the structure seriously enough for their injuries to be remarked, and just one fellow, a painter named Curtis, had died.[29] When one considers the numbers involved, and the coordination of the whole, this is a remarkable record.

The machine was properly to be viewed from afar, from the scaffold seating that would be built where I stood. From here 'twould very much present a fine aspect, though close up, 'twas not as pleasing. Columns, pediments, mouldings and other details were carved in wood to an approximation. All the stairs and balustrades up the front were done fairly rough and in haste, for they were to be used on the day only for the fire lighters and for closer inspection of the machine by the great powers. And our timber was not of the best quality. But there was never a need for fineness in much of what we did; distance from the structure made detail wasteful of time, for the whole effect on the eye, from the scaffold at 500 feet, was what was called for. Though Mr Frederick might wax both poetical and architectural over it, certainly, my old man would've looked askance at the roughness of it.

I made the long colonnades 'tween the central temple and the flanking pavilions with a wood frame overlaid with canvas, rather than in solid wood; same with the wide, flat surfaces on the central temple. It is easier to make them thus and thrifty of materials. Then, to make our wood structure and our canvas sheet infill resemble stone, we used whitewash, a lime and water mix, which is easy to apply and resists the weather somewhat.

So, standing there by the Queen's Walk, it all began to look very fine indeed.

Curious, though; pictures of the machine were being hawked on the streets already, unfinished as it was. The artists had conjured what it might look like, but what they show is not what was there. As an example: you see that bloody great cartouche right at the top with the Lion and the Unicorn holding up the Crown? It's on the drawing that George Vertue made later and on all the prints and paintings. Well, we never put it there; 'twas too big and heavy to make, Servandoni's crew didn't have the time to carve it, and we'd not the lifting gear or procedure to set it into place, spite of what I'd let on to him. Anyhow, the great girandole with VIVAT REX written upon it would have been impossible to erect with that thing in the way. Only with that cartouche did the king's ambition o'erstep his reach. In its stead, Servandoni painted it on a flat board and smaller.

'My condolence upon your loss,' said his Grace the Duke of Montagu, who was visiting the site one forenoon. 'Your father was a fine architect, and his kind are few.'

'I thank you, Your Grace, and truly appreciated your presence at the funeral.'

''Twas the least I could do for such a fine man. Now,' and he clapped his hands together, all business, 'what of the timber? It meets the need?'

'Truth to tell, Your Grace, we have plenty, but it wants seasoning.'

'How so?'

''Tis milled wet and brought straight into use. Thus, we have to nail it up tighter than normal lest it curl and twist.'

'But you can make do?' He was very solicitous for a man of his station, one who should know naught of timber and care less. I quite honestly preferred him to the Fredericks of this world, who can not mind their own damned business. You'd never see his Grace poking his nose in with ideas and suggestions; he was there just to see that all was well.

'Aye. As I say, perforce we need to nail it, which is costly in iron. Nails are quicker, but they ain't cheap.'

'What quantity of nails do you require?'

'Well, I'd have to calculate it out, but 300 pounds, at least, to be getting on with.'

With this he seemed satisfied and so taxed me upon other matters of time and readiness before he took himself off in the direction of the palace. 'Twas three or four days later a consignment of nails was delivered to the site, but they were certainly not from the stores in Woolwich. I'd run them down already. Passing strange that a cove of his station would concern himself over timber and nails, but what would you?

I was happy to have had very little intercourse with the decorators, as we had each stuck with our tasks, one out in the Green Park in all weathers and 't other in the comfort of the Haymarket. This was an excellent arrangement because Servandoni had taken a dislike to me and I to him. Perhaps I was too blunt on first acquaintance, but when you come poncing around my worksite in all your powder and finery and peer down your nose at me, well... what would you do? The main cause of the rub, to my way of thinking, was that the design was all cut and dried. The king had done it up and left precious little further to create for one who was fond of having it all his own way. I don't know how they do these things for King Louis in France, but here in England, we're told what's wanted, and we get on with it.

The most precarious of our many operations was the hauling up and installing of the framed transparencies, painted inscriptions and sculptures prepared by Servandoni and his crew. We made the wooden panels—for such things as the Latin inscriptions, the bas relief sculptures, and so on—and then packed them off to the Haymarket on drays drawn by a pair of horses. They would paint, carve and decorate as wanted, then have them carted back to us. These are great unwieldy things: the frieze over the central arch with GEORGIVS II REX painted on it—which was to be lit from behind with lampions throughout the playing off—was fully twenty-five feet long and four high.

There was one other feature, the central transparency of His Majesty Giving Peace to Britannia, that Servandoni insisted on framing as well as painting in his workshop. He told me our wood wasn't up to the mark, and he would find better. It was the biggest piece, being twenty-eight by ten, and was made in four frames for the linen to be stretched over. He wrote the sizes down direct from my notes. I know he did; I saw him do it. I wasn't to know it then, but discord would follow.

Mr Frederick came out of his office to watch the first of the big panels—the one on the left as you look, situated above a pair of Doric columns—being hauled into place. Servandoni appeared, having accompanied the dray from Haymarket with the panel loaded on it. I was not surprised to see Mr Frederick, for now he was everywhere and taking tremendous interest in the work, but my heart sank at the sight of the Frenchman.

I would have liked to see to the installations myself, but Monsieur Servandoni had other ideas. Our method was to rig hoists attached to the top of the machine and cantilevered outwards, then sling block and tackle from them. Two hoists were needed for each piece, one at each end. We'd swathe the piece in sacking where the ropes might bite, lash it around with rope, and then inch it aloft with the tackle, keeping an eye for level. If it doesn't go up level, the ropes can slip off. Once the piece was up to the height, men on the scaffold would swing it onto temporary supports whilst the rope and sacking were taken off, then slide it into place, and secure it with wood pegs or nails. I make it sound simple, but it wasn't. It needed care and good timing, but most of all, it needed one boss. Whilst Servandoni largely agreed with the method, he insisted on being present for every installation, but not just present; he was inclined to run the show. Or try to.

So, on that first day, we had the dray situated below our tackles, and I was just instructing my men on the procedure we'd follow, showing how the padding and ropes would be tied, when Servandoni strutted forward.

'*Attention!* Take care, take care! We have laboured hard over this work!'

'I know you have,' I snapped, 'and so have we.'

'Be careful how you tie these ropes.' This, not to me, mark you, but to one of my men. 'Do you know nothing of correct knots? Here, let me show you.'

And damn me if he didn't start tying the rope contrary to the way I had just shown. Mr Frederick, who was standing by, must have spotted the smoke pouring out of every hole in my body, arse included, because he stepped forward smartish.

'Thank you so much, Chevalier, but tell me, have you seen the work we have lately done on these columns…?' And so drew him aside with a hand on his sleeve, Servandoni looking over his shoulder the while. We continued with the lash-up, slung the ropes through our sheaves, and began the lift. The piece was not ten feet off the bed of the dray when the monsieur dragged himself away from Frederick and came striding back.

'*Lentement! Lentement!*' he yelled. 'Slowly, you at that end!' and he waved at one of the rope men who, being an obedient worker, slacked off somewhat. Now the piece was out of level and set to slip its ties. I stepped forward, called a halt, and had the men at each end balance their work again. I was more concerned with saving the job than I was with anything else. Behind me, Mr Frederick was again interceding, talking, charming and drawing the man away whilst my blood boiled. I bridled in no way whatsoever until we had her hoisted up to the level and secured in place. The last thing I needed on such a delicate operation—and the first of many—was any loss of temper. However, once it was secured, I turned around and walked over to him.

'Now listen,' I said, quietly and calmly right into his face. 'Fact is, this is my structure, and I am the one to order the work. And if you're in England, you'll bloody well do it my way.'

'What Mr Morris means,' intervened Frederick, buttery as buggery, 'is that we might strive to establish a clear circumscription of roles.'

'Just so,' I said as Servandoni was about to bite back.

'I am sure Chevalier Servandoni would agree that, as Mr Morris hath assumed this side of the work, some financial compensation might be forthcoming...' and so drew him away again, dangling the prospect of sovereigns.

Bloody foreigners.

Chapter Twenty-Seven

John, 2nd Duke of Montagu (1690 to 1749)
Master-General of His Majesty's Ordnance

In which gloating triumph is unrequited, and the workshop of the stage designers is visited to the duke's education

Construction of the machine going apace, I realised that it had been some weeks since I had seen Servandoni and his crew installed in the undercroft at the Haymarket. I had seen the hoisting of some finished decorative parts and had heard how Charles had successfully intervened against French and British antipathies, but naught had I seen of the decorator's art in their workshop.

'Twas high time to check upon progress. That's what I told myself. Truth was, whilst there it would be most apposite if the foul Foote were present to be pissed upon, with scorn and contempt, as a low buffoon. To score against an enemy such as he is rewarding of itself, but to observe at first-hand the worm wriggling adds spice to the cake. I took my carriage from Whitehall and was pleased to see some greening of the parks, an effort by the plane trees to put forth bud, and an overall harbinger of ease and serenity to my poor old joints. It had been a harsh winter and one that I would have preferred to spend nigh to warm fires, with a glass in my hand. Though the project of the fireworks had so far profited me well enough, 'twas not without some cost to my agèd constitution.

Arrived at the theatre, I was met at the door by John Potter and conducted through the building. It warmed my heart to see the destruction of the interior still evident, vindictive bastard that I am, and how little work of reconstruction was yet undertaken. Potter knew not that I was the instigator of the Battle of Bottle Noddles, but had he known, he would have thanked me mightily for his acquisition of the night's proceeds. I doubly thanked the Lord—and the solidarity of my co-conspirators—that Cumberland knew nothing of my part, for I doubted the king would find it in his heart to forgive me. The sun shone out of his son's arsehole, and to mock him was to mock the sovereign. Had I known the crown prince would be gulled into attending, I might have thought better of the jape. Frederick, yes, I could see him being drawn in, for he lives in a different world.

'What a terrible set of consequences,' I remarked as we made our way to the back stair. 'Such wanton destruction.'

'Aye,' replied Potter. 'I wasn't to know how 'twould turn out when I booked 'im. Nice sort of fellow, he seemed.'

'I heard there was some complaint upon the takings,' I said, all innocent-like. 'This fellow who collected the money absconded.' I couldn't resist the temptation to watch his face. I was rewarded.

'Ah, as to that... ah, well...' he stuttered. ''Twas a very confused situation...'

'So confused, I'm told, that when the hapless customers sent the day following for their refunds, there was no one present to accommodate 'em.'

'I know nothing of it, sir,' he waffled, and I was content to push no further. I simply nodded. It was all in his face to see. Before we descended to the workshop, I paused at the top of the stair.

'Bye the bye, where is your master, Mr Foote?'

'He hath taken a visit to Paris, sir. I know not when he might return.'

Damnation! My whole intention in coming here was to see his fat, bibulous face and gloat upon the misfortune written upon it, and the scoundrel was off to Paris with my money. *My money!* I controlled my face; 'twas not seemly to appear concerned. The bastard! The cowardly worm to go pissing off when London got too damned warm. Nothing for it but to be content with the wreckage I could enjoy all around me.

The undercroft was a hive of busyness, with Servandoni's three assistants, de Cleremont, Casali and Soldi, each working on separate parts of the great edifice and each supervising teams of workers. Against one wall, Soldi was overseeing the painting on linen of a vast wooden frame with figures rendered to look like marble, whilst beside it was the same exactly but rendered in colours. A stack of such frames awaited painting, each with its counterpart. In the centre of the room, Casali was mixing great quantities of French plaister and guiding his workingmen into pouring the liquid into moulds of clay. Dust, confusion, mess and noise; out of this would come, by the alchemy of workingmen, the decorations of the machine. It was unimaginable to me that anything of worth could emerge from this chaos and all that in but the span of a couple of months. Why, I wondered to myself, am I here at all when this is all of a world I know not? Would I have dreamed some few months past that I would witness this? The things I do for my king. Still, like little Jackie Horner, I do pull out the odd plum.

Servandoni himself was seated at a high desk with paper, pens and instruments before him. He swung round and stepped off his stool as I entered, sweeping towards me, dandyish to the highest degree. Unlike the craftsmen, he had not a touch of dust or dirt upon his fine clothes. There are those who perform and those who issue instruction. On this point, and upon no other, we were kindred.

'Ah, Monsieur *Le Duc de* Montagu, come to observe the great work?'

This exercised me a little, as the great work was actually under construction in the Green Park in Morris's able hands. What was happening here was mere decoration.

'No, I was there yesterday. I came to see the lesser work today.' God damn his windy, puffed-up opinion of himself.

'It is only a great work,' he rejoined down his long nose, 'when it is graced with fine decoration and marvellous contrivances of art and mechanism.'

On a long table beside him, he had several finely made drawings of plan and elevation of the structure. I remarked upon the fineness of them.

'I employed William Jones to make a fair and more accurate copy of the rough draught you gave me from the king. And more of the details besides.' This was the drawing that His Majesty and I had worked upon with the draughtsman from the Ordnance. Rough draught be damned, but these were more complete and detailed.

'Well and good,' I replied, 'for that is the need of your craft, save that no change be made in His Majesty's desires upon the choice of elements.'

He assured me that the sovereign's desires—nay, requirements—were well accommodated and that no change would be made, and with this assurance, I was most comforted, for I dreaded the thought of what explosions might occur if my master's will in this matter were crossed. We left the drawing table and passed across to the wall where Soldi was slapping paint upon a frame of transparent linen in what I took to be a highly careless manner. Ignorant though I am, I was minded to comment upon this but held my tongue. Servandoni, seeing my expression, taxed me upon my concern.

'You consider our work slipshod? I see it in your face.'

'There is not...' I ventured to say, 'much of a fineness about it...'

'You see it from close! You see it but sketched in with large sweeps of the brush. There are seventeen more of these.'

'Eighteen altogether?' I couldn't credit the number.

'Yes, eighteen. Nine each side. Should we execute this work with the accuracy one would apply to intimate works in a fine art gallery... *alors*, we would never have it done!'

'So, you must hurry to get it finished in time?'

'No, no, no,' he cried, clearly addressing a child or a barbary ape. 'One stands back; one stays 500 feet from the front, and then one sees the grandeur of it all. Details matter not.'

Now I did see his point. It is all designed to fool the eye. Sitting in a gallery of the opera house, one sees the impression, not the substance. It was the same here. I nodded.

'See here,' he continued. 'This art was devised for the stage. It is through theatrical productions, which must be staged at short notice, that we have refined what is essential to show and what is superfluous.'

Now I recognised these eighteen frames that Soldi was daubing. I had seen them in the king's drawing, and Servandoni had described them when we all met the king. They were to be painted to seem like carven stone, as one would see upon the face of any building. Why, then, would there be another eighteen in colour? Before I could pose the question, Servandoni answered for me.

'You will recall I told King George, these eighteen great transparencies appear first as bas reliefs, painted in *grisaille*, but as the fireworks are played off, they are removed by machinery and replaced with their counterparts in colour.'

'Ah, yes, I mind you said so. But machinery?'

'Yes, machinery. Ropes, pulleys, sheaves. Manpower. This is where my team of scenery specialists are involved. You must send for them directly, for they have to be trained and made ready. May I assume you have made arrangements to reimburse their travel and other expenses?'

'Of course. You asked me to send for them, and I have done your bidding. That was never in question. They may stay in the tents and will mess with the Ordnance artificers. Now about this machinery…'

'The machine is transformative; as the spectacle progresses, so goes its disposition.'

'How are the colour pictures made visible?'

'They appear by sliding the bas reliefs aside, and as they do so, a great number of lampions are lit up from behind. The machinery and fireworks run together like the finest of clockwork.'

Only now did I begin to understand the complexity of the machine. Only now did I begin to see what a Brobdingnagian undertaking this was. And the more I thought on this, the more I wondered how in God's name all these damned foreigners could possibly be made to cooperate with their British counterparts in this endeavour. It seemed to me then that all my feasting and regaling at Christmas was but a brief ceasefire, a détente, which soon came to an end with the last wipe of a napkin, the last muffled belch. Servandoni and Morris were shit and sugar, Ruggieri and Desaguliers were at a fragile truce, and Frederick fussed twixt 'em all, liked by none.

I thought of the Peace of Aix-la-Chapelle and what a cobbled together piece of squabbling patchwork it was, and could only compare it to its counterpart made manifest in the Green Park.

Like one, like 't other?

Chapter Twenty-eight

Charles Frederick (1709 to 1785)
Surveyor-General of the Ordnance

In which a meeting is called of all participants, and plans are put in place for the creation of an official drawing and publication

'The king is mighty displeased with this rash of scurrilous drawings, prints and descriptions, which depict the machine as it never will be and are sold for pennies on the streets by unscrupulous dealers.'

Thus said John Montagu at a meeting of the Board of Ordnance convened by me at his request. Around the board table were Captain Desaguliers, William Rawlinson Earle, the Clerk of the Cheque, and our sturdy artificer James Morris. Giovanni Servandoni, Gaetano Ruggieri and Giuseppe Sarti were also invited because our discussions would have great influence upon their work and their reputations.

Morris raised his hand for a word. 'If I may? Artists have been out in the park for some time making sketches of the machine, though most is swathed from the eye by canvas.'

'Aye,' said Montagu. 'They can but draw the outline as it stands and so should return to the site as more detail is visible. But no, they render a false likeness from the mind's eye.'

'There's great licence in the finishing of 'em,' said Earle. 'There must be, for the draughtsmen must have 'em to the printers in time to sell.'

'Not, I think, from the mind's eye,' said I with a nod to Montagu. 'The work is far too detailed. It is my impression they have somehow gotten a copy of other drawings.'

'Your working drawings?' asked Montagu of Servandoni. 'What of them?'

'I have had drawings done by William Jones, as you know,' said Servandoni, quite offhand. 'That others may have seen them is no fault of mine.'

'I agree,' said Ruggieri. 'By now 'tis common knowledge. I think you say "the cat hath left the sack?"'

Just by the way the two of them exchanged glances, I wondered at some collusion. It was clear that Servandoni was displeased at the completeness of the design presented to him and lusted for greater authorship, and Ruggieri and Sarti would benefit greatly in reputation by widespread acknowledgement.

'We need an official drawing,' said Servandoni, 'so that no mistake may be made upon the *true* authorship of the machine *and* of its firework effects.' Ruggieri nodded and Sarti smiled.

Now I was sure. They'd leaked the pictures to force our hand. Nevertheless, ownership of the project was best made official anyhow, and Captain Desaguliers was the first to voice this.

'The thing to be done... if I may?' he said, '...is for the board to take ownership of this endeavour. When I was visiting St Petersburg, I remarked how the Russian savants produced official plans and descriptions and passed laws against unofficial representations.'

'In effect, a royal patent upon this project,' I observed. This would make the cavalier uncomfortable if he'd made his drawings widespread, not that the Crown could proceed against him, of course, even if he had.

'It would require an Act of Parliament,' said Earle, 'but I do feel it should be brought forward.'

Servandoni was quick to speak and clearly expressed his own views and those of Ruggieri. 'Absolutely must our names be protected, for it is upon such things that reputations rise and fall. I am ashamed to see some of the *ordures* being sold on the streets.'

'May we vote upon it?' I asked the table at large.

All hands were raised. 'So moved. Make a note, please,' I told the recording secretary at a side table, 'for the production of a drawing to be an action item.' A minute of the entire meeting would be prepared for me, which I would then circulate to all parties before forwarding it to the parliamentary secretary.

'And, *apropos* of this,' continued the cavalier, 'is the need for a written description of the machine.'

'In words as well as a drawing?'

'Yes, such a description as Captain Desaguliers refers to when he cites our Russian friends.'

'We have,' said Ruggieri, with a nod to Servandoni and Sarti, 'taken the time to write a description of the machine, its decorations, its operation and the entire unfolding of events upon the day.' He withdrew some papers from a document case.

Of course, you did, I thought. You and your damned *fait accompli*. Jumped the gun on us, did you not?

'Give me the copy,' I replied shortly, 'and I will see to it that it is laid before Parliament as soon as possible. Once the act is passed, we will have the printer to the Board of Ordnance produce copies for sale. All other descriptions will then be rendered illegal.'

'Illegal?' said Servandoni. 'Will you make the drawings of William Jones also illegal? What nonsense is this?'

'His working drawings,' I replied, tasting the lees of what little patience remained at the bottom of my cask, 'are not at issue, for they have not been disseminated... Have they? Hmm? But an official drawing in elevation and plan, and as detailed as possible, must be made for public information and purchase. A draughtsman must be employed...'

'The drawings exist already!'

'*Working* drawings, yes. Official, no.'

'Then Jones may be employed to complete the work,' he replied. 'Make it *official*.'

'We would prefer,' and I laid accent upon "prefer," 'that the draughtsmen of the Board of Ordnance be employed in this task, as in all others the same. Mr Jones may make his drawings available to our draughtsman, and he will be recompensed. I am sure this is satisfactory?' 'Twas not truly a question.

There was a long silence before Servandoni nodded, gracelessly at best, but there was naught he could do upon the matter.

'I move, then, that this board assign a draughtsman and a copywriter to assist Cavalier Servandoni, and Signori Ruggieri and Sarti in the execution of these designs. Do we agree?'

Captain Desaguliers raised his hand. 'I feel it incumbent upon us to give credit in both the drawing and the description to His Majesty's Train of Artillery, the Royal Laboratory and the Master Carpenter, for without these, the celebration will not take place.'

'Due credit must surely be awarded,' I agreed, 'upon the drawing and in the description. His Majesty would not have it otherwise.'

By a show of hands, the motion was carried. Instructions were sent to commission the draughtsman who had followed the king's designs to make a fair copy of the drawing and see to its engraving and printing. Mr George Vertue was charged with this task. Mr Bowyer, printer to the Board of Ordnance, was commissioned to work with the artisans in producing a description of the machine and its operation. Copies of the drawing could later be had at the printer's in Pall Mall or Paternoster Row for a shilling, whilst a water-coloured view of the machine would be half-a-crown. The booklet produced from the description was also made ready to sell, but even so, these works all belied the actuality, being produced quite before the day.

It had oft been remarked by all the contractors in this endeavour, foreign and English, that division of their duties betwixt diverse workshops was counter to efficiency. Nevertheless, whilst the body of the structure, the elements of decoration and the pyrotechnics were being separately created, there was no need of close association. We had put couriers at the disposal of both parties, so swift communication between the Green Park, the Haymarket and Woolwich could be undertaken. Indeed, geographical separation had offered a level of quarantine from the Yellow Fever of discord that had so marked relationships to date. I feel 'twas a remarkable Christmas feat of John's to bring 'em all together to eat and drink, to play japes, and not one word of discord. Since then, though, the parts had flown asunder in discord. And now, around this table, the parts of the whole began to come together again, and work in some sort of cooperation.

Or so I hoped.

George Vertue's drawing of the machine for the Royal Fireworks

The title page of Ruggieri and Sarti's book

CHAPTER TWENTY-NINE

His Majesty King George II (1683 to 1760)
King of Great Britain and Ireland

In which King George is persuaded that music is wanting for his fireworks

I hate music. No, that's not true at all; in its place, I am as fond as anyone. My family and I have patronised the King's Theatre for years, and the daughters in particular wait on the latest Italian opera or, lately, English oratorio. It's not for nothing that Mr Handel is paid a handsome pension drawn from the crown purse and is charged with the musical education of the princesses. Certainly, I understand the structure, I can hear the notes, and can appreciate it in its entirety. I don't have tree fungus for ears! No, it's not the melodic part of it; it's just that it's so damned obtrusive. Of course, having music for all occasions is essential to a royal court, but music should be an entertainment set in its time and place. And then there are these blasted violins. Once Louis XIV had his *quatre-vingt violons du Roi,* everybody had to have them. And our Mr Handel is as bad as most, mayhap worse, with this blasted French fashion. All we seem to hear is his damned fiddles, and as I am his sovereign, he would do well to heed my likes and dislikes. His head's too damned big for his wig.

Handel's as German as I am, but he's taken on English colouring, or British I should say since we absorbed the Scots into our realm, God blast their Papist hearts. George Frideric; more English than the English. They say he wrote his *Water Music* to curry favour with my father, but that's so much hog swill. When Handel came to London looking for fertile musical ground, he got to writing for Queen Anne. Now there was a cloth-eared ninny for you! She only knew music from farts because it didn't stink.[30] And they say Handel knew not that George of Hanover, his old patron, would get the nod to take the crown as soon as the dropsical old queen's toes turned up. So, word had it he near shat his hose in terror, falling all over himself to write something to appease the king. The rubbish that gets taken for truth! King George I was delighted to have Handel in London and would likely have commanded him here had he not already taken root. Not but I ever asked the old bastard.

All this to say that when Montagu entered my office one forenoon some time in February and told me—*again*—that music was wanting for my celebration and that Handel was just the man, I damned his eyes. Handel, bloody Handel!

'Damnation, no! We have discussed this!'

'I really feel, Your Majesty, that if Handel were to…'

'No! Every time I bring a fork to my mouth, there's music. Every time I entertain, there's music. Every time I go to holy service, there's music. You'd have me shit to music! Enough!'

He became insistent. 'Mr Handel hath ever given you satisfaction in his music…'

'I know! I know! In its place! And he hath oft o'er stepped the line.'

'Surely, his music is ever of its time and place…'

'What? Look what the bastard did at my coronation!' He had writ a soft and gentle piece for his precious fiddles, lulling the entire assembly into a stupour, then of a sudden blasting us to death with trumpets and drums and a full yelling chorus.[31] It half blew my bloody head off. I think the Archbishop near fouled himself, and half the congregation was close to pissing their drawers. Bastard! 'No, I want none of it, and there's an end to it.'

'His *Te Deum* for your Highness's victory at Dettingen was most well received…'

'It is glorious, it is gorgeous, but in its *time and place*. I desire no music for my fireworks, d' ye hear? Are you bloody deaf?'

'Such a prestigious celebration,' continued this oily weasel, as if I hadn't said a deuced word, 'will be observed throughout Europe, and comparisons might well be made…'

Yes, well they might. The devious swine. Bringing Servandoni and Ruggieri away from King Louis was a thunderous fart across the Channel, no error, but if I were to use them to purchase the hearts of the English vulgar, music needs must be part of it, else we'd bear poor comparison to the French. And Montagu played full well on Handel's great prestige. Thousands flock to hear his concerts in Vauxhall Gardens with that dratted hornpipe and dead march and whatnot, whilst in the King's Theatre, there's never an empty seat. More and more, he's become the voice of English music, German that he is. Music of Handel's would beguile the people, not a question of it. Curse Montagu; he sees me too clearly.

'I'll have none of his damned fiddles! D' ye hear me?'

'I am sure, Your Majesty, that martial instruments most suitable to warlike sentiments…'

'Be sure. Be very sure, for I'll have none other.'

'I will direct Mr Frederick to meet Mr Handel and state your terms.'

I dismissed him with a wave and tried to resume my reading of some dry rubbish put before me by Henry Pelham—in whose broad bottom I needs must have total confidence—but my mind was out of it.[32]

Music!

Chapter Thirty

John, 2nd Duke of Montagu (1690 to 1749)
Master-General of His Majesty's Ordnance

In which the duke crosses the Thames upon a matter of some delicacy

Now, the need for music with the fireworks being sown in the king's mind, there must surely be a public rehearsal. There was profit to be made, if I'm any judge, and where better to hold it than the gardens at Vauxhall? A visit to my good friend Jonathan Tyers was called for. He is the owner of the Pleasure Gardens there, on the south bank of the Thames. He is a highly serviceable man of business, portly, florid of face and as sharp in his practice as ever could be. He's always on the lookout for advantage and hath his nose—a veined and bulbous one that speaks to his love of snuff and strong drink—into every nook and cranny of the entertainment business in London, both legit and not so. By patronage, by influence, by money well placed and debts honoured, and by an uncanny eye for the main chance, he's made an empire for himself at Vauxhall. If you've had your family done in oils by the likes of Francis Hayman—one of our most accomplished painters of the likeness—you can be said to have taken a place amongst us. So, though he is from coarse roots in Bermondsey amongst the tannery trade, he's given Vauxhall and himself an air of refined respectability. Withal, the coarse speech of his youth is not lost, or perhaps he chooses not to refine his enunciation in order to have it as a badge of his proud and solid roots in trade.

Years ago, when Jonathan Tyers took over Vauxhall—called the Spring Gardens at that time—it was a den of iniquity, a place of hedge whores and cut-purses, said to be no more than a brothel set in the countryside. It is now perhaps the greatest enterprise of entertainment in the capital, for there is music and dancing in the pavilions, fountains and tended gardens, and food and drink to be got at booths and stands.

At night it is all lit up with hundreds of lampions in glass globes hung amongst the trees, and it is all quite magical. 'Tis the resort of the gentry and the well-to-do, a place to be seen. But when the lampions are doused and the gentry have taken their leave, the old function of Spring Gardens again rears its head. Tyers is no fool; he caters to all walks of life, and if there's coin to be taken for assignations of a less open kind, he's not the one to miss the chance.

Tyers stages many works by Handel, Thomas Arne, William Boyce and others who write in the English fashion for the bandstand in Vauxhall, making it an English-speaking counterweight to the Italian operatic nonsense they got up to at the Haymarket. He hath made an exhibition gallery for paintings by the likes of Hogarth and Hayman, all in fine good taste and most genteel. This whole enterprise is particularly supported by both his grace, the Duke of Cumberland, and by Frederick, Prince of Wales. Prince Frederick owns the property upon which Tyers carries the lease. 'Tis clearly to Tyers's advantage that the prince is so popular amongst fashionable society, for everywhere he goes, so go his hangers-on; all those who wish to be with him and to be seen with him. It is also highly convenient to Kennington Green where the prince will repair to play cricket, of which he is uncommon enamoured. The loathing of the royal family for this most popular of them seems not to influence the political colour of the place; Whig and Tory alike leave differences aside when they cross the Thames.

I stepped from my house in Whitehall, which lies on the Thames bank, and took a wherry to a dock close to Vauxhall, for the bridge at Westminster was still not open. I had a need of haste, and a carriage ride by way of London Bridge was too far out of my way. I should say this: though Tyers sits well amongst fashionable society, it is only when society finds itself *south* of the Thames that mixing and hobnobbing take on an altogether different cast, if you take my meaning. 'Twas not to one's advantage to be seen together too often on the London side of the water, for people do talk. This is why I found it necessary to see him, rather than have him come see me. Besides, as I had need of his cooperation in this scheme I had in mind, 'twere better I came to him.

There had been a light rain at the start of the day, but by the time I'd crossed and alighted at the south bank, it seemed to be holding off.

Tyers came down from his house to the dock at Vauxhall Stair, gave me his hand as I stepped onto the wood planks, and led me up the road to the gardens.

'What brings ye to the unfashionable side of the river, my friend?' he asked ironically as we strolled upon a gravelled path amongst flower beds.

'A matter of some delicacy…'

'Aye, that's why they calls it Fucks-hall, them as knows what's what. 'Tis a fine and private place, and many I think do there embrace!'

He gave a deep phlegmy guffaw and hawked prodigiously into a bush beside the path.

'No, no, you mistake me, sir.' He walked on a little. ''Tis about the king's fireworks…'

'Yers, talk o' the town. 'Tis bruited about everywhere.'

'You know that I am charged with the execution of it.'

'O' course. Who doth not? Wot of it, and why come t' me?'

'Here are my thoughts…'

Chapter Thirty-One

Jonathan Tyers (1702 to 1767)
Manager, Impresario and Entrepreneur

In which Mr Handel is contracted to rehearse his music at Vauxhall before he yet knows he is to write it

Well, damn me, Montagu's a match for me and no error. I've ever had an eye for a good chance, for to take guineas from folks' purses in exchange for diversion and entertainment is my way of life. Now, if this scheme of his comes about, we'll both be the better for it and no one the wiser about how it might have been brought about. Same as the highly profitable caper of sawing timber that the old rascal told me about. As we strolled the paths amongst the gardens of Vauxhall, he laid out his scheme to me.

'As you know, the fireworks want music, and I have persuaded the king so and will also Mr Handel in due course.'

''Tis nothing to me. 'Twill take place in the Green Park, surely?'

'Aye, just so. And for such a staging, I will need precisely the people, the material and the skills you employ here at Vauxhall. We will need many lampions and lamplighters, crowds must be controlled and carriages parked, tickets issued, and entrance money taken. There must be a temporary scaffold with seats for the gentry. And what of food and drink? None of these things are to be had at the Green Park, and the Ordnance hath not a blind clue on the organising of such spectacles. How could it?'

'I know all this. 'S wot we do 'ere every night o' the season.' I started to see what he was driving at, least I thought I did. 'And ye can hire them orf me as occasion demands, if that's wot yer arter. But they don't come cheap.'

I spent a minute running the numbers through me head as we strolled along the gravelled ways. 'Don't hold me to an igzak figure, but I reckon that lot 'll cost you around seventy quid.'

'Seventy pounds? Hmm… I think the Ordnance could well support such a fee.'

'Course, numbers like that do… grow in the telling, do they not?'

'Depends who you tell them to,' answered Montagu.

We crunched on gravel a little time in silence.

'How would it be,' Montagu said slowly with his gaze far off, 'if Handel were to rehearse his fireworks music here first?'

'Here? Now, that might be a diffr'nt story.' Dreams of golden sovereigns danced behind me eyes. An out-of-season bonus. 'I lend you the stuff for free, and you have him play here?' He nodded. 'He'd do it, wouldn't he?'

'Never one to avoid a sovereign, if you take my meaning.'

'Oh, aye, the king'll come. And he'll bring Cumberland. Not but what he'd come anyhow.'

'Oh, Cumberland!' says Montagu. 'He'd attend the opening of a door if someone told him it squeaked musical.'

Made me laugh, that did. 'An' if he comes, 'arf o' society comes with him.'

'Why, Cumberland's Handel's best suitor. He was ever the conquering hero since Handel honoured him.'[33]

'Aye. And Prince Frederick will bring the other 'arf o' society. Don't play politics 'ere.'

'No,' he replied, glancing my way with what I took to be a most avaricious eye. 'Society's all one when it comes to their parting with cash.'

'Shillin' a head, six mebbe seven thahsand souls, makes a pretty penny.'

'My head for numbers,' Montagu replied quickly, 'makes it nearly 300 quid.'

'Course, especial occasion, ye might push it to 'arf a crahn.'

'Indeed, you might. Half-a-crown is imminently reasonable. And you would get all that coin for the loan of a few lampions, a crew of workingmen and sundry other small things. A very lop-sided deal… if you catch my meaning.'

'Hmm. So, we might arrange a lil *quid pro quo*, as we Latinists would put it.' See, that's what I'm driving at; ever an eye for profit, Montagu. Man after me own heart.

'Indeed, we might. For example, how do you count heads at your concerts?'

'Pre-sell tickets to the nobs in the enclosure, day or two before,' I said. 'The rest at the gate. Simple. Take the money, let 'em in, take the money, let 'em in… Count the heads arterwards by the take.'

'Your word? My goodness, how slipshod.'

'Yers, quite shocking how careless these things are managed, ain't it?'

'Oh, true! So much room for taking advantage.'

'Not that anyone would…'

We shared a pinch of snuff and wandered slowly through the gardens within our own thoughts. The rain had held off nicely, and it wasn't too cold. Many of the flowers was coming out along the beds, although 'twould be some time before anyone saw 'em, the season being a month away. Montagu knew what I was thinking; I knew what he was thinking. He cracked first and broke the silence.

'What cut?'

'Forty you, sixty me.'

'And the lampions, workingmen, all I'll want?'

'Done.' And we shook hands, which is all two gentlemen need.

Another shot of snuff and a turn around the Octagon Bandstand and the Organ Building before we spoke again.

'Fly in the ointment's my friend Handel,' I said. 'What if he don't bite?'

'Oh, he'll bite,' replied Montagu. 'The king's purse pays his fee on the nail and, as I said, there are sovereigns to consider. Master of the one kind, servant of the other.'

'Aye, so be it. He's bin a good friend to me, and we've done concerts here for years.'

'Exactly,' said Montagu. 'He'll be here, for His Majesty hath commanded it. Now let us set the date.'

I thought about this a bit. I'd have to get the staff together earlier than what I usually do, clean the rubbish of winter, prepare the grounds. 'Not before mid-April.'

'How is Monday the seventeenth of April?' he asked. 'There's no other great function in London that I know of that day, so people will not be drawn away.'

'Seventeenth it is.' I made a note in me mind.

'Just between ourselves for the nonce.' He tapped his nose. 'Not noised about.'

'And the informing of Mr Handel?'

'Frederick will be charged with that duty', he smiled. ''Til then, not a word.'

'You, sir,' I says to him in all sincerity, 'are a man arter my own heart.'

With this we returned to the wherry dock and woke up his boatmen. As I watched him set out downriver to Whitehall, I bethought myself how mighty convenient 'twould be to have a bridge hereabouts. But the one at Westminster's lately subsided, and it's cost hundreds of thousands so far. Idle thought.

Chapter Thirty-Two

George Frideric Handel (1685 to 1759)
Composer and Impresario

In which Mr Handel is persuaded against his better judgement to provide music for the fireworks, and discord rises upon its nature

Commissions from the king are ever fraught with peril, and this one came at a damned difficult time. The early months of 1749 were amongst the busiest I remember. I'd opened the season in February with *Susanna* for four performances, then went straightway into *Hercules*, which needed much reworking. Then I planned to revive *Samson*—long a public favourite—and so on to *Solomon*. And betimes I would tutor Princess Mary, oversee the writing out of parts by my trusty copyists, and deal with the interminable squabbles and airs of my singers. I felt guilt, also, that I had somewhat neglected my duties with the Foundling Hospital, for I wished to compose an anthem to be played there. And there is never enough time in a day for one's own work when one needs must oversee the huge team whose efforts keep my enterprise afloat.

Of course, I had seen the temple rising in the Green Park and knew the king's plans for a vast firework show—all London, indeed, the whole realm knew—and I had also heard that music was wanting for it. In January some ink-smitten pamphleteer had broadcast "plans" for forty trumpets, twenty French horns and God knows what hautboys, drums and whatnot.[34] Music? You may call it music if you will, but I'd not grace it with that word. For certain I'd have nothing to do with such monstrosity. There are not above a handful of trumpeters who can do my bidding with any satisfaction, nor horn players neither, and as for the rest, whoever organised such a rabble would need to drag the taverns and bawdy houses for them. Let some band from the army put it together; 'twould not be me.

So, when Charles Frederick, Montagu's Surveyor-General, knocked upon my door at Brook Street in late February with his plans for some sort of musical accompaniment in the Green Park, I was ready to damn his eyes for his impudence.

''Tis fashionable to have music before the fireworks,' he began. 'And the king is convinced.'

'Oh, aye. Certain! Y' mean Montagu hath convinced him.' I felt sure John Montagu was at the bottom of this, him being not one to miss the main chance.

'I know not. I assume the direction comes from the king, as I have no intelligence to the contrary.'

'Hmm? So, the celebration wants music from *me*?' I asked, knowing the king wouldn't give a tinker's curse who wrote it, if he wanted it at all, which I doubted. 'Hath His Majesty taken a liking to the coarser arts, then?'

'You take liberties, sir, with your sovereign. Have a care lest such untoward implications find a less forgiving ear than mine.'

'What? You disagree?' Damned impertinence!

'He is regularly in attendance at Covent Garden, and music graces St James's Palace,' Frederick snooted, 'as you well know.'

'Aye, but I said *coarser*. There his ears are regaled with *fine* music. Precious little of that he'll hear in the Green Park. There's talk of a braying mob of bandsmen, drums, military rubbish. Have Arne do it or Boyce.'

He tut-tutted and shook his head, knowing I spoke true. 'I am sure His Majesty's musical sensibility will be better served with music of a refined nature.'

'So, by what alchemy doth the king decide that it should be me to write the music to accompany his grand design?' Although I smelt subterfuge, it was only afterward I learned that it was, indeed, Montagu who'd convinced the king and not t' other way round. 'And if I were to refuse? Tell him I had not the leisure?'

'It would not go well with you.' He eyed me knowingly. 'You know as well as I do that reputations and employment rise and fall upon royal conceits.'

'Very well then. When is this wanted? And who pays my receipt?'

'Before late April. William Rawlinson Earle, the Clerk of the Cheque at the Ordnance, is comptroller of the purse for this endeavour, so you have no concern upon that score.'

'Good. I'll wager Montagu's got some damned thimblerig with the king's purse, though. I see through him, my friend, and I'll have none of it!'

'God forbid that John Montagu would think to profit.'

I smiled at that and gave Frederick a hard stare, more penetrating than perhaps he would have liked, for he shifted a little, and his eyes went every which away but mine. Then I nodded slowly.

'I will give it my attention then. Tell me, what form of music,' and here I eyed him knowingly, 'does the king desire?'

'Well, it would… um… he… he places the decision in your hands.'

Certain now it was that the cart was before the horse. If I knew my sovereign at all, I would know that what would most suit his fancy for this occasion would never suit mine.

'So be it. I will set about the task and send notice when a draught is ready.'

So it was that I set aside some other work and got down to writing the sketch of a suite of music to grace the occasion. A sketch would suffice because it was certain that revisions would be necessary. Editing and correcting the sketch would be simple; I write music as swiftly as another would write the line of a letter, especially when the purse of the Ordnance is opening its strings to me. And 'tis a great attribute of mine that, although I might find a task distasteful, I will not give it less than my best. There is no room in my world for quick and off-the-cuff works, for you never know whose hands they may come into, to your later detriment.

Nevertheless, I left it as just a sketch for a few days; damned if I'd look all that eager to please. There was work yet to be done on *Solomon*, a concert for the Decay'd Musicians charity, and divers other intrusive but important duties. It must have been a week before I sharpened a quill, pulled out the ruled paper, and finished the job. Naturally, I would score for the full string ensemble and add wind instruments—a pair of hautboys, a couple of trumpets and horns, and such like—as occasion demanded in the texture of the work. My *Water Music*, written some thirty years before, showed a fine model for the disposition of the instruments. I reused some writing for horns from a concerto I'd half-worked some time before; good work and not to be wasted. Keep it simple, I thought, for it is to be played outdoors in God knows what weather and played by some who perhaps sight-read music not too well. I did the whole damned thing in D-major, thumping military stuff. It started with an overture, of course, with a segue into an adagio and an allegro. A bourée followed, then a largo, which I did *alla siciliana*, a mood I much fancy, and called it *La Paix*. An allegro, *La Réjouissance*, followed, and then I threw in a couple of menuets to round it off. Quickly done, a mere sketch, but satisfactory to the task.

Outdoor performance is ever perilous. The weather on the day would make this work a wager, as it is almost impossible to maintain tuning in inclement conditions, let alone the composure of the musicians. I reckon above half of the outdoor performances I have ever overseen at Vauxhall were ruined by rain. Ruined to my ears, that is; outdoor audiences are ever forgiving or ignorant, and most are so busy chatting, swilling and scoffing, or making groping discoveries amongst the crinolines, to heed the music. And even when clement, the variations of damp in the air play havoc, especially with the strings. But for an outdoor occasion, the small discerning fraction of the audience must perforce be tolerant of wayward tuning and know that what they hear upon that occasion will be all the better when appreciated indoors.

Frederick wrote twice before I had got to finish the work, and it was some satisfaction to put him off. I relished the thought of keeping His Highness waiting, though I was convinced the order for music came not from him in the first place. When Frederick wrote the third time, I was ready for him. I invited him to Brook Street and thrust the pages at him ere he'd taken a chair. He drew out his reading glasses and scanned the sheets quickly. Though he knew naught of music, he saw that the parts were labelled. He looked up at me over his glasses.

'I see a preponderance of violins,' he remarked cautiously. 'Violin I, violin II…'

'Well? Doth the king not want the best of musical fashion?' What was he driving at? I felt a small alarum.

'The king thinks more of martial instruments…'

'I've given him horns, trumpets! Damnation!'

'But the fiddles…'

'What of 'em?'

'I don't at all doubt but when the king hears it, he will be very much displeased.'

I lost my temper with the man. 'Take it to him! Show him! Tell His Highness that if he wishes music from me, he'll take what's offered.'

'Mr Handel,' he flapped his hands in front of me, 'you can not think that I would so approach the king.'

'It's not my blasted problem how you *so approach* the king,' I shouted. 'Take the music. Show him,' and I ushered him out to the stairs.

Horns, trumpets, hautboys, drums, instruments of war! Damnation! Yes, it was perilous to score for strings outdoors—one was so much at the whim of the elements—but fine music was demanded for a fine occasion, and military brass and drums and whatnot would hardly suit. If I was to write anything, it would be the best I could do. As I said, one never knows where one's music will end up.

It was not a week before the Duke of Montagu himself came fussing into my writing room, all a quiver with the music sheets clutched in his hand.

'His Majesty says he wants none of your damned fiddles,' he started without preamble, 'and he is mighty exercised over it.'

'The strings hold the foundation! They guide and solidify.'

'His Majesty…'

'Well, in damnation,' I cried, 'have another do it then!'

'No, no, no,' Montagu cried, all in a fluster. 'It must be you. No other. It must be you.'

'Why? Why me? Why no other?'

'The… the… king would be most displeased…' He was prevaricating, and I suspected why. 'Royal pleasure… king's wishes…'

'Blast you to hell! What would he have me do?'

'He hath expressly requested martial instruments.'

'Martial instruments? Well, here's a blessèd irony,' said I. 'The instruments of Ares to celebrate the peace of Eirene? Better have flutes and harps, I warrant. Peace, my nether eye!'

'He wants a dozen or more of trumpets…' Montagu continued as my barb at his hypocrisy quite flew over his head.

'A dozen!'

'And of horns, the same...'

'Damn and blast!' I had perforce to cool my choler, for I had not the choice now the king had spoken. 'Oh, damn you and blast you. What option have I? To hell with it!'

'Royal pleasure... King's wishes...' he said again.

I smelt some stinking subterfuge, but resistance to the king's bidding could only go badly with me. 'I'll do as bid and score for his damned metalwork.' 'Twas hardly wise to make a great scene of it. I almost shoved Montagu to the door, so keen was I to see the back of him, thinking he was done, but he paused.

'What then?'

'His Highness is very much taken with the serpent...'

'The serpent!' I roared, again quite losing my temper with such coarse buffoonery. 'It be the serpent what seduced Eve! I'll have no black monstrous Satan in my band!' God's balls, of all the instruments, the serpent is the lowest of the low. A mooing, braying, rasping bass devoid of musical quality, all coiled up in a black leather skin redolent of sin and the Fall. A base, farting monstrosity.

'The king doth so wish...' I sat silent with arms crossed. 'And his displeasure...'

I took the path of least woe. 'He shall have his blasted serpents. Now leave me in peace.'

He scuttled quickly down the stairs, and the door bang-banged at his going. I felt a mite sorry for the old fellow. He was caught 'twixt a rock and a hard place, but all the shuttling to and fro was really at his charge. I swear 'twas he who suggested music to the regent in the first place. As ye sow, so shall ye reap.

Still, something stank.

So, of necessity and risking royal displeasure, I transposed and simplified all the string parts for hautboys and bassoons, eased melodic lines for the horns and trumpets, and added a thundering squad of drums. It was hateful to squander my work; to take a fine piece of art and despoil it in this way. Imagine, like my friend Hogarth, to create a fine painting in oils and, when quite done, to besmirch it over, daubing coarse colour over fine line and shade. Tear the canvas, and rip off the frame. That is what it is to render one's work base. So, I scored for nine horns and the same number of trumpets—damned if I'd add any more—because I know only too well how few of the players at my disposal can play in tune. Long gone are the times when I scored for the brasses in oratorio and opera and could count on the likes of John Shore to grace my lines. He is now long retired, and though Mr Snow follows him well, in playing this work, he will be beset and run aground amongst inferiors. A ship of the line amongst bumboats.[35] Perforce, I would need to employ bandsmen, and whilst they may be able to square-bash on the parade ground or blow George's head off at banquets, I'm damned if they can play music. Oh, blast it all! I even included parts for two serpents, just so the king could see 'em in ink, but I was God damned if I'd have 'em play no matter what the displeasure. Oh, this would be a noisy, discordant affair but, in all hope, masked by the roar of the mob and never to be repeated where finely tuned ears might apprehend it.

What a horror!

Play it once; get it over with.

I had my man Smith and his family of copyists prepare fair scores of the work and sent one set post haste to Frederick.[36] Let him show it to the king, serpents and all, and be damned to it. But I would keep my preferred scoring and have Smith write it out fine, my lovely strings being a testament to what the music should have been. Perhaps, in the fullness of time, I would have it played before the Foundling Governors in the chapel at Lamb's Conduit Street?

The score copied out for the fireworks could go to the devil, for all I cared.

CHAPTER THIRTY-THREE

Charles Frederick (1709 to 1785)
Surveyor-General of the Ordnance

In which a rehearsal of the music is proposed to Mr Handel, and fireworks of another sort result

John Montagu bade me speak to Mr Handel on the subject of a rehearsal for the fireworks music. John had plans for it to be held at Vauxhall Gardens and had apprised the king of this, finding His Majesty much enamoured of it. He had not, though, broached the subject with Handel himself yet. I thought this to be folly, though I forbore saying so. Handel was ever a porcupine, and I knew that Montagu, having been pierced with his quills more than once, was of mind to have me broach the subject in his stead. However, I was as loath as he to speak to the composer, knowing what squibs and serpents might be directed my way. Though I would never tell Montagu so, I felt it somewhat poltroonly that he not do it himself. I asked myself why he so desired music at all, and had persuaded the king of the need of it, against the royal wishes. Then he further wished it rehearsed and quite probably contrary to Mr Handel's desire as well. 'Twas a pit he himself had dug. There was no understanding him.

On a forenoon, I made my way from my workplace in the Green Park to Brook Street and was shown up to the chamber where George Handel did his work. His servant told me that he had this moment returned from a visit and might be ill disposed to seeing me. I could have fled, for here was the pretext I had wished, but I thought it better to bite the bullet; I would anyway be obliged to return later. Therefore, at my insistence we went up, the door was opened with caution and myself announced. Handel remained seated behind his writing desk and pierced me with a gaze of irritation mixed with impatience. He was wigged and dressed for company, and I guessed he had at that moment picked up his quill to write. Caught in the midst of inspiration, he put not the quill down.

'To what is this pleasure ascribed?' he asked, though pleasure it clearly was not, as I stood before the desk. 'Was not the score of the music all that was wanted?'

'No, no, yes,' I replied. 'All is very well with the music. You have retrenched the violins and made much of the martial instruments, so the king is not at all out of humour.'

'Why then do you accost me, if all is well?' He thrust his quill aside.

''Tis on the subject of the rehearsal...'

'I shall have it rehearsed in good time.' He addressed me as if I were impertinent. 'Why think you I would not have it ready, and what business of yours is it how I go about it?'

'No, no. I mean the *public* rehearsal.'

'*Public rehearsal?* There is to be none! The piece will be played but once before the fireworks, and there's an end to it!'

'The king wishes a rehearsal...' Before I could finish, the man stood up, tearing the wig off his head and flinging it to the floor in a cloud of powder.

'No, no, no! Damnation, I will not hear of it!' Such was his sudden choler I feared for his health. 'You tax me o'ermuch, damn you! *No public rehearsal!*'

'The king hath set the date...'

'Set the date? *Set the date!* I gave no by-your-leave to set any date!'

'His Majesty hath decreed,' I said in as calm a voice as I could muster, though I was all aquiver within, 'that the rehearsal will take place on Monday, the seventeenth of April.'

'Damnation to *any* rehearsal where others may hear it!'

'It is both the king's wish and that of the Duke of Cumberland.'

He took a deep breath and gathered himself. 'Well, if we must play it before them, we must. But let it at least be privy to them and not in a place where any of the public may hear it.'

'Ahh... It is to be at Vauxhall...'

'*Vauxhall!* No, no, no! Not Vauxhall! Get out, get out!'

He seized my coat cuff with a surprising strong grip, spun me around, and thrust me to the door. I had no desire to bandy more words, so I quickly left but paused on the stair with heart a-beating as the door slammed shut. There were thumps and bangs within like unto a mischievous spirit and curses of a far more corporeal nature. I heard the fall of something fragile, fragile no longer. I had thought to return to the room once his choler had subsided, but I thought better of it and made my way hastily down the stairs.

'He wants not a rehearsal,' I told Montagu, when I accosted him in his office later in the day. 'Indeed, he is violently opposed. The king must hear of it, and I don't doubt but he will dispense with the music altogether, or it might easily be supplied by another.'

'No!' replied Montagu with force. 'He must neither dispense with it nor have it done by another. Handel continues to express his zeal to His Majesty's service by doing what is so contrary to it! No, it *must* be Handel, and it *must* be Vauxhall.'

'But why so? If he is so intractable and the king indifferent?'

'The true reason must not be given. Content yourself with the rehearsal proceeding as required.'

'So, shall it be you who takes the lion by his beard? For I shall not!'

Montagu sighed, rose from his desk, and paced the room. 'Charles, Charles. Handel can not resist the command of the sovereign, froth and foam as he might. Go you back to his lair, and tell him that he durst not refuse this commission.'

'I can not,' I said, the wrath of my latest encounter fresh on my mind.

'You can, and you must,' he smiled with an ironical rise to one eyebrow, 'for I'll not go. Here is one circumstance where you can not delegate. And it must be... expeditious.'

So, I returned to Brook Street the following day in the afternoon all unannounced—having spent the forenoon winding myself up to the task—half hoping that Handel was elsewhere, or engaged or mayhap indisposed. None of these three possibilities came about, and I was shown again into his room. He stood as I entered and waved me to a seat. I found him not at all angry, nor exercised in any manner but quite resigned. He poured from a carafe, handed me a glass, and sipped from his for some minutes.

'Forgive me,' he began, 'for earlier thrusting you from these rooms.'

'On my part, I am sorry if I gave offence, though 'twas far from my mind.'

'Y' see, I am twixt the devil and the deep sea. His Royal Highness hath decreed a rehearsal of the music in Vauxhall Gardens. Upon his favour rests much. I am his servant; I do his bidding. Why, think you, do I find this charge vexatious in the extreme?'

'I know not, for if it were the matter of payment, your fee would be well covered.'

''Tis not for money! I lack for nothing in *money*.'

'Then have you not the time to devote to it?'

'I am ever as busy as it is possible to be, yet I find time when 'tis needed. I can assemble my forces in Vauxhall as ever I do through the season. So, no.'

'What then?' I could not conceive of his concern over the playing of a piece of music and said so.

'The king hath decreed great forces of martial instruments, and I have bent to his will. *This is not music!* And few of those who will play it are musicians. Do you comprehend me?'

'But surely, it is to be played in the Green Park, whatever.'

'Aye, by all means, play the damned thing when there are guns and salutes, merriment, drink and fireworks. That's one thing... but not Vauxhall!' he moaned. 'Please, not Vauxhall. The most prestigious, the most popular, the most refined locale for fine music, that it be so debased by such a roaring cacophony.'

'Surely,' I said, 'is it not true that music is but a passing sensation, and that the ear fails to remember discord?'

'Oh, wax not philosophical with me, sir. Ears that hear discord drive scurrilous pens. The music may evaporate, but their foul ink doth not. I have critics enough already. To have such music the centre of attention, standing strip't as Eve but as discordant and ugly as she is fair? No, no, no!'

He poured us more from the flagon, sipped and sighed. Of a sudden, a shaft of sun shot through the dust of his window and laid a lattice pattern upon the music sheets on his desk.

'But twixt Satan and the sea, I have no choice.'

I kept silent, for what could I say when we both knew we were confronted with the will of the sovereign?

'Tell me,' he mused after a spell, 'what part has Montagu in this?'

'Part, sir? He, also, is the servant of his master.'

'Come, come. 'Twas he put the notion of music in the royal ear and not contrariwise. Is that not so?'

'Perhaps he mentioned to His Majesty that a musical overture to a firework is the very fashionable thing?'

'And perhaps he *mentioned*, also, that the only other person sitting with you in this room was the one to see it done? The only one?'

'Both he and the king hold you in very high regard.'

'I'll not be flattered! Anyone can see that music, so-called, to accompany burnt gunpowder and drunken, groping oafs could be served by any clod. No, Montagu's playing some thimblerig. He gains somehow, or why take such trouble?'

'I am sure the Duke of Montagu would not stoop…'

'Oh, aye! He'd not take advantage. And my arse is the dome of Wren's great church! What d' ye take me for?'

Chapter Thirty-four

John, 2nd Duke of Montagu (1690 to 1749)
Master-General of His Majesty's Ordnance

In which the duke joins his friends for cards, coffee and a pipe, whilst a scurrilous pamphlet is passed around

'Twas joy unalloyed to relieve my coffee and tobacco friends of their pledges when we met again in our box at the Bedford for a pipe and a few shillings at whist, and quite a jingling purse of guineas it was. They handed over the loot in good face, for so soon as Fielding had put forth the advertisement, 'twas a foregone conclusion the jape would be pulled off. Once they'd read the playbill he'd set up, they might as well have paid up there and then. Yet, ominous as a storm seen from afar when all seems calm was the cloud of Cumberland. I think, in retrospect, that I'd not have thrown out the challenge of the affair had I seen his face in it. 'Tis all well and good to part the unwary from their cash, and bring the flush to their cheeks to boot, but such a one as the Butcher made the soup just a trifle too rich. If he were to discover the engineer of his disgrace, would his word in the king's ear carry weight in my disfavour? But, on 't other hand, should he bring forth a complaint, would he be showed in a bad light, even though he knew it to be me? I could not guess. But I deemed secrecy was still vital, so I moved to swear them again to the bond. It was a month and more since we'd last met, for I felt it wise to let the smoke of the affair blow thin.

'Damn me!' cried Portland, laughing. 'He's not chased the culprit. Be seen as all kinds of fool, should he be so unwise.'

'More than he is yet,' said Leone, who was with us at the Bedford that evening. 'He'll do naught lest he come down a peg.'

'Not a word has come from that quarter since,' said Henry Fielding. 'Proof of the pudding. You're safe.'

'Even so,' I replied, 'it is my arse that's over the brazier, so I'll have you swear anew. Place your hands on the board, all of you.'

They all did that, and I swore them again whilst my bag of guineas sat by my side upon the table and mocked them. Then we took to recounting the great event, lingering over each scene as though 'twere a drama we'd lately taken in.

'Oh, the sword from the Scheuldt!' roared Portland. 'And the demolished smock petticoat! I liked to piss myself when I first read it.'

'A hasty retreat from the Battle of Bottle Noddles,' chuckled Chesterfield. 'What wag penned that, I wonder?' We all roared again, as we had roared before, whilst curious faces popped over the wainscot of the box, drawn to the stir. I waved my table quiet, still concerned it would be bruited about, and the curious faces withdrew about their own business.

'Now here's something equally comical,' said Fielding as our mirth subsided. He withdrew a printed booklet from his vest, passed it to me, and said with a wicked smile, 'Cast your eyes o'er this.'

' "An account," ' I read on the cover page, ' "of the Famous Sieur Rocquet, Surgeon, just arrived from Paris…" Oh, Christ, this is Ruggieri! How did you come upon this?'[37]

'They're scattered everywhere about. I had it at Slaughters this forenoon.'

'The villains! They are making sport of Ruggieri!'

'Yes,' he cried, seizing the book from me and opening the next page, 'your firework man. Here, listen: "This is to give notice that the Sieur Rocquet, surgeon, is lately arrived from Paris and hath brought with him fifty assistant surgeons, who will attend at the ensuing Royal Fireworks…" '

'Stop! Stop! This is scandalous. Calumny!'

'Read more! Read more!' cried two or three of the assembled, banging their cups and glasses on the board and shouting down my objection. 'Go on! Read!'

' "…as near to the several scaffolds as can be done with safety; where they will be ready to assist all persons of quality and distinction; and to prevent imposition…" no, shut up, Montagu,' as he waved me back, ' "…he engages to perform the following chirurgical operations, at the lowest prices, viz." and then,' he turned the page, laughing, and spread it before us, 'look here, he gives a list. A butcher's bill! See, here they're cutting off a leg for a guinea...'

Chesterfield seized the foul pamphlet and read aloud, 'Here's a new nose for ten-and-six, realistically scarr'd with smallpox.'

'And it's only five shillings to carry off and bleed a corpse,' cried another, reading over his shoulder.

'Cutting off a thigh (leg included) is a guinea...'

'But half that price for a leg below the knee!' roared Leone, exploding in mirth.

I sat back, astounded, as they passed the damned thing around and read extracts in turn. This was the foul journalism, so-called, that Frederick and I had worried over. Lampoons abounded since His Majesty's Grand Conceit was first noised about, but this foul edition stood upon a pinnacle of defamation.

'Returning a corpse to a relation's only half-a-crown!'

'Or they reserve the corpse for anatomical lectures!' cried another. 'And pay not a farthing for it.'

'Hand, foot, thumb, toe... teeth at a guinea the dozen...'

'Clearing out a bruis'd eye...'

'Oh, Jesus! Listen, listen,' crowed Fielding, seizing back the paper and waving their laughter to silence. 'Here's something for Charles Frederick.' He took an oratory stance, holding the paper before him and thrusting his other hand into his bosom. 'Sieur Rocquet, "hath also brought over with him a quantity of *Kevenbuller* cotton for the ears, which will entirely prevent any ill consequences which might arise from the noise of the cannon; absolutely necessary for ladies, gentlemen and officers of the fleet and army, not used to sudden and frightful explosions." '

By this time, the entire assembly was roaring with laughter, and the eyes and noses from the adjoining box had appeared again above the wainscot.

'Here, here,' he read above the din, 'even selling "a most agreeable volatile salt, highly useful for such gentlemen of the Train, as can not bear the offensive smell of gunpowder!" '

Observers from the adjoining box brought forth another copy of the pamphlet, found right here in the Bedford, and jostled each other for a look, or passed it amongst themselves, reading snippets and splitting their sides. As I sat listening to the raucous, roaring laughter around me—watching the other boxes emptying, their occupants coming over to ours with glasses in hand and pipes in mouth, to share and join the merriment—I went through a strange change of mind; a mental transformation, if you will. Appalling as this was to be bandied about, and detrimental to good governance, there was a devil in me that sat upon my shoulder and whispered in my ear: "What did His Majesty expect when he so slenderly knows his own people?" And when some court toad brought a copy to him—which was bound to happen—he would rail at it, and then he would see to it that I got an unholy earful. But he was hoist with his own petard whatever.

The more I thought on this pamphlet, then, the more I appreciated a particular breed of wit that grows up only in these British Isles. What other nation on earth could craft so bold a conceit or bring it off in a printing with such style? And who fronted the printing of it? And how many might be spread abroad? Then I bethought myself of my very own prank, which sat there, concrete, in the purse of guineas before me, and I knew myself to be one with the anonymous wit who penned this dreadful account. 'Tis not too great a stretch to say that a sense of pride grew upon me… or was it only the coffee, the tobacco, the good company?

There's an infection in laughter; 'tis the smallpox of our daily intercourse, and it passes quickly from one to another. 'Twas not long before I was roaring with the rest.

Chapter Thirty-Five

James Morris (c. 1700 to c. 1760)
Master Carpenter to the Office of the Ordnance

*In which friction amongst French and English allies causes
delay, and Mr Frederick is all powerless to reconcile them*

The truth was there for all to see, but the monsieur was hardly one to admit his error. Fact is, the panels didn't bloody fit. We had hauled all four sections of His Majesty Giving Peace to Britannia up to the niche they were to be fitted in—right at the top, front and damned centre of the whole creation—and found the pieces too tall by about six inches. The men called me, and I climbed up the ladder to the scaffold, where they showed me the framed-out space above the cornice. They had the four linen-covered panels stacked precarious and secured from tipping with a rope. I was baffled, so I went back down and checked my notes and drawings. Sure enough, all measured out and noted, with a sketch as well, twenty-eight long by ten high in total. No error. These were the frames that Servandoni insisted they build at the Haymarket; the rest we had made here and sent 'em off by cart. I recalled he'd taken the dimensions off my notes, or at least I'd swear he'd done. There was nothing for it but to haul all four sections down again, and only then did I discover how hard it was to lower pieces down, having 'til now just hauled 'em up. Charles Frederick was in his little lean-to office, so I fetched him out and showed him one of the framed panels, lying flat over a couple of trestles, and explained the problem. I asked what he thought, more out of politeness I will say, because I didn't think his opinion would be of much value.

'Can you not enlarge the space?' he asked.

'No, sir, I can not, for it is framed already.' I took him out and pointed up at the place with its cornice above and its base below. The space was framed out, and that was that.

He tut-tutted something fearful. 'Signor Soldi will have to do 'em again. But we have not the time! Oh, goodness, what are we to do?'

'I could easily cut 'em to fit. Pull the nails off the linen, lop off six inches from the bottom of the frame, reattach the cloth. By my judgement, you might lose Britannia's right foot and the tip of the king's boot. Better than off the top 'cos you'd come close to His Majesty's head.'

'Don't be impertinent, sir! We must consult Chevalier Servandoni. Send a boy to the Haymarket for him.'

'Begging your pardon, sir, but it might be wise to leave the chevalier where he is and deal with this as our problem, not his.'

'We must consult. I insist upon 't.'

'It were better…'

'No, no. You may not do aught without he knows. Send for him directly.'

I should have argued with him but, whatever his abilities, he was my superior in both rank and station. So, I sent a boy running with a note to the Haymarket to bring the monsieur here for a consultation. As I'd spelt out the problem in my note, when Servandoni arrived, he'd already had time to concoct his excuses. Should have kept it cryptic so I could see his first impression.

'They're all ten-foot-six high,' I began as soon as he had come across the grass and mud to me, tricked out in all his finery, sword included. 'Don't fit.'

'You gave me the measurements yourself,' he replied, so quick I knew 'twas fictive.

'Not so,' says I, 'for here are my notes and sketches. 'Twas you wrote 'em down.'

'I never did. You wrote them for me.' Now here was a bare-faced lie, but I had no proof to counter it.

'I'll not admit error in this,' I said. 'Every other frame was made here, and every one of 'em fits perfect. Just the ones made by your crew are in error.'

'You gave us the wrong sizes!'

Frederick intervened at this point with the sensible observation that, whosoever was in error, remediation was needed. 'What are we to do?'

'One of two things,' I replied, all practical. 'We can cut the frames down, or we can have 'em painted again.'

'No, no, no!' shouted Servandoni. 'You ignore the third choice: make the space bigger! It is obvious.'

'Look you,' and I pointed as I had done for Frederick, 'the niche is built and framed, and we have it finished and whitewashed. This work can not be easily undone, and even should it, the proportions would be all wrong. Is that not so, Mr Frederick?' I called upon Frederick because I knew of his classical dabbling and his knowledge of balance and form. He might be a meddler with old coins and papers, but he knew architecture.

'It is true, Chevalier,' he said, rising to my bait, 'that the classical form of the temple demands true balance and clean line...'

'What is this? You side with the carpenters against the artists? We'll not repaint!'

'Then we must cut 'em down...' I said.

'No, no,' Servandoni shouted, swinging his right hand to the hilt of his sword. 'The space provided is too small. It is impossible to do justice to the subject in such tight confines.'

'Perhaps then,' put in Frederick, with mighty hand flapping, 'we might, after all, compromise upon the proportion of the niche...'

I should not have cut across a man of his rank and station, but I was sorely vexed. 'What's this? Am I to demolish my work? Are then the classic proportions to be sacrificed for *his* error?'

'It is not *my* error!' cried Servandoni. 'It is yours!'

'Not mine! D' ye think I don't know good English measures? What measures d' you use where you come from?'

'Please, please, gentlemen,' said Frederick, 'let us be reasonable...'

'It is *raisonable*,' replied Servandoni, 'to enlarge the space to accommodate the work of art.'

I lost my temper at this nonsense, for I saw no way forrad at all. We had here a three-way "love affair" that would've graced one of Foote's plays. I called to one of my carpenters engaged on a balustrade behind me: 'You! Bring me a pair of pincers, a cross-cut saw and a chalk line!'

'Do not dare to cut them!' yelled the Frenchman. And then to Frederick, with spittle flying from his chubby lips: 'Do you not understand that this is to be seen from a far distance and is to serve but one use?'

'What of it?'

'It matters not in the slightest how it shows!' He was working himself to a passion. 'It is all in the *impression*.'

'Well, then,' says I, all practical-like with the saw in my paw, 'that being the case, it'll not matter a bishop's fart if the top and bottom are lopped off.'

'*You will not!*' he yelled, and this time the sword began to slide out of the scabbard.

'Gentlemen, gentlemen,' said Frederick coming between us, fearing the dissolution of the Peace of Aix-la-Chapelle right here in the Green Park, 'this is not seemly.'

Neither was it, when most of the construction crew had laid down their tools and were watching this high burlesque with great grins on their faces. I took the steam out of the affair by turning my back on the monsieur and waving angrily at the men to get on with their work. Whilst my back was so turned, Servandoni strutted off the field with Frederick trotting along behind him and prattling away. I had the strong impression that a bribe of coin was being put forward.

I went back to my work in the lean-to tent or tried to. I was mighty distracted and disturbed, not just at the stupidity with Servandoni but with the way I had snapped at Frederick. He was my superior, and he held my position in the Ordnance in his hand. He'd not dismiss me whilst the work was underway, but at the end of it—after the great show in April—who knew? I didn't have long to stew, for he came back shortly, waved my two men out of the tent, and stood before me with his hands on his hips.

'Well, Mr Morris? Well, sir?'

I decided as he stood there that I was in no mood to be contrite, no matter what the cost to me. I had been lied to, he had been lied to, and I would stand my ground.

'I apologise, sir…'

'You do? And so you damned well should!'

'I apologise, *sir*,' I repeated, then paused for a few heartbeats, 'for not insisting that summoning Chevalier Servandoni to the park might make things difficult.'

'Why so? What do you mean?'

'Did the Duke of Montagu not describe our earlier problem with the assignment of roles, sir?'

'He told me of a problem with hoisting pieces, yes. I know not the details.'

Nor wish to know, I thought, but said naught on that head. 'It was made clear at that time, sir, that regarding the decorations, Servandoni would be in charge in the Haymarket, and I would be in charge here. The duke offered the monsieur some guineas as a surety of our separate roles.'

Frederick coloured at this observation, so 'twas clear he'd done the same today all unsuspecting.

'Had I lopped those frames myself,' I continued, 'he'd never have known, and we would have been saved a heap of waxing theatrical.'

'Nevertheless, I have been shown in a bad light by this behaviour.'

'By *his* behaviour, yes.' I would go that far.

'You gainsaid me!'

I played my trump. 'If his demand were to be carried out, sir, I would needs remove much of the upper work. Or Soldi would needs redo all four paintings. In short, either way, the job would remain unfinished, for we've not the time.'

This played upon his greatest fear and that of Montagu as well. We, all three of us, would mock King George II in our failure, and it would go hard with us. I watched him crumble; not a pretty sight to see in a man in authority, though he masked it well as those of our class are trained to do.

'Do what you must do,' he sighed. 'Enough time hath been wasted thus far. We can ill afford more.'

He turned and left, doubtless to report the episode to Montagu and doubtless, also, to place himself in a better position with him. I could hear him already: "I had Morris cut them down, for I deemed it the more *expeditious* course." Me, I have to say that I took great pleasure in personally lopping those frames down to size. I laid each of 'em across a pair of trestles, took the linen off the bottom with a pincer, and sawed away with the joy of a boy on first walking out with a girl. I'd not have any of my men do it; the job was mine.

As I've said before, I knew Servandoni's trouble far better than he did himself. Fact is, he had no control over what he was employed to do, and that, I think, is what he mostly lusted after. He was one who designed theatre sets, produced spectacles and made fine buildings, but here he'd been given the king's grand plan *fait accompli*, as he would've said, instead of creating the works himself. Then his relationship with me, a workingman (or so he saw me), was all topsy-turvy in his world; it sat ill with him that he was cast as a labourer working in an undercroft. It suited not his fancy. Add into this his foolish error in measurement—forgivable and correctible in a less haughty man—and you have the perfect concoction. Of course, yours truly wasn't so blameless, but that's neither here nor there.

By this time, I'd looked over draught copies of the official Ordnance drawing and the booklet, so I'd seen therein the full public credit our Frenchman craved. And he was filling his pockets with coin, paid out to shut 'im up. When this was all said and done, he'd not suffer in either fame or purse.

Still, I doubted we'd had the last of his tantrums.

CHAPTER THIRTY-SIX

His Majesty King George II (1683 to 1760)
King of Great Britain and Ireland

In which the king satisfies himself upon preparations for the fireworks

I enjoy my court days at St James's Palace; there I host and entertain people of my choosing, their spouses and their close friends, knowing in all certainty that what passes betwixt us must be inconsequential. No business of the state gets done on those days because I'm damned if I'll have the likes of Pelham and his political cronies there. The last thing I need is to have my eating, drinking and social intercourse spoiled by those who would run the country in my spite. Let them do their damnedest for themselves—and injury to each other—in Parliament and leave their pettifogging to my office days when I needs must entertain their tedious policy-making.

It was on such a Sunday early in April, I recall, that I had around me my son William, the Duke of Cumberland, and my dear Lady Yarmouth, one or two of my son's close intimates, and old Montagu, whom I particularly wished to question on the matter of the fireworks. William was ever my favourite son, for he takes after me in so many things. We have carried arms together for the defence of my realm, I entrusted him in seeing to the rebellious Stuarts in the Highlands, and in all things, he has served me mightily. He is a large, imposing man, a mite taller than me, and carries himself as a prince and hero should. In all of this, he is quite unlike his brother, my heir, who is unwelcome in this house. I would that things could be otherwise, but… Aye, well.

Though of a fine and even bearing, howsoever, William is prone to getting above himself in our presence. But I must say—to my own and privy amusement—that I have only to murmur the words "Bottle Noddles" into his ear to bring him back into line. Though it sets him into a fine distemper, he durst not show it. I mind I did this once a week or so past when John Montagu was in attendance. The expression on the duke's face was hard to read but, surely, did I not see fear...?

The talk that Sunday came to the music for the fireworks, the organising of which had vexed me not a little. William knew of my irritation but was fully a supporter of music, for which he hath an inordinate fondness. I was ever of two minds as to whether music was wanted at all.

'Damn you,' I said to Montagu, 'you have inflicted me with music and then double inflicted me with Handel and his damned fiddles!'

'It is all well now, sire,' he replied palms upwards, 'and Handel is quite satisfied that...'

'*Satisfied? Handel* is satisfied! A pox on him! It is *he* that satisfies *me* in this!'

'I mean to say that he is doing your bidding...'

'By Christ's bones, he'll do no other. The man gets above himself. Any more of these shines on his part, and I'll have another do the music. Or better, have none at all.'

'I have this very day,' put in Montagu mighty quick, 'by his hand, the score of the music.

'And he hath done as directed?'

'Yes, indeed. He hath scored for nine trumpets and an equal squad of horns...'

'Nine only?' Was Handel still cheese-shaving me down? 'I had said that there were to be twelve at least of each.'

'But many, many hautboys and bassoons,' he put in quickly, 'and such great drums...'

'So, a big band?' He nodded. 'No damned fiddles?' He nodded again. 'Well, then.'

'Music,' said my son, perhaps observing his father's indifference on this occasion, 'will be essential to the celebration. In this John, Duke of Montagu...' and he bowed slightly in his direction, 'hath it quite correct.'

As I say, my Cumberland is a lover of music; wherever there is fine entertainment, he goes, and the court and society with him. He is a great frequenter of Vauxhall Gardens, where Handel draws large crowds, and is one of the man's greatest admirers. Scarce remarkable when the scoundrel flatters him so. It was no surprise, then, to hear him next raise the subject of attending the rehearsal, for he would be hardly content to hear the piece but once.

'It will be fine,' he continued, 'to hear the *Musick for the Royal Fireworks* rehearsed at Vauxhall. Montagu, you must tell Handel to prepare the music and the musicians in good time.'

'That I will do, sire,' replied Montagu. "Twas set for Monday, the seventeenth of April, but Mr Tyers, the master of Vauxhall, said 'twas too soon to have the gardens ready. They are yet in their out-of-season state and must be brought up. So, we set aside Monday the twenty-fourth, and it was so advertised.'

'That'll not serve,' snapped Cumberland. "Tis my drawing-room day. All Mondays are, so the twenty-fourth will not serve. You had need to consult with *me* before setting the date.'

'What date would better serve your grace?' asked Montagu.

'I have not my day-book here,' he replied. 'If my memory serves me, the Friday before is free, but see Napier of my household, and have him write it up.'

'I will send someone directly,' said Montagu. 'And on a related matter...' he turned to me, his regent, 'the Green Park must be lit by lampions as the sun falls. There will be crowds to control, carriages to park, tickets for the gentry. Food and drink. None of these things are to be had there, but they can be borrowed from Vauxhall. Seven hundred pounds is the assigned...'

'Seven *hundred* pounds! Paid from the Ordnance?'

'No, no, Your Majesty,' he flapped. 'That is but the *assigned* value. Tyers agrees to lend them *pro bono* in exchange for having it at Vauxhall.'

'So, 'tis *quid pro quo?*'

'Exactly so.'

'Aye, but where Tyers is concerned, I wonder what part of *quid pro quo* most interests him. Eh, Eh? Not the *pro* nor the *quo*, I warrant!' They all laughed but Montagu with a sense of relief, or I'm no judge.

'I'll see to it,' he said.

'Now, what of the machine?' I asked. I could watch my Temple of Peace a-building from the window of my library but was sore concerned about the pace of it.

'Yes,' spoke up Lady Yarmouth, 'whenever will it be done? The noise and mess are driving us quite mad, and the park is ruined! It is both irksome and vexatious.'

'Will it be finished on time?' I said. 'That's the point.'

'But the mess...' said Lady Yarmouth.

'Will be dealt with!' I waved her back. ''Tis the pace of work that is of concern to me, not the damned mess. Well?'

'Mr Morris is working well, sire,' said Montagu, 'and hath all the materials, labour and assistance he requires.'

'Don't mince words with me, sir! I asked you if it will be finished.'

'Yes, yes, Your Majesty. Morris assures me that work is in train and that all will be ready.'

'And what of Servandoni? Are his works also meeting satisfaction?'

'Ah, yes. Yes, indeed,' answered Montagu, with some sort of hesitation, I knew not why. 'All is well and is well... er... ordered.'

'Good. After this we will all go directly to the great temple and make a surprise inspection. I want to see Chevalier Servandoni's work, and the man Morris needs to know that his king is watching closely, lest he falter.'

I ordered my equerry to make arrangements for the visit but not to inform the labourers of our coming. It was not raining, thank God, else we'd have had stayed in. I'm damned if I'll have the Robinsons out unless there is no other recourse. They may shelter from the weather, but they're a bloody laughing-stock.[38] I signalled for more wine and led the entourage to the buffet where were laid out some choice viands and uncommon fruits.

'And what of the fireworks?' I asked Montagu.

'All proceeds... well...' he said, swallowing quickly the pastry he had half eaten, his head bobbing like a pigeon's, '...in that case...'

'Proceeds well? How well?'

'Signors Ruggieri and Sarti, and Captain Desaguliers are in... good time to produce all the desired elements...'

'And what of their installation upon the machine?'

'Much of it needs must wait until close to the day, for fear of ruination through moist weather.'

With this I had to be satisfied. It irked me that fabrication of all the fireworks must take place at Woolwich and that to visit and inspect involved a laborious rigmarole that would take a whole day I could ill afford. Whilst I trusted Montagu's assurances that all was well, there was about him a reticence that troubled me. But if I could not trust him, there was none other I could, so perforce I had to be content.

I swallowed my wine and waved to them all to eat up and drink down. Then we would be away to the park.

Chapter Thirty-Seven

John, 2nd Duke of Montagu (1690 to 1749)
Master-General of His Majesty's Ordnance

In which the king again inspects the great machine, and Cumberland surprises with a date for rehearsing the 101-gun salute

The entire train of us tripped down the staircase, left St James's Palace by the front door, and processed out to the Green Park. I chastised myself for forgetting the Duke of Cumberland's dratted calendar; I should have known he'd be the first to whistle up his carriage and not spare the horses to Vauxhall. Tyers and I had discussed this very thing. Slipshod of me. And Handel would have his choler raised all over again when told of yet another date change, he being still under the impression it was the second Monday. Still, the attendance of Cumberland now being guaranteed, this did signify a very great popularity for the show. I would send directly to the man Napier and suggest the date of Friday the twenty-first. It would be just my luck there'd be a scragging at Tyburn that day, though I'd heard naught of any miscreants slated to dance the Newgate hornpipe. That'd trump Handel's composition of the same name, no error.

I must say that, when one saw the Temple of Peace in all its splendour, the sensation again was of awe and astonishment that so great a structure could be conceived and built in so short a time. It would look far better, of course, when the village of tents, the waggons and horses, and the hundreds of labourers were away and all the covers thrown off. That, I suspected, would not happen until the very last day for, even though I had assured His Majesty that all was in train, Frederick, Morris and I were sore troubled at the pace of it. The job today would be to conceal any concern for tardiness from royal eyes and to assure that all was well. The king being ignorant of any single feature of the craft operations, this should not, I hoped, be too difficult to effect.

Another task today would be concealing the absence of Frederick. I was more than slightly concerned that his absence would be felt; he had sent me a note saying that on this very day he was to visit Woolwich to learn more of the craft of candles and gerbs. He was expected to be at his post and on call, and I knew this would not sit well with His Majesty.

When last the king had visited the site, the ground had been muddy and foul, but this time I had Morris called over to get his men ready to lay out the walkway he had invented. The sovereign was intrigued to see four men humping a great bale of staves and rope, only to be highly amused as he watched it roll forth in front of him like a mighty wooden carpet. So, we progressed above the mire, turn and turn about with each twenty-foot walkway, until we had arrived at the stair in the centre of the machine.

All was madness; hammering, thumping, the ring of tools and the yells and oaths of the men at work, until one man on the structure above us noted our presence. Of a sudden, a wave of stillness passed over the site as tools were downed, ropes were slackened, and men stood to attention. Although the deference was well meant, His Majesty was mighty exercised over it and waved the men angrily to get on with their labour. Reluctantly, and at first quietly, they picked up their tools and continued work.

'John Montagu tells me you are working well,' said the king to Morris, who had come to his side, 'and that you have all the materials, labour and assistance you require.'

'Yes, indeed, Your Majesty,' replied Morris. 'All is well in train.'

'In train, you say? When, then, will the machine be finished?'

'It will certainly be finished...' I began, when the king interrupted me with a slice of his hand.

'I asked Morris! Please be silent, and let him speak for himself.' I retired, mortified at the king's mercurial change of mood since the smiles over the walkway.

'We have, Your Majesty, a written calendar of functions,' replied Morris steadily, 'and every day I mark those that are done and review those that need to be performed for the day following.'

'And what *date* on this *calendar*, Mr Morris, shows where the machine is finished?'

'I estimate, sire...'

'Estimate? Estimate? I asked you the date!'

Now, Morris, Frederick and I had met and discussed the progress of the building and were sore put to say whether it would be ready in time or no. Now the sovereign had fixed his gunsight point-blank upon poor Morris, being in my estimation a great deal more informed than I had thought. I crossed my fingers behind my back that Morris would not let deference get the better of him and speak a truth the better left unsaid. But he stood taller, did Morris, even in his working clothes and with sawdust upon him and spots of whitewash, and looked his king right in the eye.

'It is my bounden duty, Your Majesty, to have this structure complete in time. It will be complete. I have been given this task, and I will not fail to fulfill it!'

I couldn't resist supporting Morris. 'Yes, indeed, he wi...'

'Hold your deuced kittle-pitchering! This man is as perfectly capable of speech, as you have a surfeit of it. Well, Morris?'

'Nothing is wanting, Your Majesty. My men work swiftly and well.'

'Good. Then let us all ascend and examine the work at close quarters. You will conduct us.'

Three sets of stairs led up to the platform before the central portico, and it was quite the operation to get all the entourage in their dress clothes, swords and crinolines up all the flights, as the work was but rough-finished as befitted the planned scarce usage. A good number of Servandoni's sculptures and paintings were now installed along the flanks of the central temple, including the picture in the centre of His Majesty Giving Peace to Britannia, which had been so troublesome. All decorative works were swathed in oilcloth against the weather. By this time, the decorator Andien de Cleremont had been employed on the site, and where before there were bare white walls of wood and canvas, there was now much-painted decoration.

The royal entourage paused at the top of the first stair, and the king had Morris lift the covering off the plaister sculpture of Isis reclining upon an urn. Cumberland then unsheathed his sword, winked at one of the cronies who had accompanied the group and, to the horror of all, began poking at the sculpture with its tip as if to test the worth of the plaister. Seemingly satisfied, he smiled at Morris and had him cover the work again. Once up to the platform, the king had several other works uncovered and remarked immediately upon their slap-dash execution. I thought to explain the "theatrical" quality of the work, as Servandoni had laboriously explained it to me, but rather forbore. I would not speak until spoken to and, besides, why defend the cock's-comb in his absence? Rather, let his work speak for itself.

I had not visited the platform level of the Temple of Peace for some time, so it was as surprising to me, as it was the king, to see the mechanisms behind the façade. As the firework progressed, the bas relief panels would be replaced by fully-coloured paintings, and here sheltered from the outside weather, one could see the system of ropes, pulleys and sliders that would be employed to effect the change. Such mechanisms I had not imagined, nor the royal party neither, so we were intrigued by the complexity of it.

'Seeing all this machinery,' said the king, now addressing me directly, 'I begin to see the coordination of it all. The movement of the pictures, the lighting of the illuminations, the timing of the fireworks. Yes, Montagu, you may speak.' I had been nodding, silent.

'As you know, Your Majesty, Chevalier Servandoni is in charge of the choreography of the machine and hath lately sent for his team of skilled operators from France. Meanwhile, Captain Desaguliers and Signor Ruggieri will instruct selected men from the Train of Artillery in the lighting of the fireworks. 'Tis a highly coordinated endeavour.'

In making this assurance, it struck me I had told the king a falsehood. In avoiding mention of the business with the chain of command and Ruggieri's team from France, I had committed a crime of omission. Howsoever, I'd not have got this far were I unable to dissimulate. The less known upon that subject, the better.

'And Frederick? Where is Charles Frederick in all of this?'

'It is he who directs and organises the whole.'

'Good,' interrupted Cumberland, 'for it is he who will organise and direct a review of the guns for the salute.'

This was the first I had heard of any review and, watching King George's face, 'twas the first he'd heard of it as well, though it was clearly to his liking.

'A review, sire?' I asked Cumberland in all politeness.

'Aye, on Wednesday the nineteenth of April,' he replied. 'We would review the guns and have 'em perform a timed load-and-fire exercise. They've been stood-down too damned long.'

'I will send to Mr Frederick directly.' Jesus God, that would send Charles into a tizzy, I doubted not. He was apprised of the activities upon the day, of course, and had ordered the mustering and training of the Artillery, but what seemed like a whim of Cumberland's would throw him widdershins.

'And where the devil *is* Frederick?' demanded the king, casting about him of a sudden as if we had the Surveyor-General somehow hid behind the woodwork. 'Why does he not attend us?'

Cumberland broke into a laugh. 'Dabbling with squibs!' And he elbowed one of his cronies, who barked with laughter.

'Tell him to stop dabbling!' huffed the king at me. 'It is unseemly to be so engaged.'

'Mr Frederick doth so with the best intentions, Your Majesty,' I replied. 'The firework Laboratory at Woolwich...'

'He should be here! Woolwich be damned! And keep his hands clean. Squibs!'

'Doubtless the multifarious administrative details of this very far-reaching and complicated...'

'Enough of your waffle.' He waved me to a halt. 'From now forward, when we discuss the fireworks, Frederick will attend us as well.' He made for the stairs. 'Morris! Convey us on your magical raft safe to dry land.'

With that, the entourage descended the stairway and waited whilst Morris's men unrolled the walkway. His Majesty smiled at James Morris and pressed a small leathern purse of coin into his hand, though the latter durst not at first take it.

Chapter Thirty-eight

George Frideric Handel (1685 to 1759)
Composer and Impresario

In which the composer discovers a subterfuge and takes steps to ensure that no scurrilous word is written in review of his music

It stank. This commission for the fireworks carried all the marks of a Montagu swindle; how else had the king come to the view that music was wanted and that none but me could provide it? And that it was required to be rehearsed at all, leave alone at Vauxhall. And I was so damnably busy; the end of the oratorio season was but a few days past, having done *Hercules*, *Samson* and *Solomon* in quick order, then another *Messiah* at Covent Garden and a concert for the Decay'd Musicians at the Haymarket. Now there was work to be done on a benefit for the foundlings and my good friend Hogarth. (I had in mind to have an organ installed in the hospital; I had set aside the funds for it.)

With all this, and much more of a routine kind, I had now to see to the assembling and rehearsing of a most mis-assorted band of so-called musicians. My premises at Brook Street were far too small for rehearsal, so I must rent a hall and use my agents and connections to cast about for players. Drag the alehouses, more like, and scour the barracks for stood-down cavaliers. This was all a most vexatious imposition. I was obliged to do His Majesty's bidding, of course, and I would be very well rewarded for my work, of course, but withal there was a niggling worry. Simply put, I could not produce my best under these conditions—far from it—and my critics would make great play of it.

I resolved to discover more of this business because it was a flea in my brain; an irritant that kept me from the close study I so rely upon when I sit down to write. Reluctantly, I set aside work on an anthem for the Coram Foundlings—"Blessed are they that considereth the poor and needy"—and decided forthwith to cross the river to Vauxhall and set my mind at rest. I sent word to Jonathan Tyers that I was to visit and took a wherry from Whitehall Stairs. I mind it was Tuesday the eighteenth of April, just a few days before the rehearsal. Tyers was of the view that I was visiting to discuss the arrangements for the music and to make all things secure, and I resolved to open our meeting on just these premises. He met me at the dock of Vauxhall Stairs, and we walked together up the hill.

'The gardens want but a little to bring 'em up,' he began, waving his hands about. 'Y'd no need to come over. There's nothing we've not dealt with before.'

''Tis a big band,' I said. 'I wonder upon the disposition of the players, accommodation, the sufficiency of music stands…'

'All is taken care on, I tell yer. And ye stand to make a deal of coin.'

'Touching upon that,' I replied, 'I trust that you, too, are richly rewarded?'

He paused in his walking and turned around to face me. 'Come along, my friend, we've known each other a good while. Y're not 'ere to talk abaht bloody music stands!'

Yes, he saw me clearly, as I saw him. Our association follows many years of mutual satisfaction and benefit, to the point now that he is more friend than business associate. My prevarication upon the arrangements was transparent.

'Aye. I must cut to the chase. Where is Montagu in this?'

''E wanted lampions, fences, labourers, food and drink; all the things that y' don't see a lot of in front o' the king's palace. So, we did a deal; we 'old the music 'ere, I lend 'im all the gear.'

'There's more to it than that!' I cried. 'I see it in your eyes, you avaricious old shark.'

'There might 'a been talk of some adwantageous difference twixt the value of the goods supplied and the coin we'd… *I'd* take at the gate…'

'Yes, there might well be! And knowing you, my good friend, there *was*. And Montagu fixed it up, did he not?'

'He told me that it was at His Majesty's command and the great desire of the Duke of Cumberland. Come, I'd not have agreed else!'

'Whether His Majesty commanded it or no, are you to tell me that John Montagu arranged this from the depths of his kind bosom?'

Jonathan looked every which away but me, then of a sudden, took some mighty interest in the well-being of a small bush beside the path. I began to laugh.

'What turns out so comical?' he asked as he relinquished horticultural attention.

'Montagu takes a cut of the gate else he'd not have put it forward. Come now!'

'Aye, so he does, and what of it?'

'Simply this, Jonathan. Simply this. That if he chooses to dispense my services to the lining of his pocket, he must pay the fiddler.'

'You'll dun him for a cut?' And he laughed loud and phlegmy and hawked into the bush he had shortly been so solicitous of.

'No need. I am well paid enough and need not the coin. No, he will serve me in another way…'

I'd not say more, but Jonathan Tyers and I parted in the best of spirits. I took the wherry across to the stairs next up from Privy Garden and walked thence to Whitehall.

I chanced catching Montagu in his office without introduction and considered it worth risking the time wasted should he be absent. As luck would have it, he was there when I presented myself. I wished to trap the rascal unawares, for truth flies first out of mouths ere lies have a chance to be concocted. He rose from his desk and came around it to greet me. The last time we had spoken, I had roared at him about the king's damnable serpents. Since then we had but exchanged letters, though the score of the music had proved satisfactory to His Majesty else I might have seen him sooner.

'Mr Handel,' said he, all smiles, as he waved me to a chair and reached for a decanter and two glasses, 'what an excellent surprise. Knowing the music is all well and satisfactory to our sovereign, may I assume this to be but social?'

'You may so assume,' I replied, taking the proffered glass, 'for it hath no bearing upon the music I supplied or upon the generous fee for the extra performance at Vauxhall.' I took a sip. 'For which I thank you.'

'I am pleased that all is well and that you are satisfied with the fee. I do look forward to the rehearsal.'

'I think perhaps you do, y'r grace, though 'twould not be the music that so beguiled you, as the count of heads passing through the gate and relinquishing their coin.'

'How so?' he asked, looking quizzical but with a wary cast to his eye.

'This whole business was of your confection, damn and blast you! No, no, no…' I held up a hand before me, '*I* know it is so, *you* know it is so, and there's the level of it.'

I had his cullions in a pincer. He knew it, and I could see passing across his face a resolution to display his hand. 'I confess. But in my defence, I did mean you well. And you have just thanked me for the generous fee…'

'Aye, that is so, but here's the rub: this thing you have made me do is a torment. You are a musical man, are you not? Have you not twice invited me to hear your Ignatius Sancho?'

'Indeed, yes, I appreciate fine music, as you are fully aware.'

'Well, you'll hear no "fine music" on that day, nor at the eve of the fireworks neither, and you know it! 'Tis a blasted cacophony which will be forever my shame and chagrin.'

'I am sorry to hear this,' he said, placing his glass most gently down upon the desk, 'and could wish it otherwise. Frederick hath spoken to me of your feelings. If there were any thing I could have done to repair the fault…'

'Oh, there is yet.'

'How so? We may hardly inform His Majesty that there is to be no music.'

'Oh, there will be music, of a sort. But the pens of those foul journalists who report upon such things will be silenced. And it is you who shall see to it.'

'*See to it?*'

'Just so. I want none of these London Avisons raising a single murmur on the topic of the *Musick for the Royal Fireworks*.'[39]

'You're asking me to *nobble* the horses?'

'Nay, *telling* you. You know 'em. You and that Bedford coffee crowd of yours; Fielding, Chesterfield and whatnot. You know the editors, know the critics. Take 'em aside, cross their palms with the pieces of silver you stole from King George.'

'But, Mr Handel…' It seemed clear he would baulk at the task if he could. 'Twas time to squeeze the grips of the pincer.

'Mr Handel, nothing.' I rose from my chair and looked him in the eye from my height. 'His Majesty would be most displeased should he hear…' and I jingled some coins I had loose in my pocket.

'You wouldn't…'

'Would I not? Are you ready to wager on 't?'

Whether His Majesty would take my word on Montagu's was a moot point, though did he but know by what wiles the music was brought about… Damned sure it was the Duke'd not risk it.

He held up both hands, palms out, with a grin of capitulation mix't with a roguish twinkle. Blast me, the man was incorrigible!

'Enough said. I will see to it.'

I left John Montagu's office in Whitehall in a much-refreshed frame of mind, returned swiftly by two-wheeler to Brook Street, and let the music pour out upon the ruled paper more happily than it had done these two weeks past.

Chapter Thirty-Nine

Charles Frederick (1709 to 1785)
Surveyor-General of the Ordnance

In which King George inspects the artillery for the 101-gun salute, and tragedy strikes

I know first-hand what great store our king places in his artillery; directly after my appointment, he had me up to his office in St James's Palace and there regaled me upon his Train of Gunners that were the pride at Dettingen in June of 1743. The British had ninety-eight guns, he told me, and it was the cannonading of the French cavalry and foot that turned the tide. George II was never more proud of the steadfastness and order of his gunners that day, as they loaded and shot again and again to afford his cavalry and infantry a way forward. The road was cleared and victory over the French assured. I felt quite puffed up to be charged with the overview of these doughty lads.

My study of the workings of our artillery (before Montagu warned me off for meddling) stood me in good stead later, for when the king had ordered the 101-gun salute to open the fireworks, I was ready to attend him and his entourage knowledgeably. Since Montagu informed me last November of the sovereign's plan for this salute, I had sent the requisite orders to the colonel at the Tower, demanding the readiness of the captains and had them see to the training of their gunners in this deployment. I needed do no more; all was in hand. Similarly, the gun captains had detailed their men to work with Captain Desaguliers on the firing of the show, so I needed do no more than review their work as required.

But then, His Majesty decided to review the Train of Artillery this Wednesday, so I ordered that they were to be called from stand-down in the Tower to muster in the Green Park and to be ranged along Constitution Hill. I was, of course, called to attend His Majesty. Prince William, Duke of Cumberland, and Frederick, Prince of Wales, accompanied the king on the inspection, along with Montagu and other of the usual hangers-on. Cumberland, His Royal Highness's warrior son, strode along right smartly with his head in the air, as he was ever a military man like his father. The sight of the guns warmed him, and he was all smiles. (It was never spoken, never mentioned, never *hinted* that Cumberland was amongst the most incompetent of commanders ever to bestride a horse; he only vanquished the poor Scots at Culloden because they were not an army but an ill-equipped, starving rabble, whilst his wilful ignorance at Fontenoy and blind stupidity at Lauffeld have made him a cross twixt a wilful murderer and a popular laughing stock.)

Poor Frederick Lewis, the detested heir, must have been dragged away from some cricket match or other for all the enthusiasm he showed. As heir to the Crown, God help the nation, the king must have him along, though it went hard with the sovereign's temper. The poor fool damned well had to attend and, moreover, be seen to attend. I harboured a secret hope that the blasting of the cannon would cause the ninny to wet his drawers.

Ah, they were a fine sight spread wide atop the hillslope, our cannon: seventy-one six-pounders, twenty twelve-pounders and ten mighty twenty-four pound guns. Behind them were the shot crews, their limbers unhitched from the horses, which had been stabled in Horse Guards. The salute would not be fired on this day, for this was an inspection only. We strolled along their rows, their gun crews standing as straight as their ramrods, their gun captains aglow to be so close in our king's presence, and all the equipment spotless clean and as exactly arranged as the cutlery and crockery on the royal dining table. I took pride in commenting upon details of design and fabrication, noting certain innovations in workmanship, technique and discipline. His Majesty, and Cumberland too, would nod wisely, agreeing upon points and perhaps pleased at my engagement in an enterprise upon which I was but a political appointee.

For the salute on the day, all guns would be readied beforehand blank-shotted, then fired in sequence, so there would be no need of reloading between shots. Nevertheless, it was Cumberland's intention and the king's pleasure on this day to observe the reloading practice and to encourage a demonstration of how often a crew could load and discharge a cannon in the space of a minute. The king and Cumberland stood atop the hill, Cumberland with legs astride and with a pocket watch in his hand, ready to time the sequence. Slightly downhill from him, in a place set aside from the line of guns, a select gun team of five men with a six-pounder was drawn up: the gun commander, the sponge- and rammer-man, the loader, the vents-man and the match-man. The gun commander and the match-man held ranks above the three matrosses, which is to say assistant gunners, who were but common soldiers. On the command of "one," the sponge-man would swab the bore with a wet mop on a long shaft, whilst the vents-man placed his finger over the touch hole to prevent moisture from entering the flash pan; on the command of "two," the loader would swing his canvas cartridge of powder into the bore followed by a wad of cotton waste; on the command of "three," the sponge-man would reverse his pole and ram the charge home; on the command of "four," the vents-man would remove his finger from the touch hole, insert a bronze wire poker to pierce the cartridge, and fill the touch hole bore from his horn with fine gunpowder mixed with a little spirit; on the command of "five," the match-man would touch the powder in the pan with his slowmatch, and the gun would fire. Needless to say, in battle a ball, or other kind of projectile, and a second wadding would be rammed home. This sequence is paramount in ensuring rapid fire with no errors, for gunpowder is a most unforgiving element and condignly rewards those who do not respect it, as we were too soon to be reminded.

All went well for the first set of six shots, the king and Cumberland looking right pleased as they discussed the timing. Observing the drill was like watching the dance of precision marionettes on a Nuremberg clockwork; *one:* step forward, swing in and swab, step back, stand to attention; *two:* step forward, swing the cartridge in... and so on 'til *BOOM* on five. The smoke had scarce shot forth, and the echo returned from the rear of the great Temple of Peace, before the sequence began anew; *one:* step forward, swab out... It was a joy to hear the orders, watch the ballet, feel the rhythm. The barking of one, two, three, four, was like the ticks of a mighty clock that struck on five with a roar.

Tragedy struck on the second set of evolutions. On the sixth and final shot, it seemed that, even though the ramrod had seized and was not swiftly pulled out, like a great machine, the rhythm of the count continued uninterrupted so the gun discharged whilst the rammer's hand was yet in the way. It was terrible to see, a heartbeat before, how the tragedy would with certainty unfold. The clap of the gun and the scream came one upon another and, for a few breaths after, the shocked silence was broken only by the sobbing cries of the wounded and the dying echo of the shot. Oh, 'twas such a piteous sight! The hand full blown away and the arm most shattered and sundered to the elbow. King George was the first to step forward, and when I saw his face, it was brought upon me again how he prized his artillery and how much to heart he took their injuries. Whilst the men gathered around with cloths, bandages and a stretcher, the king and his entourage moved slowly back down the hill to the palace. Of necessity, I stayed until the poor man was taken away and saw to the disbanding and rolling-out of the guns.

Matross Thomas Harvey was conducted straightway to St George's Hospital, where the arm was amputated and wounds to the face and side dressed, but the man died later that night. I heard tell the day following that His Majesty was so moved that he ordered a purse of ten guineas for Harvey's family and expressed a great deal of concern to them at the misfortune.

So ended the day on Constitution Hill, and we knew not whether this was a foreboding of ill to come, or an unhappy circumstance that was got out of the way, the better to presage later success.

Chapter Forty

John Byrom, 4th Earl of Orford (1692 to 1763)
Fellow of the Royal Society, Poet and Inventor

In which our first eyewitness returns to tell us of the Vauxhall Gardens rehearsal of Mr Handel's music

Rumour had it that Handel wanted nothing of a rehearsal and that strong words had been exchanged touching the subject between him and the king. I do know that he liked not the constitution of the band, and would have far preferred more melodious forces, but the king, of course, had his way with it. Spite of Handel's reluctance, the rehearsal at Vauxhall had been much noised about, and thousands were expected to attend. That wily old fox Tyers stood to make a fortune, for April was out of season and the ticket more highly-priced as a consequence.

Elizabeth was down from Manchester on a visit, and as luck would have it, the rehearsal had been brought forward to Friday the twenty-first, else she would have missed it. I had thought it very elevating to show my wife some of the culture of this great city before she returned north, and the weather was fair and promising. We set out in our carriage in good time, to make a day of it, knowing how tedious would be the journey.

London Bridge is, without doubt, the worst thoroughfare of a city that prizes itself in horrors of wayfaring. I would fain fend off the whores, footpads and pox-ridden sluts on a stroll along Gropecunt Lane than I would take a carriage over the River Thames. All manner of wheeled conveyances must pass across there, for there is no other way save by boat. And blast that Swiss cove Labelye that his bridge of fools at Westminster is not yet done. Many of us gentry and tradesmen put in money for the lottery to see it financed, and damn me if we've not been robbed. Kent is the most bounteous of the city's gardens, and it sends most of its wealth of goods and produce north across London Bridge. This would be all well if 't were not for divers other cargoes and passengers that must go back and forth. I would say that passing over that one bridge at the best of times is purgatorial, but when anything of note is put on at Vauxhall—and there is often no boat to be had for a king's ransom—to go there is a descent into the pit of hell. Thus it was that we, and thousands of others, had perforce to cross with our carriages, for the rehearsal for the fireworks music was not to be missed. The news-papers reported that over 12,000 souls attended Handel's rehearsal, and though this number might well have been overstated, to see London Bridge that day, one would be inclined to lend it credence.

We had not gone more than a quarter of the way across when we were held up by a commotion ahead. The view was jam-packed with vehicles of every kind, impossible to go forward and impossible to see, so my footman snared an urchin and promised him a farthing to seek out the inconvenience and report back. The wheels of a dray, the waif told us, loaded with great hogsheads of beer had become snared with those of a carriage, and an altercation had ensued. Some duke's bully boys—the urchin knew not whose—had descended from the carriage and were dividing their labours betwixt sweating to untangle the wheels and beating upon the poor tradesman, for all it was no fault of his.

I decided to quit the carriage and force myself forward amongst the press, whilst at the window of every carriage I passed, querulous questions were thrown out. Arrived finally at the scene, the altercation had now become a pitched battle with flung fists and one or two cudgels. The language would blister the lacquer off a carriage door. Panicked horses were being restrained by grooms and drivers, and a couple of fellows were down upon the cobbles with boots swinging at 'em. As I watched, a troop of toughs of some sort from the Southwark side waded into the fray and, with swishing sticks and fists, quelled the riot and commenced to establish order. The wheels were soon unsnared by dint of labour, but then perforce the dray must be pushed backwards off the bridge to give way to the carriage. No amount of beer may impede the passage of a titled gentleman. The jam of carriages, sedans, drays, horsemen and walkers surged forward, and again wheels became locked, and tempers shortened. It was fully three hours before our carriage could pass off the bridge and into the streets of Southwark, and in that time, I learned some highly choice vocabulary, whilst beside me Elizabeth stopped her ears whilst her face turned a beguiling rosy hue. Sadly, I have no company in which I might employ the language I picked up, so my learning of it was an exercise in scholarship only.

We were extremely anxious that we might come too late, but by good fortune, few missed the rehearsal because the Duke of Cumberland was himself quite ensnared and so sent a runner on to convey a message to Handel that the playing be delayed at all costs. The passage from the Southwark side of the bridge to Vauxhall was less eventful, even though the way was thronged with vehicles and people on foot and horse. Our carriage was parked suitably close to the east gate of the Gardens, and we passed through, having first relinquished our half-crowns to the gatemen, who were doing a roaring business. I frankly thought half-a-crown pretty steep for the rehearsal of but one piece of music of perhaps twenty minutes, but one would hardly turn about and go home, and those rascals knew it.

Mr Handel had assembled a mighty force of musicians: twenty-four hautboys, twelve bassoons, nine horns, nine trumpets, three pairs of kettledrums of the usual size, two vast double drums borrowed from the Tower, monstrous to behold, and four side drums with snares. It was a manifest impossibility to situate them all in the raised Octagon Bandstand, so perforce the larger number of the reed instruments stood before the building on the sward, whilst the brasses and some of the drums played from above under cover. It had proven impossible to lug the great double drums up the narrow stair, so they were placed on the ground behind the bassoons. Handel stood on a high platform in front, the better to command a view of the entire band.

King George, the Duke of Cumberland and Prince Frederick were seated in an enclosure close to the band with many ladies and gentlemen of the court, and I noticed John Montagu and Charles Frederick, who were ever close to this endeavour. It was difficult to come anywhere near the front due to the press of visitors, but even from our place to the side, we could see that Handel had a most dyspeptic look about him. I know he had been ill some time since, and had recovered most wondrously, but yet he seemed quite out of sorts. He appeared to have great trouble organising his musical forces and was obliged to step down from his podium several times to instruct or to admonish. Some few harsh words drifted our way, whilst upon each return to the podium, his disposition became more choleric. Finally, all seemed to be ready. He called for silence, raised his hands and commenced upon his *Musick for the Royal Fireworks*.

Good God, it was a phenomenal din! Vauxhall had never heard the like, nor any other venue of fine music in the nation's capital or yet further afield for all I know. We know Handel; we know his music and have so oft been beguiled by it, but here was a great blaring, thundering, roaring wall of sound so unlike him in its essence yet, paradoxically, essentially *him*. It could not have been writ by another, but it was fantastical that he could have written it. Even in the sections for the reed instruments alone, the sound was gargantuan and disproportionate, but when the brasses and percussion cried forth, the very walls of Jericho might have fallen. It was what the king had wanted, and by God, he got it. To my way of thinking, it was a great damn-your-eyes aimed directly at the sovereign; a mighty gesture of the raised indecent finger. Not that King George saw it that way, I am certain.

The music was not well played; how could it have been when so many musicians must be marshalled, and when so few are at the height of their craft, especially the horns and trumpets, ever fickle even in finer music? And we could see Handel's dissatisfaction with the proceedings in the fury with which he conducted, the angry gestures, the sweeping of the arms and the stamping of the foot. Certainly, these histrionics were lost upon the king and Cumberland and their entourage, for as last blast was yet dying, His Majesty signalled to a bowing Handel that he must play the piece over. The enthusiastic and deafening applause fell silent on the instant. The composer looked his sovereign right in the eye, paused a long moment, then turned upon his heel and waved to the musicians to find their first sheets and prepare to start again. This was well for the rest of us; half-a-crown spent on two short rehearsals is nigh on robbery but 'tis more so with but one! The second iteration was scant improvement upon the first, whilst the redoubled fury from the conductor's platform was well manifest. At the close of the performance, Handel bowed perfunctory towards the Crown and took himself off to the ground floor of the Octagon. The immense crowd roared and cheered for his return—Han-del, Han-del, Han-del—but he came not out of hiding, so presently, the hubbub died down, and the people began to disperse. I'd have expected grumbling at the price paid, but there was none of it. Most appeared to have been awed by the audition and well satisfied for their half-a-crown, save for those upwind who complained of not hearing well.

I'll not dwell upon the return journey, save to say that it mirrored the outward one, but not in frustration. We wisely held back from returning to London directly, so bided our time a few hours in the gardens, which is ever a pleasant occupation, even when not quite into the high season. Thus, the return coach ride across the bridge, whilst slow and tedious, was without alarums and altercations.

Spite of the poor rendition of the music, I looked forward mightily to the playing of it as a prelude to the fireworks just a week hence. I have resolved to write to Elizabeth upon it, as she will be back to Manchester before then.

Chapter Forty-One

Jonathan Tyers (1702 to 1767)
Manager, Impresario and Entrepreneur

In which Mr Tyers delivers his contribution to the fireworks and is amazed at the scene he encounters in the Green Park

I mind it was the twenty-fifth of April, a Tuesday. My men loaded all the stuff Montagu had ordered onto a couple of drays, save for the scaffold of seating, which I'd sent on a week or so past. We set off by way of London Bridge (I'll not mention that poxy so-called bridge at Westminster again) and so made our way by the long route to the Green Park. I don't venture much over to the fancy side of the river, but I had a hankering to take a look at this great temple that was all the talk. The sixpenny picture I had of it made it look pretty and fine, all set in the green grass and trees, ladies in crinolines sporting parasols and gents in their finery strutting around. Oh, right! When we rolled up, 'twas more like a scene out of Bedlam. The building was impressive as hell, oh yes, but there wasn't no greenspace to be seen, all churned up to mud it was, and the noise of sawing and hammering, shouting and going on was carried on the air. Building stuff was scattered every which away, and people were to-ing and fro-ing like a kicked ant's nest. The Temple of Peace was railed off, and fusiliers were standing sentry about a hundred feet apart all round.

We wheeled our drays through the gates of the park and rolled up beside the fence along the Queen's Walk. Montagu spotted us and came strutting over from his place by the machine. The rehearsal of Handel's music had gone off something wonderful; there'd hardly been any roughhousing amongst the riff-raff, and though some duke's footmen had a bit of a set-to, there were no drawn swords nor cudgels. The primped-up ladies and gents up at the front were seen by all, the king and Cumberland and Prince Frederick lapped it all up, and old Montagu was in his element. I could see his eyes lighting up from halfway across the garden as more and more people poured in. According to the *Gentleman's Magazine*, there were 12,000 there, but those rags always pile on the horseshit. And they said there was a hundred musicians there, but damned if I counted even as many as three score. So, in my reckoning, there wasn't above 10,000 folk passed through my gates, but at half-a-crown a head, it was a tidy take. Of course, I gave Montagu his cut in coin, though I gave the numbers a little colour. We'd shook hands as gentlemen, I know, but there are levels of gentlemen in my world, and I'm not above halfway on that scale, even though I take their news-paper.

"Ere we are then,' I cried as he hove to and I swung down. 'Got all the stuff 'ere. Lampions, frummery to hang in the trees, some fences to keep the riff-raff orf the gentry, cushions for their tired arses, the whole lot.'

'Excellent! So you came too?'

"Ad to. Couldn't resist seeing this thing, see what folly my stuff was being wasted on.'

'Wasted, be damned. We'll have your men string up the lights and whatnot and have 'em bring the fences over there.' The scaffold of seats I'd sent along had been set up along the Queen's Walk, not 400 feet from the machine. 'We'll have the fences around the scaffold, and seats in front on the grass.'

'Call that grass? Never saw grass so brahn and downtrodden. I can have that done real nice... for a small recompense,' and I winked.

'Hmm, we'll see to that anon.' He smiled. 'Now, as to ticketing, we'll want your help in putting us in the way of it. That whole scaffold...' he waved at the erection '...is for those who hold tickets and none other.'

'What are they charging? 'Arf a crahn, like Vauxhall?'

'Half a *guinea*, my friend. And more if they want a cushion to ease their bums.'

'What about the rest, without the fence?'

'The public enter the park with no charge.'

Me eyebrows shot up at this. 'Well, if that's how the sovereign runs 'is affairs, no wonder the merchants in the city are all a-lather. Good God, that's throwing money away, that is!'

'This celebration is for the people,' he replied, a bit snotty 'and is provided by His Majesty from the purse of the Ordnance in goodwill, thanks and beneficence for the Peace.'

'Peace?' says I. 'Piece of my arse!' But I couldn't do more 'n laugh really, 'twas so against any principle I ever held, holding off from soaking people for coin.

'Now,' he continued, ignoring my ribaldry and pulling a paper from his satchel, 'here is the list. Privy council members twelve tickets, every peer four, every commoner two, and the Lord Mayor, aldermen and trading company directors will get a batch as well. Can you get 'em printed up? Perhaps 400 all together? You'll need to tally exactly.'

'Aye, I'll have the seats in the enclosure counted, get a more useful number of how many arses'll want a ticket.'

'And what about food and drink?'

'The suppliers I use for Vauxhall are apprised. They have booths they can bring and set up, though not until the very day. All in good 'ands.'

'And your men, to see to the carriages, the crowds?'

'All in good 'ands, I told yer. Christ! We *'ave* done this afore, y' know. Now, lemme have a look at these fireworks.'

'They are like nothing you will ever have seen at Vauxhall,' said Montagu with a fine pride in his voice. 'Greater by far than anything this realm hath yet seen.'

'Wossat smell?' says I, sniffing the air. 'Oh, I know. 'Tis horseshit. That's what it is!'

'Come, see for yourself, you pox-saddled lobcock. Follow me.' And with a nod to a sentry, he led me through a gate and across the mud right up to the machine.

He wasn't jesting. Nothing we ever put on could match this. I've seen rockets, wheels, candles and all those things with French names, but one of Brock's shows would fit into a Bethnal Green shitehouse compared with this lot. The whole of the machine was festooned with fireworks, tied into place, attached to wood slats, stuck on dowels and all connected with fuses going this way and that. The great pictures had hundreds of lampions behind 'em. Wished I'd known; could've sold them the oil, as I'd bet they'd paid premium. God bless the clement weather I thought, for I dreaded to think of the time and effort needed to shield this lot from the damp. I minded the time some years past when Brock had been washed out at Vauxhall. That was a year of thunderstorms, and I don't recall what else. Made hardly a penny that year. Funny how changeable things can be; boiling our thingumabobs off in the summer, skating on the Thames in the winter, then being pissed on the year following. There's no accounting for it. Well, this year God was shining on the king in all his folly.

We walked along the length of the machine and passed round one of the flanks to the back. There, all laid out flat on the ground, was a firework structure larger than could be imagined. 'Twas a great wooden wheel—must ha' been forty mebbe fifty feet around—and all covered in fountains, gerbs and whatnot, tied in place with strings, fuses everywhere. Uncountable numbers and more being attached as I watched. This was the sun figure I'd seen in my sixpenny print, but you have no idea until you see the thing. Yes, I'd mocked old Montagu with this fireworks nonsense—and we'd both profited from it mightily—but only now 'twas brought into my face. This was monstrous.

'How in Christ's name is this lot going to be hoisted up yonder?' I asked Montagu, pointing up at the top of the machine.

'There's our Mr Morris,' he said, waving to a group of gents. 'Chief Carpenter, the one chatting with Mr Fredrick. I'll get him over.'

Morris was a solid and doughty cove, no nonsense and a handshake like a blacksmith's vice. If he could get this lot together in the space of a few months, here was a man to be reckoned with. I could use his sort at Vauxhall, no error.

'It'll get hauled up the back of the machine, upsy-down,' he told me. 'Then we'll attach its base to the roof with a swing pivot and haul it upright with ropes.'

'With all them fireworks attached? Must weigh tons.'

'No other choice. Once 'twas upright, no one could scale it to attach 'em. Have to do it all on the ground and haul it up complete. Then there's the boxes of rockets after.'

'It is quite wonderful,' put in Frederick, who had walked over with Morris, all bubbling enthusiasm, 'what prodigies we are performing here!'

Morris was having none of it. 'Ah, once you've hauled up the masts of a ship of the line, and you've the practice of it, it's not that different. Easier if anything.'

'Oh, you do yourself down,' he replied. 'You have worked wonders here!'

'Aye, well,' was all he would say before excusing himself and returning to work.

'How are ye lighting this monstrosity, right up there on the roof?' I was more than curious, for I'd never seen a thing close to it. ''Tis gargantuan!'

'Signor Ruggieri,' called Montagu, 'may we presume upon you?'

The man who was busy sliding rockets into holes in a square wooden box stood up and came over.

'How's it lit?' I asked him after an introduction. 'I don't see how 'tis done.'

'Up the back of the machine are ladders.' He pointed up at rope ladders, what they'd call ratlines on board a ship, leading up from the platform to the roof. Loosened my arse to even think of going up one o' them, particularly in the dark with stuff exploding all around. 'The men must scale the ladders whilst carrying their portfires. The leads are led from the fireworks in the sun figure, and from the boxes of rockets behind it, and attached to the roof edge of the structure.'

'How do they see 'em?' says I, peering up. 'There'd be darkness all about and smoke and glare from the fireworks.'

'The place of the lead is marked with a square shingle of wood, whitewashed, and the lead will be set in a pile of loose gunpowder.'

'Looks bloody dangerous.'

'Aye, 'tis not for the… faint in the heart.' He smiled. 'One must be nimble and obey the commands instantly. There are few who can do it, and I am certainly not one of them!' With that he smiled again, bowed quickly, and returned to his work.

Montagu took himself off to his office soon after we'd met but not before a promise that we'd see to that grass together. The whole of that day, I wandered around the park, stepped up onto the platform, asked questions, and poked me nose in, all unaccosted the while. I talked to more of the fireworks men seeing to their set up. They had a storehouse built for 'em inside the north pavilion of the machine, so I took a look in. You never saw so many fireworks! The Italian fellow told me it wasn't unusual in France, but I wondered if he wasn't just putting me on. The French designer chap rigging up his devices was too busy for me, but I stopped and watched as ropes and pulleys and whatnot were being rigged so these big wooden frames with paintings on could be slid aside on greased rails. It all struck me as being a lot of labour and construction for just one show, but that's how it's done on the Continent so, of course, we must have it here. Damned if I'll ever lower the standards at Vauxhall for such vaudeville entertainment. It lacks refinement, in my view.

Off to one side, to the north of the machine, were three of Newsham and Ragg's water engines of the fourth size, the 120-gallon ones, for putting out fires. I had two of them at Vauxhall, and handy they were, as insurance couldn't be gotten without 'em. Never had to use 'em, thank God, but 'twould only take one fire to pay for 'em. I eyed the reservoir up on the rise and hoped they had a good bucket brigade 'cos they'd empty their cisterns in a minute. Then I looked back at the machine and thought of all those fireworks; 'twas pissing into a nor'easter should the need ever arise.

All through my wandering that day, Charles Frederick was ever present, popping from one thing to another like a grasshopper. For a file who had his nose more into his books than his desk or his constituents in New Shoreham, he was a surprise. I heard tell he was so enamoured of gunpowder that he pestered the artificers ragged with his questions. Someone told me he even started to making his own squibs and would have thrown off his coat and helped with the fuses if he hadn't been restrained.

Takes all kinds, don't it?

Chapter Forty-Two

Charles Frederick (1709 to 1785)
Surveyor-General of the Ordnance

In which Mr Frederick brings all the players together and sees to them rehearsing their parts

It was April the twenty-sixth, the day before the great event, and fear was loosening my bowels. John Montagu had done sterling work for months in organising the entire spectacle—from rental accommodations, to securing materials, to ordering, negotiating, mollifying—but now the reins and whip were mine. I was the director of the fireworks on the day, and it was in my hands that the programme was lain. And so, largely as John had inculcated, 'twas a simple matter of delegation: Servandoni was to run the machine, and Desaguliers and Ruggieri were to order the lighting. I had but to stand and watch. Hah! Lucy would tell me this whenever I woke in the night, tangled in the sheets and muttering about gunpowder and lumber, hands blown off, whitewash and fat French cavaliers with swords. I knew I need not fret so, but I was yet fearful. Nothing in my life had prepared me for this.

Now, on the eve of the thing, the ground before the machine—twixt it and the scaffold seats on the Queen's Walk—was well cleared and the grass made as clean as possible, though 'twould need much repair after the event. All traces of continuing work, such as wood piles, whitewash crocks and ladders, had been moved behind the machine. Finishing touches were still being made to the machine itself, and whilst not yet frantic, Morris was becoming increasingly urgent. The final setting up of fireworks would continue until the very hour of their firing, but in Ruggieri and Sarti, I saw order, method and great *aplomb*, as they would say. Tom Desaguliers had been an unknown element before this great enterprise, but he now worked well with our foreigners, and I saw none of the fractious behaviour twixt Servandoni and Morris. The cavalier and his three assistants were all done with their preparations and decorations so could only wait, though Servandoni divided his time between drilling his machine team and meddling in the affairs of others. Yesterday, Montagu had done me, and the works in general, a great service by taking him away and plying him with fine food and drink 'til he had to be helped back to Curzon Street and tucked into bed by his man Gaston.

I continually prayed to whatever gods of fire I could conjure in this endeavour—Hephaestus, Hestia, Helios, Vulcan, Fornax—that they would smile upon us, as they had 'til now done. I even prayed to Thor of thunder that he might hold off.

Upon the eve of the thing, I called together all the players to my lean-to "office" behind the Temple of Peace and gathered them around the table, on which were laid schemas of the operations, the order of service and the detailing of duties.

'In the late afternoon,' I began, 'at about seven o' the clock, the royal party will visit the machine. I expect all of you to be in attendance and as well turned out as can be.'

'Will there be time to change our clothing after?' asked Servandoni. 'For I'll not work the machine dressed in my finest.'

'Oh, yes. We have a tent.' I thought of Gaston fussing with brushes and combs and powder whilst fireworks boomed all around and could scarce stifle a chuckle. 'That's all the facility we can offer.'

'I will not change my apparel in a *tent!* This means, then, that I must, indeed, wear the same clothing for my work.'

'Quite so.' I was a little irritated that the discussion had already run askew. 'I am sure you may doff your hat and wig and set aside your sword, should you so desire.'

'Why must we attend the king anyhow? Have we not met him some months since?'

'His Majesty sets great store by good manners. He expects his servants to attend him, and he would feel ill-served else.'

I forbore to inform him that the sovereign oft times carried small leathern purses of coin about him and was wont to press them upon those who served him well. I'd half a mind to have the king told that he should pass by the fat one with a sneer on his clock. I took a deep breath and continued.

'As soon as the king is done with his inspection, one single skyrocket will announce the start. Captain Desaguliers?'

'All in order, sir. We have one rocket of six pounds weight set to one side. With a report in its head.'

'Good. You must wait until the sovereign and his party have returned across the sward and are seated and ready. I will accompany them to their seats and signal to you with a wave of my kerchief.'

'I will keep a sharp lookout, sir, from our position on the platform,' the captain replied, 'for 'twill be growing dark.'

'It will be a white kerchief. You'll mark it well. Mr Handel is apprised that, as soon as he hears the report, the overture is to begin. This is the signal for us all to take our stations.' I reminded myself to select a clean kerchief on the morrow and not use my habitual snuff one, which was crisp with dried snot and tobacco stains. 'I shall make my way from the royal enclosure to my horse, hitched behind the machine, and will ride quickly to Constitution Hill to be on hand to command the salute, which follows directly upon the overture. Yes, Mr Morris?'

'Sir, begging your pardon, but do not Mr Handel's musicians play from the platform before the central arch?'

'They do indeed.'

'They will, I think, need a good deal of time to quit the stage and descend the stairs, for they must pack up all their instruments and devices ere the firework begins to play off.'

'Will there not be enough time whilst the salute is fired on the hill?'

'I know not how long that would be,' replied Morris, 'not being a military man myself. But if they were not down in time, they'd be discommoded by the smoke and fire about them.' He looked to the pyrotechnicians for their approbation.

'Yes,' agreed Desaguliers, 'we on the platform are used to it, but musicians might find it irksome!'

'Thank you, Mr Morris,' I replied heartily, 'I was about to make exactly that observation. I will wave with my kerchief again when the musicians are down and dispersed.'

'So, I will look for your signal from Constitution Hill?' asked Desaguliers. 'Shall I see you that far? And shall you see the musicians?'

Oh, blast it, I thought to myself, I am presenting as an ill-tricked ninnyhammer. How could I signal that the musicians had left when they were at the front of the machine, Desaguliers was on the platform, and I was up the damned hill?

'Perhaps, if I could forward a suggestion?' said Desaguliers. 'We could position one of my gunners at the front of the machine with a whistle. My men are not occupied at the beginning. Thus, when the musicians are away, he would blast a signal to Signor Ruggieri for the firework to commence.'

'A perfectly workable suggestion. I thank you,' says I, trying to regain composure. I hoped my colour showed not. 'Please assign a man to this task. I have informed Mr Handel of the order and will communicate this change to him. Now, once I see the firework beginning to play off, I will ride back from the hill and take a position of command at the rear of the machine.'

'Oh, sir,' cried Desaguliers very quickly, with nods from Sarti, Servandoni and Ruggieri, 'you need not trouble yourself to be so close, for our actions are now well-rehearsed.'

'I agree,' said Ruggieri. 'We would not wish you troubled, for the cares of your office are now discharged.'

'My colleagues speak true,' put in Servandoni. 'We have the reins now. It is for you but to watch.'

'Nevertheless, gentlemen, I will take a place close by. I thank you for your solicitude, but I am most up to the task before us.'

I knew they meant well—and I was touched by their solicitousness—but, as Surveyor-General, I felt the need to be close by lest something untoward came to pass where my leading role would be of advantage.

'Now, ah… Morris,' I continued after a long pause, 'please tell me that work is near done. Yes?'

'Yes, sir. There's a deal of rope, lengths of timber, suchlike stuff. Rather than cart it out o' the park, we've shoved it under the palisades for now. We have but finishing things for the morrow. Some tidying up.'

'Thank you. His Majesty will be as happy as I am. Signor Ruggieri, are all fireworks now ready?'

'No, sir. We work until the last possible moment, but all will be well.'

This concerned me, but there was naught I could do or say. 'Very well. I understand your team is to start the firework.'

'Yes, sir. We commence with 120 rockets, and mortars with air *ballons*, but you need not more detail. Captain Desaguliers, Signor Sarti and I have charted out the progress extensively, and our men are well drilled.' He shuffled the papers he had before him and spread them out. 'The schemas here upon the table show the order of it.'

'Aye,' agreed Desaguliers. 'We have been drilling our teams these weeks past.'

'And Lieutenant Jones is a member?' I asked. I had been most impressed with Robert Jones and had sued for his advancement.

'Yes,' replied Desaguliers, I thought somewhat sourly. 'He is. Now then,' he stood and leant over the papers, 'our teams are mustered at two stations in the rear of the machine. Here and here. We play and play about, each team coming from its station and returning as our assigned sections are fired. Signor Ruggieri's team starts the firing, and they also see to the lighting of the higher pieces, including the great girandole to conclude the spectacle.'

'Though the captain's men are now well drilled,' said Ruggieri, 'it is my team that will scale the… rat lines, is it?… and light those higher pieces. They have the way of it from long practice.'

'Yes,' said the captain, 'my men are gunners, not sailors!'

'And what of Signor Sarti?' I asked with a nod in his direction.

'I ham finish wid my work,' he replied in an English that was progressing by leaps and East London bounds. 'All fochan done. I see to watch now.'

'Good.' I smiled with all around the table.

The less I needed to be concerned with the actual firing, the better I felt. Here was truly a place where I could happily delegate and simply be the supervisory presence. Though I was in fear of conflict between the French and English crews, it was between the captain and the signori and damn all could I do.

'Cavalier Servandoni. How is your role organised?'

'Very well, naturally.' He stopped. I waited. He looked puzzled, then there passed a so false dawning comprehension across his face. 'Oh, you wish me to describe it to you?'

'If you would be so kind.' I vinegared. 'As I am the comptroller of this *extravaganza*, I must know all that passes. I would most appreciate a detailed description of your functions.'

'Me and my team will be situated within the machine where we have close access to the lampions and machinery.'

'Within?'

'Just so. My table will be under the central arch, to one side, with my men beside me to take instruction,' he replied. 'Now, here is the schema of the day.' He spread more paper upon the table. 'You have seen this before in the booklet we produced, but here it is simplified. As you can see, the functions are written out by the hour. The large transparency over the central arch with GEORGIVS II REX writ upon it is lit at the commencement.'

'Before the firework begins to play off?'

'Yes, just as the cannonade ceases. Then, after one hour...' his finger showed the place on the paper, 'the lampions of the first of the eighteen *grisaille* transparencies are lit. Then they continue to appear one after the other as the firework progresses. At the climax, when the grand girandole is fired, my men withdraw all eighteen frames, thus revealing the full-coloured works beneath.'

'So, after the large transparency is lit, you have no duty for the first hour?' He nodded. I could not resist what followed, though I wished as soon as it was uttered that I could bring it back, but *laisser passer l'eau sous les ponts*, as Servandoni would himself had said it. 'Oh,' I cried gaily, 'then mayhap you'd have the leisure to return to Curzon Street so Gaston may help you dress more appropriately?'

I believe there were fewer vessels under extreme pressure during the entire firework display than there were around that table after my utterance. I can not fathom how Sarti, Ruggieri and Desaguliers contained themselves, and I can only marvel at their restraint. Morris left the lean-to briefly and returned momentarily with face composed. Sarti, I noted, was comprehending the native tongue very well to judge by the bottled near-explosion in his face. It was several long, extended moments before the cavalier spoke.

'I shall stay and observe the unfolding of the spectacle as is ever my wont.'

I do believe my indiscretion precipitated what followed the next day.

I must confess that I remember very little of what passed after this, save that I was rewarded by the knowledge that all was in hand and that I need not fret further upon the unfolding of it. I fretted further nonetheless and would not cease to do so until the spectacle was played off and I could be back to my business in Whitehall.

Tomorrow would unfold as it would.

Chapter Forty-three

John, 2nd Duke of Montagu (1690 to 1749)
Master-General of His Majesty's Ordnance

In which the great day dawns, and the Green Park is all a-buzz with activity

Thank God the great day was finally upon us. These months since the king first sprung this thing upon me had been the busiest and most ill organised of my life. Though His Majesty rightly charged me with bringing it about—as perhaps the most diplomatic and connected of his many courtiers—it is still one I could well have done without. Were it not for the slight financial recompense that accrued upon the discharge of my duties, I could be said to have benefitted naught from the endeavour. I say this because success of the spectacle would rest with the king, and failure would be charged to our foreigners. I would sit in the middle and be merely the humble servant, a cog in the mighty regal mill. *Virtus ipsa pretium sui*; let virtue be its own reward. This is how I have kept my head above the treacherous waters of court politics and intrigue for all these years.

The twenty-seventh day of April dawned sunny, the sky presaging that all would be well; but mayhap to one less cynical than I. Nothing in London, aside perhaps from a whore's affection, could be more changeable than the weather from one hour to the next. It would be my duty to attend King George and his court at St James's Palace in the afternoon and to accompany them to the machine for an inspection. Frederick would have all the artificers awaiting to be presented. Then I would escort the royal party to the special railed-off enclosure most suited to the viewing.

I stepped down from my carriage at the gate of St James's Park not long after noon and walked slowly towards the machine. The Temple of Peace was railed off all round and well guarded by sentries, but without the fence, the press of people was extraordinary. Already I was sure the numbers were greater than those who had attended the music rehearsal, and it was early yet. People were making a day of it, and the vendors were doing great service in food and drink. One sodden gentleman, far gone in the proffered beverages, was being hauled out of a small pond, though his rescuers seemed unsure if they had saved a soul or recovered a corpse. Some young scamps had climbed trees, though I saw not how they would keep their perches until the fireworks should commence. The Green Park, and St James's Park also, had never been places of entertainment; they were locales of trees and grass for walking and riding with no amenity of any kind, so to see the park tricked out with all the fineries of a Vauxhall or a Ranelagh was a sight indeed. Tyers had worked magic with his garlands and lampions suspended in trees, his men had cleared and cleaned the area, and an orderly line of ticket-holders was making its way early to the enclosed seating scaffold along the Queen's Walk.

I stepped past a sentry at a gate in the fence and strode close to the machine. It gratified me that the entire place was a-buzz with frantic activity and that I need lift no finger. Charles Frederick was now the master of all I surveyed, and he had things well in hand. Truth to tell, even if he had not control of the reins, at this hour, the Royal Fireworks was an unstoppable leviathan, which would unfold as it would. I examined the firework setting-up still in progress, I walked the length of the platform, and I even poked my nose into the water engines, noting their cisterns were filled. Frederick was everywhere. He was a clock wound up with great weights whose escapement was running away, and I feared that his enthusiastic "supervision" would do more harm than good. He was better sitting back, but try anybody to tell him so!

'Is it not wonderful?' Charles enthused when I encountered him in deep discussion over some firework installations. 'Will it not be a pageant to take its place in history? How fortunate we are to be so placed as to witness it and how privileged to be the prime movers thereof!'

I smiled indulgently, remarked with him upon the fairness of the weather and the orderly progress, and took myself off to wandering further afield, whilst he dipped into each of the preparatory exercises and sowed discord amongst 'em for all I knew. It was at perhaps six o' the clock that I met Lady Mary as she alighted from her carriage at the gates of the park, and we walked sedately to the palace to present ourselves.

'Damn me, Montagu!' shouted the king as soon as we entered the room. 'Are they still working on that machine? You told me... *promised me*, that it would be done ere this!'

The man was another Frederick in his fretting. I had seen him in and out all afternoon, walking before the machine, being cheered and celebrated, reviewing the Grenadiers, saluted by footguards, never in one place for long.

'Fear not, Your Majesty, all is in train. There are things that can only be done on the very eve, and these are being attended to.'

'What things? What things?'

'The fireworks may not be fused too soon lest they be affected by changes in the moon.' I was almost embarrassed to be spouting such horseshit to my sovereign, but I sensed that his anxiousness needed slaking. 'The pyrotechnicians are at the top of their craft, so fear not.'

'Well, then!' he grumped. 'I have only your word upon it, so I must be content.' His every gesture showed that contented he was not.

The larger reception chamber was crowed with all those specially invited to attend the king and—save for the absence of the reviled Prince of Wales—it was indeed a veritable picture gallery of society, Lady Yarmouth was large and prominent in the van, with Princess Emilia and Lady Pembroke close by. Even more prominent, huge and blustering, was the Duke of Cumberland, who proclaimed to his father that he'd have Handel play the music whilst they were yet examining the machine. Hearing this, and knowing that Handel and his musicians were told a later hour, I called a pageboy over and told him to report this intelligence as soon as may be to Mr Frederick. So, there was I, yet involved in the thing! Was there a little imp of amusement that poor Charles would suffer the barbs thrown by Handel?

'Now, what in God's name will happen with the weather?' said the king to the room at large. 'The rain is yet holding off.'

'We are in the hands of the Almighty,' replied some idiot, not comprehending that the last thing the sovereign needed was any reply at all. He was rewarded with a face that spoke a royal displeasure, which words could hardly wield better.

Towards seven o' the clock, frayed with the king's fretting, the royal train left the palace and began its progress across the Queen's Walk and over the sward to the Temple of Peace. There was no call for Morris's magical boardwalk as Tyers's men had done a fair job on the grass, although much yet needed doing to bring the park back to its old state. (We would see to it between us.) Frederick awaited us at the top of the stair with the artisans beside him, all as well dressed as might be. Handel had his musicians assembled upon the centre of the platform, and with a wave from Cumberland and a look of thunder from the composer, they began to play. King George and his entourage swept up the artificers and Frederick into their throng so, as we toured the machine, we were a great gabbling gaggle of geese. The king examined much and asked many questions, yelling above the din of the music. The more the sovereign bellowed, the less happy he seemed to be with Cumberland's enthusiasm for musical entertainment. The *Musick for the Royal Fireworks* came to a crashing end as the tour was completed. His Majesty paused at the top of the stair and called forward the artisans, pressing a small pouch of coin into the hands of each. Servandoni, I noticed, was obsequious to a fault. The king then rewarded Handel in the same way. As we passed the composer on our way to the stair, he leaned close to me and hissed into my ear, '*Thrice thus far, you whoreson shag-bag!*'

'*But nary a word in ink,*' I replied, teeth clenched and lips scarce moving.

It was near eight o' the clock by the time the royal train had retraced its steps to the railed enclosure, and the king and his court had taken seats front and centre. There were tiny spits of rain but nothing to dampen enough and, to judge by the sky, likely to pass, for the cloud was moving above us, and a low light still in the west. His Majesty beckoned me and Lady Mary to come to him and then bade us sit on his left for the duration of the spectacle, with Lady Yarmouth at his right. This mark of royal favour was two-edged; certain I would be in direct line for his praise but his vilification also in the absence of our foreign artificers. Frederick waited beside the gate of the enclosure with a white kerchief in his hand. Once the king and the court were well seated, I waved to Frederick standing at the fence, and he hoisted his kerchief—white, but with a curious brown stain in its centre—and flapped a signal to the captain up on the platform.

As the sun slid behind the dwellings of Grosvenor Place to the west, Desaguliers lit a single rocket, which whooshed into the heavens and burst above us. At the rocket's report, Mr Handel on his podium bowed deeply to the king and court, turned to his musicians with raised arms, and swept them down.

Chapter Forty-four

Charles Frederick (1709 to 1785)
Surveyor-General of the Ordnance

In which Charles Frederick recounts his experiences upon the evening

I could see the glow of Desaguliers's portfire in his hand, where he stood on the platform to the south corner of the machine. On Montagu's nod, I waved my kerchief and was pleased to see the rocket soar into the sky. Before even its ascent to the zenith, I was on my way to my horse tied at the rear of the machine. As I saddled up, I called up to the captain and reminded him to have a man with a whistle in place for when the musicians were well away. I mounted and rode quickly to Constitution Hill. As I cantered across the park, behind me Handel's overture was thundering mightily along. 'Twas bold, martial and inspiring, and though explained to me, I still wondered at the man's reluctance to have it heard.

In a few minutes, I reached the crest of the hill where the guns of the Royal Train of Artillery were ranged, their gun captains and matrosses beside them. I swung down, tied my bridle to a tree, and immediately took command, calling the colonel forward for a final assurance that all instructions had been given, and the salute would proceed as planned.

'Are all cannon shotted and ready?' I asked.

'No, sir, they are not,' he replied.

'Why not, in the devil's name?' I barked. 'For it wants but ten minutes before the salute!'

'With all due deference, sir,' he replied, showing me none, 'were the cannon shotted, from this range we would likely inflict severe damage upon the Temple of Peace and also on the royal family and St James's Palace beyond.'

'Damn you. You know what I mean!'

'Yes, *sir!* The cannon are loaded with *blank shot*, and all is in readiness.'

'Good then,' I huffed, feeling foolish. And just to put him in his place, 'It's all hands to the task. And we don't want any more blown off, now do we?'

'No... sir.'

'As soon as the music stops, you may commence. But wait some short time lest it be not the end but a pause 'twixt movements.' A quick rub at his doubtless paucity of musical education.

'Yes, *sir!*' And this sarcastic bastard strode off to oversee his charges.

I have never been anywhere near a battlefield—'tis a world utterly strange to me—which is why I am Surveyor-General of His Majesty's Ordnance. I have that distance from the operation that provides a balanced overview of activities, together with the necessary access to the circles where decisions of import are made. So I told myself, though truly I was but stung from his rebuke.

It seemed an age before I heard the closing strains of *La Réjouissance* from the park below and an age again for the concluding menuets. The last bars died...

'*Fire!*' I roared, but 'twas pointless; the command was already on the colonel's lips and much more stentorian than mine.

It was glorious to be present for the royal salute of 101 shots, let alone to be its commander. Six pounders, twelve pounders and mighty twenty-four-pound guns fired in pattern with great claps that thumped the chest and smote the ears. One upon another, the blasts rebounded from the buildings around the park, setting up great swarms of birds that milled about in confusion. I lost count in the din and was quite astonished in an opposite way by the clap of silence that opened at their cease. Then I heard a huzzah from the crowd as the great transparency over the central arch with GEORGIVS II REX writ upon it began to be illuminated. Now it seemed an age again whilst we waited for the whistle. It *was* an age! Had Handel fallen on the stairs, and was he even now being attended? Had they got their big copper drums stuck halfway down? Mayhap, on hearing that he must play his music yet again, Handel had suffered a fit of apoplexy? Oh, would they *ever* be away? I fretted and fretted until, clear on the air, came the welcome sound. I liked to piss myself with relief.

The fireworks began to play off forthwith. One hundred rockets shot up in that first flight, and these were interspersed with mortars hurling charges of explosives high into the air. No sooner had the rockets ceased their flight than the machine was illuminated with a large golden sun figure, which blended into rays, shot forth sparkling fire, and gave way to four huge wheels driven around at increasing speed whilst throwing great silver scintillations. More rockets followed, and so the show continued to play.

I stood upon the hill transfixed by the spectacle as the men of the Train of Artillery packed up their equipment and made ready to depart. Would that I could have watched the whole firework spectacle from my vantage point there, but I must return to my place in the rear of the machine to oversee the playing off. I rode down the hill, reined my horse behind the central pavilion, and climbed the ladder to the table that the artificers had set aside for my use. It was by this time half an hour into the playing off, and the din was indeed terrific. Wreathed in smoke, half deafened, lit by fire and surrounded by running men performing their divers coordinated actions, I was in heaven.

I was not to sit in ecstasy for the whole show; cruel fate had other things in store. It was well over an hour into the spectacle when there took place the thing John Montagu and I had most feared; a scuffle broke out amongst the men. I waded in to help restore order, recalling my days of boxing at Westminster School and New College, Oxford. I assisted Sarti, Ruggieri and the captain in restoring order and dragging the combatants asunder. This contretemps caused no noticeable pause as the artificers, such was their skill at stagecraft, altered their order on the fly whilst the wounded were removed, and the teams re-mustered. I resumed my desk amidst the din and smoke, watching as Servandoni had his lighters scale within the machine and bring another two transparencies to light.

Not long after, a great shout went up. I watched in horror as, of a sudden, the pavilion at the north end of the machine burst into flames, caught by the jamming of one of the great fire wheels. Other fireworks fixed to the structure began to burst out in disorder, lighting the huge pall of smoke from within. Rockets traced uneven paths in all directions, exploding close over the heads of the crowd.

I ran.

I ran around the rear of the platform at breakneck speed, thinking to climb down to where the water engines were parked, take command of them and issue orders. As I passed the back of the machine, I saw a knot of men in idle chatter. These must be Servandoni's men, down from the lighting I had witnessed and as yet unengaged 'til their next sequence. I saw no sign of Servandoni, who was perhaps back at his table.

'You! All of you!' I cried in French. 'Follow me, and get these engines in place!'

They trundled the three water engines forward, as close to the blaze as might be without injury. They had scarce an idea of how the engines were worked, but a few pumps on the handles of one, and water spouted forth from the nozzle on top. The increase of the flames urged them on, six men swinging on the pump handles, whilst four more scaled the engine to pump upon the foot pedals. One seized the nozzle and directed it, and the others saw what was wanted and got all three engines working after a fashion. I rushed up to the fence and exhorted men to come forward from the crowd to help in pumping. Some did but few enough fully to man the engines. Though my crews were pumping water upon the blaze, their cisterns were emptying fast, and no bucket brigade was mustered to refill them. In vain I cried again to people in the crowd to come and assist, but the pull of the firework was too great, and few came forward, most having their attention drawn skyward by the spectacle. Presently, the cisterns were dry, and the few men on the machines had perforce to stop pumping. Their efforts had contained the blaze hardly at all, and now a wind was springing up from the north. I felt drops of rain upon my face and thought what an insult from heaven this water was for all the good it would do now.

I eyed the fire moving south to the thin wood and canvas of the palisade. As I watched, a renewed burst sent flames and smoke shooting up. I could see only one way to prevent the spread of the flames along the palisade to the main structure. Morris had said there were wood and lengths of rope stored beneath the palisade. I called to Servandoni's men to follow me.

I knew what must be done…

Chapter Forty-Five

Captain Thomas Desaguliers (1721 to 1780)
Chief Firemaster of His Majesty's Royal Laboratory

In which Captain Desaguliers recounts his experiences upon the evening

We were as ready as we possibly could be. I mustered my dozen gunners in a group behind the machine, on the platform near the south end pavilion. Ruggieri had his team of twelve nearer to the central temple. We had agreed, in a moment of great candour, that we would keep our men apart for the sake of order. This after we had both remarked hostilities and mutterings, though of a mild kind. No sense, we thought, in begging trouble. True, in all the evolutions of lighting the fireworks, the men would have to run hither and yon, and doubtless cross paths, but at least let them have their rallying place amongst their own kind. We had the charts of the show laid out on boards set over trestles—his for his team and I for mine—and we would issue orders from these and send the men running with their portfires to the site of the next ignition, then have them return and stand by. My men were generally assigned to low and platform-level stuff, whilst Gaetano's crew would scale the machine at the rear to light the high structures, as they were used to doing. He had told me—oh, it seemed so long ago—it is a concerto; it is a ballet; it is a symphony. Each part must work harmoniously with each other part for the space of three hours. That's what we had on those papers laid out before us.

Within the machine, Servandoni had his table and his team. As soon as the last blast of the cannon sounded, his men would scale the rear of the transparency with their tarred linstocks and commence lighting the hundreds of lampions behind GEORGIVS II REX. Charles Frederick would soon after come down to his table, which we had placed farther away from the centre of the action, the better to ensure that our smooth operation was not marred by over-zealous intervention. We had thought to deter him from being even this close by telling him that the noise and smoke would be terrific, but no sooner had we told him than his eyes lit up, and he rubbed his hands in delight. Yet again, I kicked myself for poor choice of words.

I left my team as Handel's music was coming to a close, walking around to the front of the machine with a whistle on a lanyard round my neck. I had suggested assigning one of my men to this task, but as Gaetano's team was to begin the playing off, I took on that duty myself. Whilst the 101-gun salute played out on the hill, Handel led his musicians down the three flights of stairs, which took a deal of time with twilight descending. They were scarce half done when the last cannon sounded and a great huzzah rose from the crowd as the transparency of GEORGIVS II REX was lit from left to right, appearing to unfurl itself.

I tried to imagine Frederick up there on the hill, all aquiver to begin the firework, all high charged with gunpowder fever, and wondering when in God's name he'd hear the whistle. Handel's great drums took some handling, two chaps running back up to the platform twice to help. Then there was a clutch of music stands and papers to be got. We'd not figured this nonsense into our planning, hoping that Handel could easily quit the platform during the guns. I wondered whether His Majesty and his guests might become exercised over the delay. Finally, it was all done, they scurried off, and the whistle could be sounded. I returned to my men as Gaetano's crew fired the first set.

I have laid enough firework shows to know what I'm about, but from the first salvo of rockets, this one outdid anything I'd done before. As those 120 rockets soared upwards into the gloaming and burst in sundry stars, I came across the final lesson in my firework education. I think I found that I was with the best in the world and that I was glad and grateful that I had been brought there.

Turn and turn about went our teams as the firework played off around us and above us in smoke, din and blaze. Giovanni Servandoni, whose team was now idle until the illumination of the first of the eighteen panels, came to observe our work and that of Gaetano, though I was busy enough that I could give him no mind, save to wish him back to his table within. It was perhaps an hour into the show, when tragedy struck. I think it was a broken stick, for a caduceus rocket of two pounds plunged on a spiralling, wavery course and struck two of my men. Both were badly burnt, one in his eyes, and worse still, it caused un-warranted outrage amongst my gunners.

'That was a fuckin' *froggy* rocket,' shouted a gunner, foolishly closer to Servandoni and me than he knew. 'Carn trust 'em!'

'Enough!' I roared. 'Shut your mouth, and get back to your post!'

Mercifully, I believe Servandoni had not heard the slur, for if he had, he would surely have made it known in no uncertain terms. He strutted away to his post, and the men scuttled quickly enough back, whilst the two injured men were carried away. Frederick arose from his stool to come over, but I waved him back, miming above the din, and signed that all was well. That breach of discipline boded ill. I had not the time to attend to the injured men; such was the pace of the show. We must continue at speed. The French crew scaled the machine again and set their pieces off—a battery of rockets, a wheel and a waterfall of fire—whilst at ground level, my team set off a mortar of nine cylinders with an air *ballon* in each and several other ground effects.

It was whilst the teams were changing places that the incendiary incident took place; one of my men, returning to his position at my table, chanced to collide with one of the French team running the other way. It was an accident clear and simple; I know that now, and I can see it still in my mind's eye. My man, knocked off his stride, slipped on the damp wood of the platform and fell to one knee. He rose immediately and, before I could intervene, swung the other fellow around by the shoulder and planted a facer. I yelled at them to cease above the roar of the rockets and explosions of *ballons*, but I might as well have held my peace for all the effect it had. The two grappled close, thumping away with fists, and almost immediately, others joined in. What had before been a muttering discontent between nations now became a full-fledged riot as more men joined the fray. As their commander, I was both furious and shamefaced, but try as I might through voice and boots, I could not make a stop.

Ruggieri and Frederick, seeing the fracas, ran over to intervene but had as much success as I. Fearing an interruption in the firing, I detailed three men, who had held off from the fray, to run quickly and see to the lighting of the next set in the order of firing. This would give Gaetano some ten minutes to muster his men for the following sequence, which was his. Giuseppe Sarti ran from his observation place at the back, and together we four waded into the battle and with redoubled voices and fists, we brought some order. I noted with some surprise the ready fists of Charles Frederick, not the most muscular of men. We dragged the combatants apart and shoved them, glowering, into two separate camps; all but four men, who lay where they had been knocked down or crawled slowly away.

'You, you and you!' I yelled at three of the less battered of my men, 'pick 'em up, and drag 'em away. Then get back to your damned posts!'

Giuseppe herded his men away, one of them being dragged by two companions, whilst Gaetano tried to bring order back. But now, with depleted forces on both sides, our order of firing was in shreds. The spectacle was on the brink of grinding to a halt once the present set was done. Thinking quickly, Gaetano decided to light two large wheels, one on the north pavilion and the other on the south, as their playing out would give more time to reorder. He detailed men to see to this, then ran over to me to confer. We had scarce seen the wheels begin their roaring turn, when we heard the cry of "fire!" from the north. We knew not how it had come to pass, but flames were shooting from the north pavilion whilst the remaining fireworks therein began to explode in the smoke, rockets going every which away as their supports were burnt off.

Charles Frederick turned on his heel and ran. We prayed that men could be mustered and the fire put out, knowing we could do naught but continue. Then, as we prepared for the next set, two awful things took place, one upon the other.

The fireworks for the Peace of Aix-la-Chapelle were on the very brink of failure. When I saw what had happened, I knew there was but one thing that could save the day…

Chapter Forty-Six

Giovanni Niccolò Servandoni (1695 to 1766)
Architect, Artist and Theatre Designer

In which Giovanni Servandoni recounts his experiences upon the evening

*A*trocité! *Foutu d'indignation!* Who was Frederick that he would think to give orders to my men? And in the wanton destruction of my work in addition? I heard the cries and saw the flames in the north pavilion from my post at the back of the machine. I ran around and was horrified to hear someone shouting at my men—who had 'til then been standing idle between lightings—and urging them forward. Amidst the crackling flames and the falling of burning timbers, I spied Frederick, and yelling I don't know what, I ran at him as he turned to face me.

Here is how this terrible confrontation came about: earlier in the evening, once His Majesty King George II had greeted us on the platform and pressed some small reward into our hands (I counted mine as soon as I had the leisure; 'twas a meagre twelve sovereigns), I took myself off to my place at the rear of the machine. As soon as the cannonading ceased, I ordered my team to scale the ladders within the main structure carrying their tarred linstocks. The central inscription, which was to be lit throughout, had over 1,000 lampions placed close to give an even temper to the light. It looks well if the illumination progresses from one end to the other, so I saw to it that my men started their assigned lighting in relays, from south to north, thus unfolding the words as one would a scroll. A fine effect, I pride myself. As the transparency made itself evident, I heard a roar of approbation from the crowd. Presently, I heard Desaguliers sound his whistle, and I returned to my place.

It would now be some time before our next illumination, the first pair of the eighteen panels, but I would hardly make myself absent for a minute. I found the jesting suggestion that I should go away and change my wearings to be despicable. Thus it was that I spent some time behind the machine, watching the teams do their work, admiring those of my friend and colleague Gaetano, and being less impressed with the English gunners. It was during my second visit to the English that the inferiority of their firework-making came home to me as two of their gunners were injured by a stray rocket, doubtless poorly made. There was much foul-mouthed and abusive language as the injured were carried away, but I heeded it not and left them to 't.

I sent my men off to the lighting of the first pair of transparencies, and once they were well lit, I had them stand down until the next set. I stepped out onto the platform, and it was whilst watching the lighting of the two great wheels on each of the flanking pavilions that I witnessed the north wheel jam, saw the drivers spray their fires upon the woodwork, and presently create a conflagration. Seeing this disaster unfolding, I decided to collect my men and take command of the water engines that I had seen standing near at hand. I looked for my men, wasting time darting here and there, but it seemed they had deserted their posts. Furious with them, I descended the back of the machine and ran towards the blaze swiftly, or as swiftly as I was able on account of the fine clothes I yet wore, my generous physique and the sword slapping at my side. I arrived at the burning pavilion to see the engines standing unused. The fools, the fools! They had engines, and they had failed to use them. Then my horror rose as I observed Charles Frederick ordering my men—*my men!*—to tear down the wooden and canvas palisades attached to the north pavilion with great staves of timber, smashing my decorative work as they did so.

'*Arrêtez!*' I cried. '*Arrête ça tout de suite, barbare!* How dare you tear down my work?'

'It's spreading, it's spreading, you God-damned idiot!' yelled this English barbarian. 'We must stop it!'

'*Suivez moi!*' I yelled to my men. '*Suivez moi, aux pompes!*'

Obviously, we would use the water engines before tearing the Temple of Peace into bits. What could he be thinking? Hearing me command them, my men desisted briefly, torn between commands.

'Get back to it!' cried Frederick, and again the men wavered. And then, to me, 'The engines are empty. Command your men to get on with it, you powdered buffoon!'

This insult, on top of all the indignities laid upon me by these vulgar English and their yokel king, was enough to make me lose my temper. And now it was coming on to rain. I regret now that I was unable to maintain *sang froid* in these circumstances, but who would?

'You dare to insult me!' I cried, amidst the roaring flames, the crackling timber, the rain on my clothes and the blasts of the fireworks. With no thought, I withdrew my sword, whizzing out of its scabbard, and ran at him with it. His look of terror was enough to sap my will and cause a wave of shame and regret, but the deed was done. Two of my own fellows seized me by the elbows and held me back, although by then my sword was slack at my side. The fusiliers whose job it was to patrol the perimeter took me in charge and led me away. The last words I heard were from Frederick exhorting my men.

'Pull hard here! Tear it away! It can't jump the space. We'll have it stopped.'

Then the rain began to come with greater intensity.

Chapter Forty-seven

Gaetano Ruggieri (1715 to 1776)
Pyrotechnician

In which Gaetano Ruggieri recounts his experiences upon the evening

What a comprehensive *catastrofe*: our men thrashing away at each other, our forces depleted by their ignorance and stupidity, and now a blaze in the machine. I'd wager it was caused by the pivot of the wheel I had ordered lit; ever the trickiest piece of woodwork and prone to jamming even under the best of circumstances. Charles Frederick took himself off smartly, clearly to take command of the firefighting. The other of the two fire wheels would play out for some minutes yet. Then there was another flight of 600 rockets with mortars laid on the platform, so if the flames could be extinguished, we might yet bring the show back to its order. I detailed my best crewman to scale the machine and await my command for the lighting of the rockets, whilst Tom sent two of his men forward to see to the mortars. Then two horrible things came to pass, one upon the other, that sent me into desperation: a further terrible accident and the onset of the dreaded rain.

No sooner had the flight of 600 rockets burst forth from the top of the machine than the man firing them cried out as the rope ladder tore away at the top. He fell to the boards with a thud that turned me sick, the ladder falling in coils about him, and as I spun to see to him, the rain began in earnest.

Whilst I was seeing to the man on the boards—finding if he yet lived—Tom Desaguliers hurried over to me from his station. By now the rain was coming on harder, and I feared for the remaining fireworks; though proofed against moisture as best we could, they'd not withstand a downpour.

'We have to fire the grand girandole now!' shouted Desaguliers. 'Bring in the conclusion early. If we wait longer, 'twill be too late. We'll send a man to Servando...' Then, on seeing the man on the boards, 'Oh, good God, what happened?'

He looked at the rope ladder tangled about, squinted up in the rain at the eaves of the temple, and his face fell.

'Yes,' I nodded, shouting through the smoke and above the din. 'Can't fire the damned thing. Can't reach the shingle! We'll have to abandon.'

'No, no, we must... how can we...? It's...' He struck his hands together, fully frustrated and close to fury. He paced back and forth, banging his fists against his flanks and swearing mightily.

I would then have thrown it in. I have seen enough shows where the caprice of the weather wins the day; enough to know that sometimes one must bend to a greater will, deep though the disappointment may be. Tom was made of a different stuff. Some call it heroic, some call it stupid, and oft times it's somewhere betwixt. In him it was genius. If there is a Muse of Pyrotechnics, it touched his mind that night. Perhaps it was Prometheus himself.

'Yes!' he cried. 'Yes!' and stormed over to me, almost laughing. 'The pumps! The pumps!'

'What in hell... Water engines?'

'No, no, no! *The fireworks!* Firework pumps. Here,' he called to one of his men above the din, 'bring me a pump from the rack at front. No! Bring me two, three. Quickly!'

Desaguliers and his damned pumps. He'd insisted on having the blessèd things even though I found them difficult to make and impossible to produce conveniently in large size. What in God's name was he thinking? Then, in a flash, I saw his plan, the mad *bastardo*. He seized one of the pumps, dabbed a slowmatch to it, and when alight held it up at arm's length and directed the stars as they burst forth, one after the other, towards the fuse on the roof.

'I can't see it! I can't see it,' he cried as the scintillating stars shot forth and bounced off the architecture. 'The glare, the glare!'

'There!' I shouted, pointing up at the whitewashed shingle where the powder and fuse lay, seizing his shoulder to turn him about. 'There, there!'

Four more stars shot out, and then the pump was done. He seized another, dashing the rain out of his eyes, and lit it from the flaming end of the first. Squinting upwards at the cornice, he aimed more shots at the place where the fuse lay.

'The last transparency!' he shouted at me. 'The lampions! Go! Tell Servandoni to get 'em lit up, then withdraw the panels. Make haste!'

I dashed through the central arch from our place at the back of the machine, but Servandoni was not at his post, or his men either. Surely, he'd not abandoned? Cursing his stupidity, I ran back outside and brought together as many of our men as I could—be damned if they were mine or Tom's, and be damned who was giving orders—and ordered them into the machine. As they were climbing up, lighting as many of the lampions as possible, Charles Frederick came rushing in with the French crew, but no Giovanni, blast him! Frederick's face was black with smuts, his clothing disarranged with sagging hose and one shoe gone, and withal sporting a most deranged expression of glee. The man was living the most bounteous and fondly cherished of his dreams. Now French and Italian crewmen, mixed with English gunners willy-nilly, dabbed blazing portfires and linstocks at anything that looked as if it needed to be lit.

'*Aux panneaux!* To the panels!' I heard Frederick cry.

Behind me I heard the *pop… pop… pop…* as Tom's stars pumped out, flared and sputtered against the cornice of the Temple of Peace, and twinkled down dying to the ground.

Chapter Forty-eight

John, 2nd Duke of Montagu (1690 to 1749)
Master-General of His Majesty's Ordnance

In which John Montagu recounts his experiences upon the evening

I could not want for a better view of the spectacle right beside His Highness but, y' know, there was a big part of me that wanted to crawl down a badger hole and never come out. 'Twas not fear of success or failure, neither yet approbation nor critique, but mostly that this was a great leviathan that had been consuming me from within. Not until I sat there, with the king on one side and Lady Mary on the other, did I feel so hollowed out and spent. The damned thing was running its course, and I was spat out, chewed and boneless.

As the last bars of the music rebounded from the palace behind us, the guns thundered out on Constitution Hill. His Majesty rose to his feet and the entire seated multitude with him. With every clap of the guns the delight in the king's face grew, 'til at last the ten great twenty-four pounders smote the London air one upon another. Then GEORGIVS II REX began to unfold in glorious light, and Cumberland raised his arms and led the great huzzah that followed the guns' silence, the entire court crying out with him in praise. We resumed our seats slowly as Handel's great kettledrums were chivvied down the stairs, watched by all in growing irritation as they awaited the suspended fireworks. Why in God's name, I thought to myself, did we not put a stair in the back?

The opening flight of rockets took all by surprise, so sudden and so majestic was their upward roar, clapping the ears with a mighty blast that seemed never to cease. Bombs shot into the air, great sheets of flame came down, and all manner of scintillating fires wreathed the entire machine. I glanced at the king, whose face was transformed; he was a child again and wholly carried away, mouth agape, eyes sparkling in reflected glare. So, the spectacle played out with a fantastical rhythm, now great effects in the sky, now fires of all sorts upon the platform, now wheels whirling fire on the shelves and cornices of the machine, about and about with scarce a pause. It was like the great panting breaths of a prodigious, slumberous monster.

It must have been well into the second hour of this bombardment of ears, eyes and senses that a light rain began to fall, though it appeared not strong enough to halt the progress of the spectacle. Few noticed it, so rapt was their attention on the fireworks. Two vast wheels then burst into activity, one on each end pavilion of the temple, but on their ignition the spectacle took a turn. Of a sudden, the one to the north stuck fast, and its fire played upon the roof. Smoke and flames shot forth and spread quickly 'til fireworks affixed to the structure ignited willy-nilly.

Now rockets, shedding their normal restraints, were free to fly outward and sideways and down. One large one came spiralling towards the royal enclosure, performing a vast corkscrew of sparks, and struck the stands with a mighty blast. One Miss Sear (oh, how apposite a name) had her clothing set on fire, but I heard tell she was mercifully spared serious injury when several stalwart lads stripped her down to her underwear, doubtless to her mortification and their delight. My bowels turned to water, and I near pissed myself at the thought of how close the sovereign had come to immolation. But whilst the north pavilion burnt, the fireworks continued unabated.

'God damn!' shouted the king in my ear. 'Those firework men don't let this stop 'em! Eh? Eh? Look at those bastards, by Christ, even now lighting more! *Huzzah!*'

Cumberland and a group of stalwarts stood up and roared whilst the king leapt to his feet, joining them in bellowing. Lady Yarmouth, at the king's side, was close to swooning with the ecstasy of it, doubtless deriving more such from the fireworks than ever she had of late from the sovereign's loins.

A group of men appeared from behind the machine and began to manhandle the water engines into position, urged on by a fellow with arms waving like a windmill. It was Charles! Damn me if Fredrick hadn't gathered firefighters together and taken command. But it was useless; I could see it was useless. The engines were no soon pumped up than they ran dry. I watched Charles leaning over the fence, waving and shouting at the crowd, but precious little good that did. Seeing he was wasting his breath, he hurried back to the engines and ordered the men to the palisade. They seized lengths of timber and ropes from below the machine and began to rip the structure down to make a fire break.

'Look at those fire-men!' yelled the king. 'By God, they'll have a purse from me ere this night is out!'

A sudden upthrust of rockets thundered into the heavens, and most attention was now drawn to them and not the scene unfolding. No sooner had Frederick's men made a start on tearing down the palisade than another figure came storming into the fray, waving and shouting (though at that distance, I heard him not). Could it be? Yes, it was! Servandoni! And blast me if he wasn't trying to get Frederick to hold off. What the deuce? Of a sudden, he drew out his sword and ran at Frederick, who was, of course, unarmed. Was he mad? My God, was there to be a murder this night? But, no, the Frenchman was seized from behind by his own men, whilst two soldiers from the fence came forward and escorted him away. I stole a glance at the king, happily seeing him entranced in the spectacle, but I did notice a grim-faced Cumberland turn his attention back as a cluster of *ballons* shot into the sky and blasted the night.

Now the rain came on a little stronger, and I knew from my talks with the artificers that this might end all. I prayed to God that Ruggieri and Desaguliers would change their order of firing, get the great girandole and the 6,000 rockets played off, and so end the spectacle with its right conclusion. The alternate course, I feared, was to have the thing fizzle to a stop. The king would be mortified. I sat there, powerless, as the rain fell, and the north pavilion crackled and smoked.

I was jolted out of these morbid speculations by the strangest of sights: from the rear of the machine, glittering stars were shooting up, one upon another, and bouncing off the cornice of the rear roof. Then the eighteen great *grisaille* transparencies that Casali and Servandoni had laboured over began to light up. Frederick, seeing this sudden illumination, waved his crew off the fire break and ordered them up the stairs and into the machine. The stars were still shooting up at the roof of the temple, but now all eyes were upon the transparencies, which began slowly to slide aside to reveal the glorious painted figures beneath.

A phenomenal explosion shook the very ground as the great girandole burst into life, and 6,000 rockets headed with stars, rains and serpents opened the whole heavens, forming a canopy of diversified fires. In the centre, and surrounded by shooting fountains and sheets of fire, the words VIVAT REX came into blazing life. The girandole surpassed all imagination for its beauty and greatness. It inspired the immense multitude of spectators with the utmost transport and banished the dissatisfaction and disappointment of the burning pavilion. Uncountable thousands of people, on a moment, drew together one great influx of breath, and let it fly out in a cheer and a roar and a hullabaloo that rivalled the rockets in their courses.

Everyone in the royal enclosure was standing, the king raising his arms and, with tears on his cheeks, acknowledging the adulations and praise showering upon him. Unique surely in the English House of Hanover was the sight of William Augustus, the Duke of Cumberland, Princess Emilia and Lady Pembroke, the divers other close associates of the court, and their wives, sisters and brothers celebrating as one with their nation and their sovereign.

Ah, the irony of gunpowder! It sunders one from another yet brings all together.

Afterword

John Byrom, 4th Earl of Orford (1692 to 1763)
Fellow of the Royal Society, Poet and Inventor

In which our first eyewitness returns to close the book

What a strange thing it is that people on one side of an affair may see it one way, whilst those on the other side have an entirely variant view. So, it was with the sovereign's apprehension of the wondrous success of his Grand Conceit upon the eve of April the twenty-seventh, 1749. The word *fiasco* hath lately come into use with us, and no word can better express the true state of affairs behind the scenes. Indeed, such is the power of this word, it might well hereafter be graven in the English lexicon. I am not sure Dr Johnson would agree, though, as 'tis brought from the Continent. But a *fiasco* it was: fighting behind the scenes, stray rockets causing mayhem, fire breaking out, a drawn sword, and then rain to dampen it all down. Thank God for darkness and the great distraction in the heavens.

All this being said, by I know not what alchemy, the doings backstage were never fully evident to His Majesty or, if they were, he chose to ignore them and see the entire spectacle as fulfilling his expectations. Is that not always the way with the theatre; front of the curtain and back of the stage as tragic and comic masques? And this success—as so it manifestly was in King George's eye—must be assigned to the heroic actions of Captain Thomas Desaguliers and Mr Charles Frederick. The launching of the grand girandole, and especially the illumination of VIVAT REX, were critical to the success of the spectacle, whilst arresting the spread of fire and the deployment of the painted transparencies merits great applause, especially when one considers the circumstances attendant upon these actions.

Popular reportage had equally variant views. Great accolades were heaped upon the spectacle in some quarters—who could not *but* be impressed by the grand finale?—but others cast aspersions upon the whole affair. Lampoons abounded, but I think they were strongly driven by an ardour that was anti-French, anti-Whig, anti-Hanoverian or anti-anything not British through and through. My good friend Horace Walpole thought the rockets to be fine enough but the ground effects pitiful and ill conducted. He also spoke of the pavilion catching fire halfway through and few being patient enough to await the end. I wondered if he had awaited the end himself. I later taxed him upon it: he'd not stopped to see the finale ere he wrote his journal entry, so he missed much.

Many a word was written of the riotous withdrawal of the populace from the park after the celebration. Crowds became dense, confused and violent, fences were pushed over by the crush, many were injured and some killed in the press. I heard of a man found with his skull split to smithereens by the fall of a dead rocket, and I myself wrestled three other men for possession of a rocket stick to carry away as a trophy. The Green Park was left in ruinous state, but I heard that John Montagu and Jonathan Tyers have seen to the rectifying of it, as a willing and selfless gesture.

The cost to the nation of this foreign *extravaganza* was much discussed in the news-papers and broadsheets. Conjectures were made that it might have cost 30- or 40,000 pounds, which sums caused such popular outrage that the following paragraph had to be inserted in the news-papers:

> To destroy all groundless reports concerning the extraordinary expenses of the late fireworks in the Green Park, we are assured from good authority, that the bills, as delivered to His Majesty's Board of Works, amounted to no more than 14,500 pounds.

It goes without saying, I think, that the mere publication of these numbers hardly caused speculation to cease, there being a wide and stinking ditch of credibility betwixt authority and Mr London Town. Besides, in some eyes, 14,500 pounds was 14,500 pounds too rich.

Though King George knew it not—or perhaps did know but cared not—fully half the fireworks never got lit. When the rain came, the spectacle was rushed to its closing, so when one reads the *Description of the Machine for the Fireworks* published by His Majesty's Board of

Ordnance, one must do so *cum grano salis*. But they were not wasted, those fireworks; the Duke of Richmond took advantage of the situation and acquired the remaining materials—I know not by what subterfuge—and had them suitably dried out and re-fused, staging his own show in May at his house beside the Thames. He even had a miniature Temple of Peace built upon the lines of the original, and the weather graced his enterprise. Charles Frederick was called in to oversee this show, and I think Benjamin Brock was charged with the firing of it.

Cavalier Giovanni Niccolò Servandoni was swiftly released from detention under the good offices of Charles Frederick and the Duke of Cumberland. Though his contrition might have strengthened whilst contemplating his lot in a cell overnight, his gratitude at being set free the next day certainly did not. That very day, he swore such retribution upon the whole enterprise—implicating the Duke of Montagu (of all people) in nefarious activities—that he was perforce bought off. He left this realm 3,000 pounds the richer, but from whose purse Montagu extracted this sum is not known; certainly not his own. He went straight to Belgium where he designed and built the façade of Lede Castle for the Marquess there. Of all the engineers of this spectacle, Servandoni was most lampooned in the news-papers.

Signor Gaetano Ruggieri took his share of lampooning too; all the foreigners did. In a serious vein, he was criticised in some quarters for the poor conduct of the whole affair but, again, we must unweave the strands of popular sentiment against Continentals from the solid facts. He was a foreigner brought here to teach granddame to suck eggs, 'tis true, but it is clear that the Board of Ordnance never had the facility to stage such a spectacle before he came. When one considers the travails that took place behind the scenes, the fact that a vaudeville nonsense became seen as a glorious spectacle must be laid to his charge. His conduct of the affair was certainly viewed with great favour in official circles, for he was instated soon after as a firework artificer at Woolwich. His colleague Giuseppe Sarti travelled to St Petersburg on the offer of a position at Empress Elizabeth's court.

Captain Thomas Desaguliers went back to his researches at the Laboratory. I wondered whether he might have been discommoded by the appointment of Ruggieri, but he told me that he took it most positively as it allowed him to concentrate more upon his researches into all manner of artillery. His premonition that things would never be the same at the Laboratory came true. He now enjoys a quite collegial relationship with Signor Ruggieri and is happy to have foisted the nuisance Lieutenant Robert Jones upon him. I think Desaguliers was of like mind to James Morris, who found a return to his carpentry department at Woolwich to be most welcome, telling me that it all appeared to him like a bit of a dream.

Mr Charles Frederick did indeed achieve his knighthood, and perhaps his conduct upon that day, and upon the Duke of Richmond's later spectacle, served his suit well. His ideas upon the spectacles of Rome, and his oft fulsome praise of all things antique, did him poor credit though. The papers and pamphlets were wont to lampoon him for his views that the great firework spectacle was a monument for posterity, when rather they saw it as the Grand Whim for posterity to laugh at.

George Frideric Handel needed have no fear of bad reviews of his music; I take many papers of both political camps, but not one word could I find of reportage, let alone critique. As the critics are many and their barbs often directed Handel's way, I found this most odd. All attention was apparently upon the fireworks, where both praise and criticism were equally to be found. Handel very happily performed his suite of *Musick for the Royal Fireworks* in May as a charity for old Sailor Coram's foundlings, of which he was a staunch supporter. This was, of course, the orchestral version, much more pleasing upon the ears and with the parts made more intricate and musical on account of their refined scoring. Handel, I think, wished the fireworks night musical score might disappear, but there were doubtless too many copies to call back, even had he the possibility. He is confident that it will never see the light of day, let alone be performed, and for that he is thankful.

John, 2nd Duke of Montagu carried off his multifarious transactions with great energy and commitment and was well praised by the sovereign for his organisation and planning of the spectacle. In truth, there might have been no other in the realm who could have pulled this off; King George knew the right man for the task and had him at the right time. Sadly, John Montagu was not long to enjoy his leisure, for he passed away just this July of a violent fever whilst at his house in Whitehall.

Perhaps I may be indulged in the last word by reproducing a poem that appeared in an Oxford news-paper in May:

On the FIRE WORKS

How! breathing peace the cannons play,
In harmless thunders hail the day;
And to like purpose powder's spent,
At *home*, as on the *continent*.
　See how the mounting rockets fly,
And, hissing, reach the spangled sky;
Marking their way with tails of light,
Aloft they beam, and banish night:
The goddess sear'd, with swift retreat,
Leaves to a mimic sun her seat;
Whilst mimic stars put out the true,
And heav'n and earth alike are new.
　See how the gaping crowd below,
Intent upon the raree show,
Survey the glories o'er their heads,
Which every squib and cracker sheds;
But whilst, with wonder struck, they gaze,
Sicks, wastes and dies the gaudy blaze;
And when played off the pageant puff,
The scene is closed in stench and snuff.
Emblems, that represent our case,
Proclaim and shadow out the peace;
A work the price of many a million!
And lasting as—a late pavilion.

Historical Notes

This is a story, not a history. Although my chosen narrators were real people, I have put some words into their mouths, and I have imputed motives and actions to them. As long as I assure readers that this is a work of fiction, I think I am entitled to get away with it. In some instances, the speech of the characters is taken almost verbatim from the historical record. Some descriptions are also a matter of record and are reproduced closely. But I would beg readers who are seeking historical truths—however they may be understood—not to see this story as a work of reference but to appreciate the historical framework as a launching pad for a flight of conjecture into what might have been, could have been and, in some cases, very probably was. Nevertheless, a brief description of which features are based in fact, and which are fiction, would not be out of place.

I have had George II heavily involved in the design of the elements of the machine and their disposition. I could find no evidence that he was engaged to the point that he would specify themes and texts in detail but, on the other hand, he would surely not have vested all responsibility in a French designer for such a quintessentially British celebration. I find it quite conceivable that he would rough out the design as I have described and be happy to have the architects, artisans and sculptors refine and execute his ideas.

It is reported that the King was less than satisfied with the playing off of his Grand Conceit, but I felt it would be kinder to the reader to give the result a positive spin. Besides, it is difficult to disentangle politically biased critical comment and cynical satire from the king's true feelings, especially as there is no first-hand account (that I know of) from the man himself regarding his level of satisfaction. Let George II retrospectively enjoy his fireworks.

The terrible accident that took place during the gun drill on Constitution Hill is a matter of record, and King George's solicitude is also documented. This gun drill was no part of the fireworks celebration, but the king was proud of his Train of Artillery and he and his son, the Duke of Cumberland, were fond of putting their gun crews through their paces.

That John Montagu was on the take whilst charged with the king's fireworks is conjectural, and he could certainly have let virtue be his sole reward, but in the age in which he was living, such altruism would have been unusual. Some of his nefarious dealings that I describe are fictitious—the rental of hotel accommodation, the procurement of lumber, the surcharge on Benjamin Brock—but others have a ring of truth to them. Whilst the rental of work space from Samuel Foote is a fiction, the vengeance in the form of the Bottle Conjuror is not. Montagu is, indeed, suspected of pulling off that jape, and it was Foote's Haymarket Theatre that was the victim of the rampage.

The collusion of Montagu and Jonathan Tyers over the rehearsal of the music at Vauxhall carries much circumstantial evidence. I have had trouble for years with the mystery of the music that George Frideric Handel provided for the fireworks. I have found it difficult to reconcile King George II's indifference to a musical overture in the first place with the equal reluctance of Handel to provide one. That Jonathan Tyers was persuaded by Montagu to furnish equipment for the Green Park celebration is a matter of record, as is Handel's fury at the very idea of a rehearsal, especially at Vauxhall. Then, when taxed by Frederick on the need for Handel, and no other, to be the composer, Montagu wrote: "The reason may not be given." I will go out on a limb and state that the scenario I have created is as likely as any. The lack of any critical comment upon the music is surprising in view of Handel's immense presence on the London music scene and the great popular interest in the event. The "explanation" I have invented to account for the silence is, at least, plausible.

The exact constitution of Handel's band remains a subject of debate. The complement of the wind section is well established, but some scholars argue for the inclusion of a string section on grounds of the numbers of musicians reported by eyewitnesses and the roughed-in parts in the original score. I tend to buck the trend for several reasons: firstly, as the number of spectators was quite probably grossly exaggerated, so too could be the number of musicians; secondly, I feel that Handel would not have gone against the king's wishes, especially as they were expressed through Frederick and Montagu in such strong terms. The third reason is logistical: assembling and organising one hundred musicians in both the Vauxhall bandstand and the Green Park firework machine would have been excessively cumbersome and time-consuming.

The friction and animosity between the Continental contractors and their English counterparts are entirely true, although the specific instances of their interactions are my creations. There were, in fact, fights between the French and English crews behind the scenes during the Green Park show. In France there were pitched battles and deaths of gunners and pyrotechnicians over the conduct of firework displays, the British example being a mite more restrained. However, because Gaetano Ruggieri was employed later at Woolwich, I decided to build a collegial relationship between him and Thomas Desaguliers. This was aided by the latter's Huguenot roots and by the fact that even though English gunners and Continental pyrotechnicians were worlds apart in their capabilities and philosophies, they would likely have seen mutual advantage in cooperation.

I am not sure if Charles Frederick's heroic action in bringing the water engines into play really happened, but the scenario I have constructed to explain Servandoni's drawn sword is at least plausible. A contemporary illustration shows the fire-fighters in action.

Giovanni Servandoni departed England in a huff but a good deal richer, so it was not difficult to portray him as a proud and prickly specimen from the start, especially considering the incident with the drawn sword. My portrayal was abetted by the knowledge that the world of theatre design he had left at the Royal Academy of Music in 1724 had degenerated greatly in his estimation. It may be unfair, but surviving portraits of him do lend themselves to the kind of description I have indulged in.

Benjamin Brock was of the second generation of that famous firm to operate a firework establishment in Whitechapel, but nothing appears to be known about its disposition at this period. This is not surprising as his business would not have been a matter of record and would continue to be illegal until well into the next century. Thus, aside from the physical address, all descriptions of the scene I have contrived are conjectural. The general condition of the streets and the behaviour of its denizens are matters of record, though, as contemporary paintings and prints attest. Hogarth's illustrations are hardly exaggerations, and neither are the many written descriptions in both fact and fiction.

The manufacture and use of fireworks in the 18th century are extensively documented, but it would be unwise to place too much reliance on the work of Robert Jones, who was a lieutenant at Woolwich during this period. Although his book on firework practice was published in London some fifteen years after the Green Park display, it is the work of a keen dabbler, not a practitioner. However, his book is noteworthy in containing receipts that indicate Continental practice, thus arguing that the techniques of Ruggieri were known to him. I have made Jones into a nuisance in 1748 to '49, but perhaps I have done him an injustice. His later career shows him to be a man of many facets, and I would urge readers interested in the history of ice skating to follow up on him.

Ignatius Sancho must have been a man of powerful gifts, although as a black man in mid-eighteenth-century London, he was extremely fortunate to have had an encounter with John Montagu. Nevertheless, even though Montagu and Lady Mary showed him great kindness, he was clearly a social talking point and an item of curiosity and wonder; an exhibit to be trotted out as a demonstration of Montagu's humanistic, but perfectly contemporary, sentiments. The Christmas dinner is a vignette of how, I am sure, the Montagu family behaved in his presence.

All that remains today to mark the site of His Majesty's Grand Conceit is an information plaque. There has been discussion of employing ground-penetrating radar and other techniques in an attempt to locate the exact footprint of the Temple of Peace. A plaque has been erected by the Royal Parks Department on the approximate site. It is a pity that the text mentions only Handel and his music and has nothing to say about Ruggieri, Servandoni and the rest of the team. This omission is characteristic of some current thinking, where prominence is given to the music, which actually played a quite minor role. One source even suggests that the fireworks were arranged to suit the music! This topsy-turvy conclusion naturally comes about because the music has continued to stand the "test of time" while the rest of the celebration was considered by its engineers from the beginning to be ephemeral. Even the contemporary illustrations show a thing of great classical beauty when, in fact, on close inspection it would have appeared as it truly was; makeshift and temporary.

I feel it is incumbent upon the Royal Parks Department to give the public the fuller story. I would gladly sell them a book.

HANDEL'S *MUSICK FOR THE ROYAL FIREWORKS*

Of George Frideric Handel's music, not one word of review of the premier performance of the suite seems to have come down to us. There are many recordings of the work now available, most of which feature the refined orchestral scoring that Handel happily provided for posterity. In recent decades, some ensembles have attempted to reconstruct the musical forces used at the outdoor performances at Vauxhall and the Green Park. Of these, my preferences are:

Handel: Musick for the Royal Fireworks; Four Coronation Anthems
Hyperion, CDA66350, 1989

> This is a fine recording conducted by Robert King with a much-enhanced King's Consort. It is one of the best and most spirited renditions of the work. Although the liner notes disingenuously profess the use of "period instruments," the brasses are actually modern inventions, but they still capture a great deal of the sonority of the instruments that would have been used at the time.

Hændel: Water Music & Fireworks
Glossa, GCD921606, 2003

> This version, by Le Concert Spirituel conducted by Hervé Niquet, recreates the wind instrumentation exactly, using reproductions of period instruments with correct tunings and musical temperaments. The effect is astounding, but an otherwise authentic concept is compromised (in my opinion) by including a string section, which would have delighted Handel but would have pushed King George II to the brink of apoplexy. I like this version particularly because it features trumpets made in my workshop to exacting historical principles.

Acknowledgements

I owe a great debt of gratitude to the many people who were consulted during the assembly of this tale. Members of the Ottawa Historical Writers group showed much appreciation and interest when the text was scarcely begun. John Bennet gave me encouragement to write the book-length tale by publishing my short account of the 1749 spectacle in *Fireworks* magazine. Patrick Burrows, Ettore Contestabile and James Duffin provided valuable initial overviews, and Ian Barclay in particular ran a fine comb over the text, sorted out some military issues and advised on contemporary practice. Mike Jones put me on track with some details of eighteenth-century pyrotechnic practice and Ron Harris proved to be a goldmine of information on historical sources. Ron was also a systematic editor of the technical aspects of the text. Simon Werret and Megan Doolittle contributed to the social and historical accuracy of the background. Donald Burrows guided my assumptions about what went on musically during the organization of this firework spectacle. Alex Binkley gave the text a final and thorough read-through before Sigrid Macdonald finished the work with her fine copyediting. Mag Carson checked my first draft of the cover art and made suggestions that transformed it. My wife Janet's contribution lies in her tolerance of my aberrant behaviour in writing about fireworks in the first place, her indulgence in my continual reference to the subject at every opportunity, and then reading and commenting upon many of the scenes. I apologise if I have omitted anyone from this list. Finally, I think it is incumbent on me to beg forgiveness of all the characters in this book, even though it cannot be acknowledged. They have lent their names to me all unsuspecting, and for all I know I may have done them injustice. But I doubt it…

Robert Barclay
Summer 2020

A Selection of Readings

Anon., *An Account of the Famous Sieur Rocquet, Surgeon* (London: J. Bromage, 1749)

Brock, Alan St Hill, *Pyrotechnics: the Art and History of Firework Making* (London: Daniel O'Connor, 1922). Facsimile: Michigan: University of Michigan Library, undated.

Burrows, Donald and Dunhill, Rosemary, *Music and Theatre in Handel's World* (Oxford: Oxford University Press, 2002)

Deutsch, Otto Erich, *Handel: A Documentary Bibliography* (London: Adam and Charles Black, 1955)

Doderer-Winkler, Melanie, *Magnificent Entertainments: Temporary Architecture for Georgian Festivals* (London and New Haven: Yale University Press, 2013)

Forster, John, *Oliver Cromwell; Daniel De Foe. Sir Richard Steele. Charles Churchill. Samuel Foote. Biographical Essays* (London: John Murray, 1860)

Glover, Jane, *Handel in London: The Making of a Genius* (London: MacMillan, 2018)

Jones, Robert, *A New Treatise on Artificial Fireworks* (London: Robert Jones, 1765). Facsimile: ECCO Print editions, undated.

Kelly, Jack, *Gunpowder: A History of the Explosive that Changed the World* (London: Atlantic Books, 2004)

Plimpton, George, *Fireworks: A History and a Celebration* (New York: Doubleday and Company, 1984)

Ruggieri, Gaetano and Sarti, Giuseppe, *A Description of the Machine for the Fireworks with all Its Ornaments* (London: His Majesty's Board of Ordnance, 1749)

Thébault, Pierre, 'Why Pyrotechnics Developed from Crafts to Professionalism and Science', in *Proceedings of the Changsha Conference*, International Symposium on Fireworks, 2013.

Werrett, Simon, 'Pyrotechnic Arts and Sciences in European History', in Smith, Pamela H. and Schmidt, Benjamin (eds.), *Making Knowledge in Early Modern Europe: Practices, Objects and Texts 1400-1800* (Chicago: University of Chicago Press, 2010)

REFERENCES

[1] In present-day popular culture, Lewis Carroll takes all the credit for Byrom's little ditty.

[2] GEORGIO. II. REGI. OPT. AVCTORI. SALVTIS. LIBERTATIS. VINDICI. FVUNDATORI. QVIETIS. PATRI. PATRIAE.

[3] Charles Frederick was a poet and a collector of ancient French currency, upon which he had written monographs. He was also a keen student of ancient architecture and had engravings of his work published by Smart Lethieullier.

[4] Young ladies and gentlemen of this social class were sent on a Grand Tour for their education, visiting and appreciating the ruins of the classical period upon which so much of their culture was based. Incidentally, my grandmother was on her Grand Tour in Venice when the Campanile came crashing down into St Mark's Square in 1902.

[5] There was an enclave of domestic firework workshops in Whitechapel at this period. The names of Pain and Brock appear, and there is a suggestion that the Gunpowder Plotters of 1605 acquired their supply from a Mr Pain.

[6] Roger Morris (1695–1749) was a prolific and very original architect, who was appointed Clerk of the Works in 1727 and Master Carpenter to the Office of the Ordnance in 1734.

[7] Robert Jones was posted to Woolwich around this time. He later published *A New Treatise on Artificial Fireworks* (1765), but his descriptions and receipts are those of an enthusiastic amateur, not a practitioner.

[8] Hogarth's *Emblematical Print on the South Sea Scheme* shows his antipathy to this huge confidence trick.

[9] Dingley's mill is known to have been wrecked by disgruntled sawyers in 1768. (E.W. Cooney, 'Eighteenth Century Britain's Missing Sawmills: A Return Visit,' *Construction History*, 14, 1998, pp. 83–87.) So, this was apparently not the first time.

[10] Although *Solomon* was written in 1748, it was not performed until March of the following year. To discuss it among themselves, the board members must have been privy to a rehearsal.

[11] A graphite mine in Cumberland was the only one in the world at this time. Bread was used as an eraser.

[12] Doubtless, Morris saw this illustration in a copy of *The Life and Strange Surprizing Adventures of Robinson Crusoe of York, Mariner*, published by Daniel Defoe 1719.

[13] This is a somewhat earlier occurrence of the derogatory term *rosbif* than has previously been known.

[14] An article in the *Gentleman's Magazine* asked readers to estimate the altitude of the Royal Fireworks rockets and to send in their observations, an early example of scientific crowd-sourcing.

[15] Benjamin Robbins won the Royal Society's Copley Medal in 1747 for his work on ballistics.

[16] Desaguliers's researches were inconclusive, and it was not until 1804 that William Congreve devised a war rocket that saw limited use in the British army.

[17] According to both Jones and Brock (see Selection of Readings), the *pot de brin* was similar to today's jack-in-the-box. However, Ruggieri and Sarti specify 12,200 of them, so it is highly unlikely that such a complex piece would be ordered in such vast quantities. I suggest that the *pot de brin* in this context was a small, long-burning flare used for illumination of the artworks on the machine and the outlining of decorations.

[18] It was not until the passage of the Gunpowder Act of 1860 that merchants such as Brock could finally operate within the law, although before that time, perpetrators were prosecuted sporadically at best and usually following an accident or explosion.

[19] Montagu was perhaps afflicted with a bladder stone, not uncommon with the diet of the period. The operation to remove it was an ordeal.

[20] The pump is now called a Roman candle, although the origin of the latter term is obscure as the Italians didn't use them. The term Roman candle is said to invoke the classical practice of setting fire to Christians coated in pitch. Although in appalling taste, the same could be said of the Catherine wheel, which celebrates the saint martyred upon such a device.

[21] Frances was married to Edward Boscawen, who represented the borough of Truro in Cornwall but who was almost continually at sea.

[22] Thomas's father, John Theophilus Desaguliers (1683–1744), was a natural philosopher of Huguenot extraction, much respected and admired by the court.

[23] Lord and Lady Montagu had educated black slaves, Francis Williams and Ignatius Sancho. Montagu chanced on Sancho while he was still in the thrall of his "owners" in Woolwich and took a fancy to him. He became a resident at the house in Blackheath some time in 1749. His compositions, poetry and letters are extant.

[24] Henry Fielding expressed the same sentiment in writing during an acrimonious exchange with Foote.

[25] Foote's play, *A Dish of Chocolate*, was closed by authorities in 1747, but influential voices at Court had it reinstated.

[26] There are many variations of this text extant, so it appears that the publicity was very widely distributed.

[27] Lest we mock these 18th century mugs, today's "bottle conjurors" have earned billions of dollars selling water in disposable plastic bottles to people with a domestic supply, demonstrating that the capacity of humankind to be gulled is alive and well in the 21st century.

[28] 'The Bottle Conjurer,' quoted in the *Sheffield Daily Telegraph*, 20th June, 1865.

[29] Reported in the *Scots Magazine*, vol. 11, May 1749.

[30] Lord Manchester is said to have complained that Queen Anne was, 'Too careless or too busy to listen to her own band, and had no thought of hearing and paying new players however great their genius or vast their skill.'

[31] His Majesty is referring to *Zadok the Priest*, played to this day at all royal coronations.

[32] George is hinting at the ongoing friction between the Crown and the Whig-controlled "Broad Bottomed Parliament" under Henry Pelham, who urged total confidence in the king's ministers.

[33] Handel dedicated *Judas Maccabaeus* to Cumberland after his 1746 victory over the Scots at Culloden. The chorus 'See, the conquering hero comes' could only refer to him.

[34] *London Magazine*, January 14th, 1749.

[35] John Shore (1662-1752) and Valentine Snow (?-1770) were sergeant-trumpeters to the royal court. Handel wrote much of his solo music for them.

[36] The copyist was Johann Christoff Schmidt, who brought his family into Handel's employ, changed his name to Smith, and worked in the Brook Street premises for many years.

[37] This text of this pamphlet (see Selection of Readings) was copied by a number of newspapers and became quite the town talking point. It was common for the authors of tracts such as this to remain anonymous.

[38] Portable waterproof covers, like cumbersome umbrellas, were called Robinsons after the one Defoe's Robinson Crusoe made for himself. They were extremely unfashionable and used only when absolutely necessary.

[39] Charles Avison (1709-1770) was a composer who lived in Newcastle-upon-Tyne. He was one of Handel's most acerbic detractors and often aimed critical barbs to the south.

JACOB THE TRUMPETER

If you have enjoyed reading *His Majesty's Grand Conceit*, I am sure you will enjoy Jacob's tale, a sweeping saga set in the Germany of the previous century. Since he first heard a herald in the marketplace when he was ten years old, all Jacob Hintze has wanted to do is play the trumpet. Apprenticed to a German cavalry unit as a teenager, he is thrown into the horrors of the Thirty Years War. Employed as a courier and secret agent by his Duke, Jacob meets love, hatred, vengeance and betrayal as around him Europe tears itself to pieces. He plays his trumpet on the battlefield to send men to their deaths; he makes music in holy service to the glory of God. Jacob Hintze's life story is a stirring struggle in which music, war, espionage and the love of a good woman wrestle for his soul on a backdrop of bloody conflict and fragile peace.

Available from:
www.loosecannonpress.com
Or online as hard copy or e-book

Ask Me About My Bombshells

If you have enjoyed reading about 18th century fireworks, fast-forward to the 21st century. You'll be intrigued by links between gunpowder and cocaine. A love affair over the mortars and Roman candles is disrupted by the imaginative schemes of a biker gang boss. Julia, granddaughter of a commercial pyrotechnician, falls for Rocco, sixth generation scion of a competing firework company, only to discover that her innocent romantic partner has been drawn into a network of drug-traffickers through coercion and blackmail. Sabotage, subterfuge, police raids, mix-ups and theft lead through an intricate gunpowder plot to an explosive thunderclap of a finale.

Available from:
www.loosecannonpress.com
Or online as hard copy or e-book

www.ingramcontent.com/pod-product-compliance
Lightning Source LLC
Chambersburg PA
CBHW031314160426
43196CB00007B/528